船舶信号

（双语）

王丹　井燕　韦国栋 / 主编

闫松银 / 主审

大连海事大学出版社

DALIAN MARITIME UNIVERSITY PRESS

ⓒ 王丹　井燕　韦国栋　2023

图书在版编目(CIP)数据

船舶信号：汉文、英文 / 王丹，井燕，韦国栋主编.
— 大连：大连海事大学出版社，2023.12
ISBN 978-7-5632-4479-9

Ⅰ.①船… Ⅱ.①王… ②井… ③韦… Ⅲ.①航海通
信—信号—技术培训—教材—汉、英 Ⅳ.①U675.3

中国国家版本馆 CIP 数据核字(2023)第 227225 号

大连海事大学出版社出版

地址:大连市黄浦路523号　邮编:116026　电话:0411-84729665(营销部)　84729480(总编室)
http://press.dlmu.edu.cn　E-mail:dmupress@dlmu.edu.cn

大连日升彩色印刷有限公司印装　　　　大连海事大学出版社发行

2023 年 12 月第 1 版　　　　　　　2023 年 12 月第 1 次印刷
幅面尺寸:184 mm×260 mm　　　　　　　　　　　印张:21
字数:457 千　　　　　　　　　　　　　　　印数 1~1000 册

出版人:刘明凯

责任编辑:席香吉　　　　　　　　　　　责任校对:高　颖
封面设计:解瑶瑶　　　　　　　　　　　版式设计:解瑶瑶

ISBN 978-7-5632-4479-9　　　定价:59.00 元

前　言

根据《STCW 公约马尼拉修正案》和交通运输部《海船船员培训大纲（2021 版）》的要求，航海专业毕业生必须具备使用视觉信号通信的能力、使用《国际信号规则》的能力及使用 IMO《标准航海通信用语》与船台、岸台进行有效沟通的能力。为有效履行以上要求，并进一步满足航海教育国际化的要求，提升航海专业学生使用标准航海工作语言的能力，以降低并消除未来在工作交流中的语言障碍，我们结合高等教育应用型人才培养的要求编写了此书。本书在内容上力求满足船舶工作的实际需要，系统地介绍了船舶信号以及船舶使用甚高频电话通信相关知识，并结合大量实用性、专业性的实践示例，以实现航海人才应用型教育知识体系与船舶适任培训工作场景的融合。本书可作为高等航海类院校航海技术专业本、专科生的教材，也可作为船舶驾驶管理人员及海上设施有关工作人员的参考用书。

本书是北部湾大学应用型教材规划建设项目、广西一流学科（船舶与海洋工程）和广西高等教育本科教学改革工程项目（2020JGZ135）的建设教材。本书由王丹、井燕、韦国栋担任主编，闫松银担任主审。在编写过程中，本书得到了广西海事局、钦州海事局、北海海事局及相关航运企事业单位的关心和支持，在此一并表示感谢！

由于作者水平有限，书中难免存在疏漏之处，恳请读者批评指正。

编　者
2023 年 12 月

目　录

Contents

Chapter 1
Introduction

第一章　绪论

Lesson 1
Methods of Communication on Board

Ship Communication is the method of exchanging information between the ships, ships and aircraft, and ships and shore stations. Ship communication is vital to the safety of ships and persons on board. Nowadays, though complex radio technology is used for marine traffic, those oldest and simplest methods such as smoke and forms are still in use, since they are more obvious and reliable.

Communication over relatively short distances can be made by visual or sound signals. Radio communication on board ship can send messages over long distances and with high efficiency. The vast majority of ship communication today is accomplished by electrical means. At the requirements of STCW 78/95 convention, officers in charge of the navigational watch should have abilities to transmit and receive signals by Morse Light, to use the International Code of Signals (ICS), and to communicate with other ships and coast stations on VHF telephone by the IMO Standard Marine Communication Phrases (SMCP). So, officers on board must acknowledge proficiency in visual signaling and radio telephone communication.

1. Methods of visual signaling

Visual signaling refers to any mode of transmission, which is capable of being seen. It includes:

1.1 Flashing light signaling

Using flashing light or pyrotechnics can send signals. The flashing light is an electric lamp used for sending messages in Morse Code.

1.2 Flag signaling

To hoist the international signal flag is a traditional method of signaling from one ship to other stations. To send messages by using signal code composed of a piece of flag or several pieces of flags.

1.3 Morse signaling by hand-flags or arms

To send messages by holding the two semaphore flags with two hands or using two arms in various positions similar to the hands of a clock.

Semaphore signals can be sent and received much more quickly than flag hoists or even flashing light using Morse code.

Note:

In case of emergency, rockets, flares and smoke are employed to indicate distress and the need of immediate assistance.

2. Methods of sound signaling

2.1 Sound signaling

Sound signaling refers to the sending of Morse signals by whistle, siren, foghorn, bell or other sound apparatus. They are used particularly in fog and similar circumstances which visual signals cannot be seen.

2.2 Voice over a loud speaker

Sending messages by shouting to the other with a loud speaker over short distances.

The number of blasts signifies the way the ship is manoeuvring or other important information.

3. Methods of radio communication

Radio communication is that the communication is carried out with radio devices over long distances, including:

3.1 Radio telegraph

Radio telegraph is a system, process and equipment used for sending messages across a distance by means of coded electrical impulses over the airways. It has been in use by merchant ships since the turn of the century. Although it has proved reliable, radio telegraph is too slow to complete such high-speed systems as radio telex. So its use in today's complex communication systems is limited, and it had stepped down from the historical stage after implementation of GMDSS in 1999.

3.2 Radio telex

Radio telex is a telegraphic method of passing printed information from one station to another by teleprinter. Today, radio telex is one of the primary measures to carry out high speed, long-range communication such as NAVTEX, NBDP (narrow band digital printer) over land or sea.

3.3 Radio-telephone

The radiotelephone, which uses radio waves to transmit sound signals (voice radio), is one of the most useful marine communication devices because of its speed and easy operation. Mariners can speak plain language or code messages over radio-telephony.

Today there are two basic kinds of radios found aboard oceangoing vessels.

(1) VHF radio

Marine VHF (very high frequency) radio requires an uninterrupted line of sight between antennas. This limits its range, and it is usually used to communicate over distances of less than about 30 nautical miles. Most marine radio traffic occurs over VHF radio, since shippers are naturally most concerned about vessels, port facilities, and hazards in their immediate vicinity.

（2）SSB radio

To communicate over very large distances, especially while a vessel is at sea, many pleasure craft and virtually all-commercial and military vessels are equipped with Marine SSB (single side-band) radio. SSB has a much greater range than VHF because it does not require a line of sight between stations. Its signal "bounces" in the earth's atmosphere, enabling it to reach around the planet's curved surface for thousands of miles. Transmitting on SSB requires a great deal of electricity compared to VHF, however, since its signal must be strong enough to travel over great distances through a lot of atmosphere.

4. Satellite communication

Satellite communication is a relatively new alternative for long distance communication. It features many advantages over conventional point-to-point radio. The satellite relays the signal to another satellite or to a receiver elsewhere on the surface of the earth.

Satellite communication is private. When you use conventional SSB or VHF, everybody with a receiver in range can monitor your conversation, and signals transmitted for satellite communication are highly directional, making them much more difficult for the casual eavesdropper to pick up. In the case of digital signals, data can be encrypted, making it extremely secure against even a determined spy. Satellite communication allows direct access to the global communication infrastructure(telephone and computer networks). SSB or VHF, on the other hand, both require an intermediary—such as a ship-to-shore operator—to make the appropriate connections ashore.

Satellite communication is not greatly affected by atmospheric or meteorological conditions. The signal does not have to bounce since it only needs to reach an overhead satellite which is always within line-of-sight. Because the signal is being transmitted primarily upward, it passes through a relatively thin layer of the Earth's atmosphere. SSB and VHF transmissions, however, must push their way through a great quantity of distortion—producing atmosphere as they travel across the surface of the Earth.

第一课　船舶通信方法

　　现代船舶在营运过程中,需要时刻与外界进行信息的交换,进而确保船舶的安全营运和海上人命的安全。

　　船舶与外界的信息交换的方法可分为:视觉信号通信、声响信号通信和无线电通信。其中,无线电通信又可以分为地面无线电通信和卫星通信。视觉和声响信号通信主要在人的视觉、听觉范围内进行,通信距离一般很近,而无线电通信可以适于不同距离上的通信,目前已在船上广泛使用。但先进的无线电通信仍然不能完全取代视觉、声响信号通信。

　　《海员培训、发证和值班标准国际公约》(简称"STCW 公约")明确要求船舶负责航行值班的驾驶员应能用视觉通信发出和接收信息,并且应具备用莫尔斯信号灯收发信息的能力及使用国际信号规则的能力,也要求具备使用 IMO 推荐的标准航海通信用语(英语)进行无线电话通信的能力。因此,视觉、声响信号通信及无线电话通信都是船舶驾驶人员必须掌握的基本技能。

1. 视觉信号通信方法

视觉信号通信是在视距范围内的通信,包括:

1.1　灯光通信

利用闪光信号灯(或类似发光装置,如:手电)发出的莫尔斯信号传递信息。根据 SOLAS 公约要求,船舶必须配备莫尔斯信号灯。

1.2　旗号通信

利用一面或数面信号旗组成不同的信号码传递信息。

1.3　手旗或手臂通信

双手各持一面信号旗或只用双臂变换不同的部位发出莫尔斯信号传递信息。

2. 声响信号通信

2.1　声响信号通信

通过船舶汽笛、号钟、雾角等发声设备发出莫尔斯信号码传递信息。

2.2　强力扬声器喊话通信

利用强力扬声器在近距离向对方喊话进而传递信息。

3. 无线电通信

现代船舶可以利用无线电设备进行近、中、远距离的通信,具体如下:

3.1　甚高频无线电话（VHF）

利用甚高频无线电话进行喊话通信,是近距离通信设备。

3.2　窄带直接印字电报（NBDP）

利用中高频组合电台(地面通信系统)收发信文,是中距离通信设备。

3.3　单边带电话（SSB）

利用组合电台(地面通信系统)收发,是中距离通信设备。

4. 卫星通信

卫星通信是利用卫星中继进行电话、电传或数据信文的收发,是远距离通信。

Lesson 2
Marine Communication Appliances on Board

Marine communication appliances on board include: hand flags, international signal flags, flashing signal lamps, and sound signal appliances, etc. The quantity of signal appliances which are equipped with on board should be in compliance with the requirements of related international convention and depends on the ship's measurement.

1. Hand flags

The hand flags are usually composed of two pieces of square flags whether like the pattern of letter-flag "O" or "P", and their side length is 40 cm. The two kinds of different colour of flags are selected to use at the different background of signaling. Visible distance of hand flag is about 1 to 3 miles (in normal weather).

2. International signal flags

International signal flags are nowadays manufactured in five kinds of different colors (red, yellow, white, black and blue) brush nylon fabric. A full set of international signal flags consists of 26 alphabetical flags from A to Z, ten numeral pendants from 0 to 9. Plus three substitutes (the first substitute, the second substitute, the third substitute) and one answering pendant, 40 pieces in total.

3. Flashing signal lamps

There are mainly two types of signal lamps on board ship. One is masthead signal light, the other one is flashing signal light which has Venetian hood.

4. Sound signal appliances

Sound signaling appliances have whistle, siren, foghorn, etc. on board ship.

Ships are generally equipped with corresponding signal equipment according to the requirements of relevant international conventions and domestic competent authorities, as shown in table 1-2-1, table 1-2-2 and table 1-2-3.

Table 1-2-1   Quantity of requirements for installation of flags on board ship

Type	LOA(m)			
	$L \geqslant 150$	$100 \leqslant L < 150$	$50 \leqslant L < 100$	$20 \leqslant L < 50$
Domestic national flag No.1	1 piece			
Domestic national flag No.2	2 pieces			
Domestic national flag No.3	4 pieces	2 pieces	1 piece	
Domestic national flag No.4		4 pieces	2 pieces	1 piece
Domestic national flag No.5				2 pieces
International signal flag No.2	2 sets			
International signal flag No.3			1 set	
International signal flag No.4				1 set
Hand flag	1 pair	1 pair	1 pair	1 pair
Related national flag and region flag	1 piece respectively	1 piece respectively	1 piece respectively	1 piece respectively

Table 1-2-2   Quantity of installation of flashing signal lamps on board ship

Type	Vis. distance(nm)	LOA(m)			
		$L \geqslant 150$	$100 \leqslant L < 150$	$50 \leqslant L < 100$	$20 \leqslant L < 50$
Portable	$\geqslant 5$	1	1		
Portable	$\geqslant 2$			1	1
Rotary pedestalled	$\geqslant 15$	2	1 or 2		
Rotary pedestalled	$\geqslant 10$			1	1
Mast-headed	$\geqslant 5$	1	1		
Mast-headed	$\geqslant 2$			1	1

Table 1-2-3   Quantity of installation of sound signaling appliances on board ship

Type	Vis. distance(nm)	LOA(m)			
		$L \geqslant 200$	$100 \leqslant L < 200$	$75 \leqslant L < 100$	$20 \leqslant L < 75$
Super whistle	2	1			
Big whistle	1.5		1	1	
Medium whistle	1				1
Big bell		1	1	1	1
Gong		1	1		

第二课　船舶通信设备

1. 手旗

手旗是用两面正方形的布或旗纱（羽纱）与两根木棍制成的，边长 40 cm。手旗分为两种，一种是信号旗字母"O"的样式，一种是信号旗字母"P"的样式。这两种不同颜色的手旗可依据通信时的不同背景选用。手旗的能见距离（指在正常天气以及使用望远镜条件下的距离）为 1 至 3 n mile。

2. 信号旗

信号旗用红、黄、白、黑、蓝五种不同颜色的旗纱（羽纱）制成，有字母旗 26 面，数字旗 10 面，代用旗 3 面，回答旗 1 面，1 套共有 40 面。

3. 灯光通信设备

闪光信号灯主要有两种，一种是桅顶信号灯，另一种是带有百叶遮板的闪光信号灯。

4. 声响信号通信设备

船舶配备的声响信号通信设备主要有号笛、号钟和号锣。

船舶按照有关国际公约及国内有关主管机关的要求，一般根据船舶的船长来配备相应信号设备。具体见表 1-2-1、表 1-2-2、表 1-2-3。

表 1-2-1　信号旗配备数量表

名称	船长（m）			
	$L \geqslant 150$	$100 \leqslant L < 150$	$50 \leqslant L < 100$	$20 \leqslant L < 50$
本国国旗 1 号	1 面			
本国国旗 2 号	2 面			
本国国旗 3 号	4 面	2 面	1 面	
本国国旗 4 号		4 面	2 面	1 面
本国国旗 5 号				2 面
国际信号旗 2 号	2 套			
国际信号旗 3 号			1 套	
国际信号旗 4 号				1 套

续表

名称	船长（m）			
	$L \geq 150$	$100 \leq L < 150$	$50 \leq L < 100$	$20 \leq L < 50$
手旗	1 副	1 副	1 副	1 副
相关国旗和区旗	各 1 面	各 1 面	各 1 面	各 1 面

表 1-2-2　通信闪光灯配备数量表

型式	船长（m）				
	能见距离（nm）	$L \geq 150$	$100 \leq L < 150$	$50 \leq L < 100$	$20 \leq L < 50$
手提式	≥ 5	1	1		
手提式	≥ 2			1	1
旋转座架式	≥ 15	2	1 或 2		
旋转座架式	≥ 10			1	1
桅顶式	≥ 5	1	1		
桅顶式	≥ 2			1	1

表 1-2-3　声响信号通信设备配备数量表

型式	船长（m）				
	听距（nm）	$L \geq 200$	$100 \leq L < 200$	$75 \leq L < 100$	$20 \leq L < 75$
超型号笛	2	1			
大型号笛	1.5		1	1	
中型号笛	1				1
大型号钟		1	1	1	1
号锣		1	1		

Lesson 3
Maintenance of Marine Communication Appliances

1. Halyard

New halyards should be stowed in dry places to keep them free from damp. Each halyard on the mast should be relaxed after sunset to prevent breaking due to its retractility. Keep the ropes near the funnel clean frequently. Generally, halyard is renewed once a year

2. Flags

All kinds of flags should be furled up and put in flag lockers in accordance with the prescription after each use, but if they have gotten wet, they must be furled after drying in the shade to prevent rottenness. When the sun comes out, flags must be taken out for solarizing after long raining or overcast. Generally, flags should be dried by airing after isolation to prevent worm-eating.

3. Lights

Clean all kinds of light signalling appliances frequently to keep the glass covers having a good transparency. Test them a time before dark every day, Check the contact conditions of power and fuse for breaking. Clean dust on the axis of rotation of hood and lubricate it frequently. Check the wearing condition of spring to prevent breaking during communication, cover the lights with boxes to avoid damage by bumping after using.

4. Sound signaling appliances

Clean and check the sound appliances(including whistle, electric sound gears, etc.) for maintenance after ship's calling at every time.

第三课　船舶通信设备的维护

1. 旗绳

旗绳要放在仓库中干燥的部位,以免受潮。桅上的各挂旗绳,在日落后都要放松,防止由于其绳索的伸缩性而断掉。靠近船舶烟囱的旗绳要经常保持清洁。旗绳一般是每年更换一次。

2. 信号旗

各种旗帜使用完毕后,应按规定卷好放入旗柜,但若受潮湿,则必须阴干后才能卷起来,防止腐烂。在经过长时间雨天或潮湿天气之后,信号旗需要晾晒。一般在暴晒之后还要晾干保存,以防发生虫蛀。

3. 灯光设备

各种灯光通信设备应经常清洁,使玻璃外罩保持良好的透明度。每天在天黑前应该测试一次,检查电源是否接好,保险丝是否完整。对遮板的转轴要经常清除灰尘和加润滑油。对弹簧也要经常检查磨损情况,防止在通信中途折断,使用完毕后应用盒盖好,避免碰坏。

4. 声响通信设备

每次在船舶停靠之后应该检查声响设备包括汽笛、电力声响装置等,并进行清洁、保养。

Chapter 2
International Code of Signals (ICS)

第二章　国际信号规则

Lesson 1
Introduction of ICS

The International Convention for the Safety of Life at Sea (SOLAS) has made it a rule that all ships which in accordance with the present convention are required to carry radio installations shall carry the *International Code of Signals*. This publication shall also be carried by any other ship which in the opinion of the administration, has a need to use it. The code was adopted by the Fourth assembly of IMCO (the precursor of IMO) in 1965. The current edition of the *International Code of Signals* became effective on 1 April, 1969. The government of PRC announced that all Chinese vessels and coastal stations should comply with this Code from July 1, 1975.

1. Purposes of the ICS

The purpose of the ICS is to provide ways and means of communication in situations related essentially to safety of navigation and persons, especially when language difficulties arise. In the preparation of the code, account was taken of the fact that wide application of radio telephony and radio-telegraphy can provide simple and effective means of communication in plain language whenever language difficulties do not exist.

2. Contents of the ICS

The ICS can be divided into three parts as follows:

The first part is the text, which consists of 14 chapters, including definitions, procedures, methods and rules of various signal communication, etc., for all communicators to comply with the implementation and use.

The second part is the generic-class signal code. It mainly refers to the signal code that may be used in communication and the practical meaning it represents for the choice of the communicator. This part is the main body of the *International Code of Signals*.

The third part is the appendix, which includes distress signal, life-saving signal, radio telephone communication procedure, etc.

In communication, the plain language should be used first as far as possible, that is, the language that can be understood by each other. However, when it is impossible to communicate in the plain language due to language barrier, a mutually agreed signal code which can represent certain practical meaning should be used instead of the plain language.

第一课　《国际信号规则》概述

根据 SOLAS 公约的规定,《国际信号规则》是船舶必备的航海出版物之一。

现行的《国际信号规则》是 1965 年在国际海事组织(IMO)前身 IMCO 的第四次会议上通过的,并于 1969 年 4 月 1 日生效。我国政府宣布自 1975 年 7 月 1 日起执行该规则。

1. 制定《国际信号规则》的目的

《国际信号规则》主要是为使各国的船舶、岸台、飞机等在各种情况下相互通信时有一个便于共同遵守的原则。因此,制定规则的目的就是在出现各种危及航行安全和人命安全的情况时,尤其是相互间存在语言隔阂时,能提供合适的通信方法和手段。即使不存在语言隔阂,该规则也能为广泛使用的无线电报和无线电话提供简便而有效的明语通信方法。

2.《国际信号规则》的主要内容

《国际信号规则》分为三个部分:

第一部分是正文,共有 14 章,包括各种信号通信的定义、程序、方法及规则等,供所有通信者共同遵守执行和使用。

第二部分是通信时可能用到的信号码及其所代表的实际意义,供通信者选用。这部分是《国际信号规则》的主体。

第三部分为附录,包括遇险信号、救生信号、呼救发信程序及安全电信的收听等,供紧急情况下参考使用。

通信中应尽可能首先使用明语,即互相听得懂的语言。但当彼此间因语言隔阂无法用明语通信时,就必须用一种共同约定的且能代表一定实际意义的信号码来代替明语进行通信。

Lesson 2
International Code of Signals

The International Code of Signals is a basic signaling publication which includes the single-letter, two-letter, three-letter signals and the methods of signaling such as flag, flashing light, sound, voice over a loud hailer, radiotelegraphy, radio-telephony, Morse signaling by hand-flags or arms and so on. The contents of this book include 14 chapters, the general section and medical section of code messages.

1. Type of communication message

Communication message is to exchange communication information with others through a certain language. There are two types of messages in flag communication, light communication and VHF telephone communication: plain language message and signal code message.

1.1　Plain language message

It is a kind of language message that both sides can understand. For example, Chinese seamen speak Chinese between two Chinese ships, and seafarers of other nationalities can use their common mother tongue to express themselves. In the ICS, plain language is referred to English, which is a common language among crew members of different nationalities. The characteristic of this kind of message is that the communication parties can understand its content directly after they hear or see it without the help of other translation tools. Therefore, the International Signal Rules require that plain language should be used as far as possible in communication, with the precondition of no language barrier between communication parties. The International Maritime Organization (IMO) promotes an easy-to-master English with less vocabulary and simple grammar in order to reduce the language barrier between ships in various countries, i.e. Standard Marine Communication Phrases (SMCP). At sea, IMO stipulates that officers in charge of navigation and watch-keeping on bridge should use IMO SMCP.

1.2　Signal code message

It is a kind of message which is expressed in signal codes or their combination in the ICS. It is used when language difficulties arise between stations in communication. Therefore, International Signal Rules is an indispensable translation tool for code-language communication. For example, when a ship is unable to express "Patient has diarrhoea with frequent stools like rice water" in plain language, it can be expressed by the corresponding signal code "MIP" in the International Signaling Rules. After recognizing or receiving the signal code "MIP", other ships can find out the actual meaning it represents in alphabetical order in the medical section of the International Signal Rules.

2. Signal code

The signal code embodies the principle that each signal should have a complete meaning. There are three kinds of signal codes in the ICS.

2.1 Single-letter signals

Each of single-letter signals which are from A to Z except the letter R has a complete meaning. They are suitable for any methods of signaling. Single-letter signals are generally used in the case of most urgent, important or most common communication, and their meanings should be always committed to memory. In which some of single-letter signals have the same meaning with the manoeuvring signals in COLREG.

Single-letter signals and their meanings are as follows：

A：I have a diver down, and keep well clear at slow speed.

＊B：I am taking in, or discharging, or carrying dangerous goods.

＊C：Yes (affirmative or "The significance of the previous group should be read in the affirmative").

＊D：Keep clear of me. I am manoeuvring with difficulty.

＊E：I am altering my course to starboard.

F：I am disabled, and communicate with me.

＊G：I require a pilot. When made by fishing vessels operating in close proximity on the fishing grounds, it means "I am hauling nets".

＊H：I have a pilot on board.

＊I：I am altering my course to port.

J：I am on fire and have dangerous cargo on board, and keep well clear of me.

K：I wish to communicate with you.

L：You should stop your vessel instantly.

M：My vessel is stopped and makes no way through the water.

N：No. (Negative or "The significance of the previous group should be read in the negative.") This signal may be given only visually or by sound. For voice or radio transmission the signal should be "No".

O：Man overboard.

P：In harbour—All persons should report on board as the vessel is about to proceed to sea.

At sea—It may be used by fishing vessels to mean："My nets have come fast upon an obstruction". It may also be used as a sound to mean："I require a pilot".

Q：My vessel is "healthy" and I request free pratique.

＊S：I am operating astern propulsion.

＊T：Keep clear of me. I am engaged in pair trawling.

U：You are running into danger.

V：I require assistance.

W：I require medical assistance.

X：Stop carrying out your intentions and watch for my signals.

Y：I am dragging my anchor.

＊Z：I require a tug. (When made by fishing vessels operating in close proximity on the fishing grounds it means："I am shooting nets".)

Notes：

(1) Signals of letters marked (＊) when made by sound may only be made in compliance with the requirements of the International Regulations for Preventing Collisions at Sea, 1972, Rules 34 and 35 accepting that sound signals G and Z may continue to be used by fishing vessels fishing in close proximity to other fishing vessels.

(2) Signals K and S have special meanings as landing signals for small boats with crews or persons in distress.

2.2 Two-letter signals

Two-letter signals in the general section have been allocated significations which follow next in importance and consist mostly in distress and manoeuvring signals, with the addition of a few general signals in common use.

(1) Arrangement of two-letter signals

They are arranged from AA to ZZ, allowing for many combination of information units. The material is classified according to subject and meaning.

There are nine parts of text in this section：

Part 1：Distress—Emergency (AC to HT)

Part 2：Casualties—Damages (HV to LJ)

Part 3：Aids to Navigation—Navigation—Hydrography (LK to QC)

Part 4：Manoeuvring (QD to SQ)

Part 5：Miscellaneous (ST to VF)

Part 6：Meteorology—Weather (VG to YD)

Part 7：Routing of Ships (YG)

Part 8：Communication (YH to ZR)

Part 9：International Sanitary Regulations (ZS to ZZ)

(2) Searching method

If a signal code is given, it can be found according to the alphabetical order in the International Signal Rules. If Chinese (English) is given, there may be two or more categorizes of the same sentence according to the meaning of Chinese (English) in the same part of the subject, if the user cannot find one of them, he should go to another category.

(3) Complement Codes

The Code follows the basic principle that each signal should have a complete meaning. This principle is followed throughout the Code.

First：In certain cases, some two-letter signals followed by a figure from 0 to 9, this figure is the complement code. When complements are used, the contents of two-letter signals will be more complete.

Such complements express as follows：

"IN" = "I require a diver"

"IN1" = "I require a diver to clear propeller"

"IN2" = "I require a diver to examine bottom"

"IN3" = "I require a diver to place collision mat"

"IN4" = "I require a diver to clear my anchor"

Second：Tables of complements. These tables should be used only as and when specified in the text of the signals.

Table 1：Methods of communication

Figure	Signification
1	Morse signaling by hand-flags or arms
2	Loud hailers（megaphone）
3	Morse signaling lamps
4	Sound signals

Table 2：Services

Figure	Signification
0	Water
1	Provisions
2	Fuel
3	Pumping equipment
4	Fire-fighting appliance
5	Medical assistance
6	Towing
7	Survival craft
8	Vessel to stand by
9	Ice-breaker

Table 3：Compass directions

Figure	Signification
0	Direction unknown（or calm）
1	North-east
2	East
3	South-east
4	South
5	South-west
6	West
7	North-west
8	North
9	All directions（confused or variable）

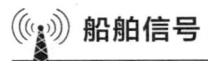

These table should be used only as and when specified in the text of the signals.

Signal Code	Signification
YR	Can you communicate by … (Complements Table 1)?
YR3	Can you communicate by Morse signaling lamps?
TZ	Can you offer assistance? (Complements Table 2)
TZ5	Can you offer medical assistance?
YB	True direction of wind is expected to be …(Complements Table 3)
YB8	True direction of wind is expected to be north.

Some important two-letter signals to be remembered.

AE: I must abandon my vessel.

CB: I require immediate assistance.

CB6: I require immediate assistance. I am on fire.

DX: I am sinking (lat… long… if necessary).

FR: I am (or vessel indicated is) in charge of co-originating search.

NC: I am in distress and require immediate assistance.

YG: You appear not to be complying with the traffic separation scheme.

2.3　Three-letter signals

Three-letter signals are concerned with medical matters and begin with letter "M" (from MAA to MVU).

(1) Arrangement of three-letter signals

There are two parts in this medical section:

Part 1: Request for medical assistance, with seven chapters

General information; Description of patient; Previous health; Localization of symptoms/Diseases/injuries; General symptoms; Particular symptoms; Progress report

Part 2: Medical advice, with seven chapters

Request for additional information; Diagnosis; Special treatment; Treatment by medicament; Diet; Childbirth; General instructions

(2) Tables of complements

There are three tables of complements which are indicated by two figures:

Table Ml—Regions of body (01−92)

Example:

MBF: The part of the body affected is…

So MBF11: The part of the body affected is heart (complement code: 11—Heart).

Table M2—List of common diseases (01−94)

Example:

MBA: Patient has suffered from…

So MBA 76: Patient has suffered from pulmonary tuberculosis (complement code: 76—Pulmonary tuberculosis).

Table M3—List of medicament（01−38）

Example：

MAT—Patient has been given... without effect.

So MAT 33：Patient has been given Ephedrine hydrochloride tables without effect. complement code：22—Ephedrine hydrochloride tables

（3）Examples for medical communication

Medical advice should be sought and given in plain language whenever it is possible. However, if language difficulties are encountered, this code should be used. Even when plain language is used, the text of the code and the instructions should be followed as far as possible.

Example 1：Request for medical assistance

Code message：MAJ35 MAM3 MBR38 MCI MCU MAA

To be decoded into plain language：

I have a male aged 35 years, patient has been ill for 3 days, temperature taken in mouth is 38 ℃, the breathing is irregular, patient is unconscious. I require urgent medical advice.

Example 2：Medical advice

Code message：MQU MRI BU

To be decoded into plain language：

I cannot made a diagnosis. You should refer to your *International Medical Guide for Ships*. A helicopter is coming to take sick.

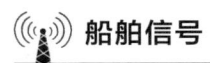

第二课　国际信号码

1. 通信信文的分类

通信信文就是通过某种语言与他方进行通信信息交换,在旗号通信、灯光通信及甚高频电话通信等通信中,有两种类型的信文:明语信文和码语信文。

1.1　明语信文

明语信文是指通信者选择一种使通信各方相互间直接能明白的语言信文。比如,中国船员间的通信可以使用汉语或汉语拼音来表达;其他国籍的船员之间可以使用他们共同的母语来表达;在《国际信号规则》中,明语一般是指英语,这是不同国籍的船员之间的共同语言。这种信文的特点是通信各方听到或看到之后可直接明了其内容而无需借助于其他翻译工具的帮助。因此《国际信号规则》要求在通信中尽可能使用明语,其先决条件是通信各方之间不存在语言隔阂。国际海事组织(IMO)为了减少各国船舶间的语言隔阂而推行一种容易掌握的词汇量较少且语法简单的英语——标准航海通信用语(IMO Standard Marine Communication Phrases)。负责船舶航行值班的驾驶员要具有使用并理解这种通信用语的能力。

1.2　码语信文

码语信文又叫信号码信文,是由《国际信号规则》中列出的信号码或其组合码组来表达的信文,在通信各方之间有语言障碍无法进行明语通信时使用。因此,《国际信号规则》是进行码语通信必不可少的翻译工具。例如,当一船无法用明语表示"病人有频繁的米汤样腹泻"时,可用《国际信号规则》中与其对应的信号码"MIP"来表达。他船在认清或收到信号码"MIP"后,在《国际信号规则》医疗部分中即可按字母的顺序查到它所代表的实际意义。

2. 信号码

《国际信号规则》的绝大部分篇幅是关于信号码组的。每个信号码组都有一个完整的意义。利用《国际信号规则》,发信人可以将信文的主题意思编成码组发送,受信人可以将收到的码组查译出明语信文。使用信号码组通信,不仅内容简明,而且通信速度快。国际信号码组分为单字母、双字母和三字母三类。

2.1　单字母信号

单字母信号是由单个英文字母组成的。在26个字母中,除"R"没有意义外,其他25个字母都有其完整的意义。单字母信号用于最紧急、最重要或最常用的内容,并适用于任何通信方法,应熟练记忆。其中,部分单字母所代表的意义与国际海上避碰规则中操纵信号完全一致。单字母信号及其意义如下:

　A：我下面有潜水员,请慢速远离我。

　　I have a diver down, and keep well clear at slow speed.

*B：我正装卸或载运危险货物。

　　I am taking in, or discharging, or carrying dangerous goods.

*C：是。(肯定或"前组信号的意义应理解为肯定的。")

　　Yes. (affirmative or "The significance of the previous group should be read in the affirmative.")

*D：请让开我;我操纵困难。

　　Keep clear of me. I am manoeuvring with difficulty.

*E：我正向右转向。

　　I am altering my course to starboard.

　F：我操纵失灵,请与我通信。

　　I am disabled, and communicate with me.

*G：我需要引航员。(但当在渔场附近正在作业的渔船使用时,它的意思则是"我正在收网。")

　　I require a pilot. (When made by fishing vessels operating in close proximity on the fishing grounds, it means "I am hauling nets.")

*H：我船上有引航员。

　　I have a pilot on board.

*I：我正向左转向。

　　I am altering my course to port.

　J：我船失火,并且船上有危险货物,请远离我。

　　I am on fire and have dangerous cargo on board, and keep well clear of me.

　K：我希望与你通信。

　　I wish to communicate with you.

　L：你应立即停船。

　　You should stop your vessel instantly.

　M：我船已停,并已没有对水速度。

　　My vessel is stopped and makes no way through the water.

　N：不。(否定或"前组信号的意义应理解为否定的"。)这个信号仅可用视觉或声响信号发出。在用语音或无线电发送这个信号时应该用"No"字。

　　No (negative or "The significance of the previous group should be read in the negative". This signal may be given only visually or by sound. For voice or radio transmission the signal should be "No".)

　O：有人落水。

　　Man over board.

　P：在港内,船将出海时,所有人员应立即回船。在海上当由渔船使用时,意为"我的网缠在障碍物上"。

　　In harbor, all persons should report on board as the vessel is about to proceed to sea.

At sea, it may be used by fishing vessels to mean "my nets have come fast upon obstruction".

Q：我船没有染疫,请发给进口检疫证。

My vessel is "healthy" and I request free pratique.

＊S：我正在倒车推进。

I am operating astern propulsion.

＊T：请让开我;我正在进行对拖作业。

Keep clear of me. I am engaged in pair trawling.

U：你正临近危险。

You are running into danger.

V：我需要援助。

I require assistance.

W：我需要医疗援助。

I require medical assistance.

X：中止你的意图,并注意我发送的信号。

Stop carrying out your intentions and watch for my signals.

Y 我正在走锚。

I am dragging my anchor.

＊ Z：我需要一艘拖船。(在渔场附近由正在作业的渔船使用时,它的意思是"我正在放网。")

I require a tug. (When made by fishing vessels operating in close proximity on the fishing groups, it means "I am shooting nets.")

注：

(1)有"＊"符号的字母信号仅在遵照1972年国际海上避碰规则第34条和35条的规定的情况下,才可用声号发送,渔船在捕鱼并与其他渔船相距很近时,可继续使用声号"G"和"Z"。

(2)信号"K"和"S"如果作为乘坐小艇的遇险船员或人员的登陆信号使用时,则另有专门的含义。

2.2 双字母信号

双字母信号由两个英文字母构成,表达一个完整的意义,属于规则的通用部分,是规则的主要组成部分。

(1)双字母信号码的编排:根据信文内容的不同主题,将 AA～ZZ 的全部信号码分为九个部分,信号码在左侧,按照字母顺序编排,意思对应在右侧。

第一部分:遇险～紧急（AC～HT）

第二部分:伤亡事故～损坏（HV～LJ）

第三部分:助航设备～航行～水文（LK～QC）

第四部分:船舶操纵（QD～SQ）

第五部分:杂项（ST～VF）

第六部分:气象～天气（VG～YD）

第七部分:船舶定线制（YG）

第八部分:通信（YH～ZR）

第九部分:国际卫生规则（ZS～ZZ）

（2）查找方法:如果给出的是信号码,可按书中字母编排顺序查找即可;如果给出的是汉语（英语）,按照汉语（英语）意思在相同主题所在部分查找,同一句子可能有两种或两种以上的分类方法,使用者如果在其中一种分类中找不到,应该到另一类里去找。

（3）双字母信号码的补充码表:在一些双字母信号的后面加上了0~9中的一位数字,这个数字就是补充码。它使双字母信号所表达的内容更完善。补充码有四种不同的使用方法:第一种已将其直接补充在规则中的双字母信号码之后。例如:

信号码	明语的意义
IN	我需要一名潜水员
IN1	我需要一名潜水员清理螺旋桨
IN2	我需要一名潜水员检查船底
IN3	我需要一名潜水员安放堵漏毯
IN4	我需要一名潜水员清理我的锚

第二种是根据《国际信号规则》中明语内容的提示由通信人从双字母信号码补充码表中选择来使用。双字母信号码内容末尾的补充码表有三个表,具体如下（参考2007年中国人民解放军海军司令部航海保证部编译的《国际信号规则》）:

表1　通信手段

补充数字	代表意义
1	莫尔斯手旗或手臂信号
2	扬声器(扩音器)
3	莫尔斯信号灯
4	声号

表2　检修

补充数字	代表意义
0	水
1	食品
2	燃料
3	抽水设备
4	消防器材
5	医疗援助
6	拖带
7	救生船艇
8	后备船
9	破冰船

表3　罗盘方向

补充数字	代表意义
0	方向不明(或平静)
1	东北
2	东
3	东南
4	南
5	西南
6	西
7	西北
8	北
9	全方向(或混乱的或多变的)

应该注意的是这三个补充码表并非可以任意选择使用。只有当信号码所对应的明语中有关于使用补充码表的提示时才可在指明的表中进行选择。

例：

信号码	代表意义
YR	你能用……(补充码表1)通信吗？
YR3	你能用莫尔斯信号灯通信吗？
TZ	你能提供援助吗？(补充码表2)
TZ5	你能提供医疗援助吗？
YB	预计风的真风向为……(补充码表3)
YB8	预计风的真风向为北

一些应记忆的重要的双字母信号码如下所示。

AE：达式我必须放弃我的船。

CB：我需要立即援助。

CB6：我需要立即援助。我船失火。

DX：我船正在下沉(必要时指明经纬度)。

FR：我(或指明的船)负责协同搜索工作。

NC：我遇险,需要立即援助。

YG：你船没有遵守分道通航制。

2.3　三字母信号

三字母信号由以字母M(medical)为首的三个英文字母组成,从MAA~MVU接字母顺序排列,专供进行医疗方面通信时使用。

(1)三字母信号的编排

第一部分：请求医疗援助

船长可根据病人的具体病情,选择适当的信号码组成信文并发给医疗指导机构,以便请求医疗援助。该部分分为 7 个子项:

　　一般情况、病人情况、病史、症状、一般症状、特殊症状、进度报告

　　第二部分:医疗指导

　　医疗指导机构的医生根据船长的请求,做出诊断并用适当的信号码组成信文对船长进行医疗指导。该部分分为 7 个子项:

　　要求补充情况、诊断、特别治疗、药物治疗、饮食、分娩、一般指导

　　(2)补充码表

　　医疗部分信号码的末尾共有三个补充码表(医学术语表)供选择使用。这三个表均用两位数字表示。

　　补充码表(M1):躯体各部位名称,补充码由 01～92 表示(详见附录 2)。

　　例如:MBF＝躯体……部感染。

　　MBF11＝躯体心脏部感染(补充码 11＝心脏)。

　　补充码表(M2):常见疾病的名称,补充码由 01～94 表示。疾病除用英文外还用拉丁文及其他各种文字表示,以便于查找正确的译名(详见附录 3)。

　　例如:MBA＝病人曾患过……。

　　MBA76＝病人曾患过肺结核(补充码 76＝肺结核)。

　　补充码表(M3):药物名单,补充码由 01～38 表示。药名除用英文外还用拉丁文及其他各种文字表示,以便于查找正确的译名。

　　例如:MAT＝病人已给……无效果。

　　MAT22＝病人已给盐酸麻黄素片无效果(补充码 22＝盐酸麻黄素片)。

　　由于大部分船员尤其是非英语国家的船员,对专业性很强的医学术语不很熟悉,这些补充码表无疑使船长在请求医疗援助时或在接受医疗援助时都得到至关重要的帮助。即使通信各方不存在语言困难,使用明语通信时,这些医学术语也有重要的参考作用。

　　(3)医疗通信示例

　　医疗指导,只要有可能,请求者和指导者都应使用明语通信。但如果遇到语言隔阂,则应使用信号码通信。

　　例 1:

　　请求医疗援助

　　码语信文:MAJ35 MAM3 MBR38 MCI MCU MAA

　　译成中文明语:我有一个男性病人,35 岁,患者已病了 3 天,口腔体温 38 ℃,呼吸不规则,病人神志不清,我请求紧急医疗指导。

　　例 2:

　　医疗指导

　　码语信文:MQU MRI BU

　　译成中文明语:我不能做出诊断。你应参考《国际船用医疗指南》。一架直升机正前去接病人。

Lesson 3
Transmission Methods of Communication Elements

Here mainly 8 elements in Signal Code Messages will be introduced, namely: names of vessels and places, azimuth or bearing, distance, course, time and date, speed, latitude and longitude and depth.

1. Names of vessels and places

Names of vessels and/or places are to be spelled out (Chinese phonetic alphabets are used for names of Chinese vessels and places).

Examples:

KN MV New Star = I cannot take MV New Star in tow.

UV Qinzhou = I am from Qinzhou.

2. Azimuth or bearing

They are to be expressed in three figures denoting degrees from 000 to 359, measured clockwise. If there is any possibility of confusion, they should be preceded by the letter "A". They are always to be true unless expressly stated to be otherwise in the context.

Example:

LW 240 = I receive your transmission on bearing 240°.

3. Distance

Figures preceded by letter "R" indicate distance or range in nautical miles.

Example:

OJ A135R5 = I have located you on my radar on bearing 135°, distance 5 nautical miles.

4. Course

Course is to be expressed in three numerals denoting degrees from 000 to 359, measured clockwise. If there is any possibility of confusion, they should be preceded by the letter "C". They are always to be true unless expressly stated to be otherwise in the context.

Example:

MG C225 = Course to reach me is 225°.

5. Time and date

5.1　Time

Times are to be expressed in four figures, of which the first two denote the hour. From 00 (midnight) up to 23 (11 p.m.) and the last two denote the minutes (from 00 to 59).

The figures are preceded by:

(1) the letter "T" indicating "Local time".

Example: UR T0820＝My estimated time of arrival is at local time 0820.

(2) the letter "Z" indicating "Greenwich Mean Time(GMT)" or "Coordinated Universal Time(UTC)".

5.2　Date

Date are to be signaled by two, four, or six numerals preceded by the letter "D". The first two numerals indicate the day of the month. When they are used alone they refer to the current month.

Example: "D08" means "on the 08th in this month".

The two numerals which follow indicate the month of the year.

Example: "D1404" means "14th April".

Where necessary the year may be indicated by two further numerals.

Example: "D101018" means "10 October, 2018".

6. Speed

Speed is indicated by figures preceded by:

6.1　The letter "S" to denote speed in knots.

Example: PZ S2＝The drift of the tide is 2 knots.

6.2　The letter "V" to denote speed in kilometers per hour.

Example: BQ V300 = The speed of my aircraft in relation to the surface of the earth is 300 kilometers per hour.

7. Latitude and longitude

7.1　Latitude

Latitude is expressed by four figures preceded by the letter "L". The first two figures denote the degrees and the last two denote the minutes. The letter "N" (North) or "S" (South) follow if they are needed; however, for reasons of simplicity they may be omitted if there is no risk of confusion.

7.2　Longitude

Longitude is expressed by four or, if necessary, five figures preceded by the letter "G".

The first two (or three) figures denote the degrees and the last two denote the minutes. When the longitude is more than 99°, no confusion will normally arise if the figure indicating hundreds of degrees is omitted. However, where it is necessary to avoid confusion the five figures should be used. The letters "E" (East) or "W" (West) follow if they are needed, otherwise they may be omitted, as in the case of latitude.

Example: OT L1945NG12015E=Mine has been sighted in lat 19°45′ N, long 120°15′ E.

8. Depth

The figure(s) is(are) preceded by:

(1) the letter "M" indicating the depth in meter.

Example: OC10M=My draft forward is 10 m.

(2) the letter "F" indicating the depth in foot.

Example: QA24F=The depth at high here is 24 feet.

The expression methods of the above-mentioned elements may be summed up as follows:

A with three numerals—Azimuth or Bearing;

C with three numerals—Course;

D with two, four, or six numerals—Date;

G with four or five numerals—Longitude;

L with four numerals—Latitude;

R with one or more numerals—Distance in nautical miles;

S with one or more numerals—Speed in knots;

T with four numerals—Local time;

V with one or more numerals—Speed in kilometers per hour;

Z with four numerals—GMT or UTC.

第三课　关键通信要素的表示方法

1. 船名和地名

信号码信文中的船名和地名用字母直接拼出（中国船名和地名为汉语拼音）。

例如：KN MV New Star＝我不能拖带"新星"轮。

　　　　　　　　　　I cannot take MV New Star in tow.

　　UV Qinzhou＝我从钦州来。

　　　　　　　I am from Qinzhou.

2. 方位

方位由 A 加上三位数字表示，从 0000～3590 顺时针方向计算。除另有说明外,该方位代表真方位。

例如：LW 240＝我在方位 240° 上收到你的电信。

　　　　I receive your transmission on bearing 240°.

3. 距离

距离由 R 加上数字表示,以海里为单位。

例如：OJ A135R5＝我已用雷达测定你船的方位是 135°,距离 5 海里。

　　　　　　I have located you on my radar on bearing 135°, distance 5 nautical miles.

4. 航向

航向由 C 加上三位数字表示。除另有说明外,它通常表示真航向。

例如：MG C225＝到达我处的航向是 225°。

　　　　　Course to reach me is 225°.

5. 时间和日期

5.1　时间

时间一般由四位数字表示,其中前两位代表"时",由 00～23 表示;后两位代表"分",由 00～59 表示。

(1)当地时间,由 T 加四位数字表示。

例如：UR T0820＝预计我船的达到时间是当地时间0820。

My estimated time of arrival is at local time 0820.

（2）协调世界时（UTC）或世界时（GMT）：由 Z 加四位数字表示。

例如：UR Z0820＝预计我船的达到时间是世界时1610。

5.2 日期

由 D 加六位数字表示。六位数字中前两位数字为"日期"，中间两位为"月份"，后两位为"年份"。如果 D 后面有四位数字，那么前两位表示"日期"，后两位表示"月份"。如果只有两位数字，则表示当年本月的"日期"。

例如：D101018＝2018 年 10 月 10 日；

D1404＝4 月 14 日；

D08＝本月 8 日。

6. 速度

6.1 用 S 加数字表示，以节（kn）为单位

例如：PZ S2＝潮水流速是 2 节。

The drift of the tide is 2 knots.

6.2 用 V 加数字表示，以 km/h 为单位

例如：SQV300＝我机的对地速度为 300 km/h.

The speed of my aircraft in relation to the surface of the earth is 300 kilo-meters per hour.

7. 纬度和经度

纬度：由 L 加四位数字加 N（S）表示。前两位数字为"度"后两位为"分"。

经度：由 G 加四或五位数字加 E（W）表示。前两位或三位数字表示"度"，后两位表示"分"。

例如：OT L1945NG12015E＝在纬度 19°45′N 经度 120°15′E 已看到水雷。

Mine has been sighted in lat 1945 N long 12015 E.

8. 水深

（1）数字加 M 表示以米（meter）为单位的水深。

例如：OC10M＝我的艏吃水是 10 米。

My draft forward is 10 m.

（2）数字加 F 表示以英尺（foot）为单位的水深。

例如：QA24F＝此处高潮水深 24 英尺。

The depth at high here is 24 feet.

以上通信要素的表示方法可归结为：

A 连同三个数字——方位角或方位；

C 连同三个数字——航向；

D 连同二、四或六个数字——日期；

G 连同四或五个数字——经度；

L 连同四个数字——纬度；

R 连同一个或几个数字——以海里为单位的距离；

S 连同一个或几个数字——以节为单位的速度；

V 连同一个或几个数字——以 km/h 为单位的速度；

T 连同四个数字——当地时间；

Z 连同四个数字——世界时或协调世界时（格林尼治时）。

Lesson 4
Ship Identification

In marine communication, there are three ways to identify one another, namely: ships name, call sign and identity code.

1. Ship's name

Each ship has a name given by her owner and is registered. It does not exist that two ships have fully identical names in one country.

Besides ship's name, the names of shore stations are usually called according to their working nature, such as × port radio, × port operation/control, × agency (Penavico ×), Qinzhougang VTS and so on.

2. Call sign

Besides ship's name, each ship also has her own identity signal which is different from any other ship's. Identity signals for ships are allocated on an international basis. The identity signal may therefore indicate the nationality of a ship.

2.1 Constitution of call sign

Ship's call sign is a group of letters and numerals which is designated and given by ship's government. It usually consists of four or more than letters or combination of letter and numeral. The first one or two letter(s) present(s) the nationality of the ship. For example:

The People's Republic of China—BAA~BZZ, 3HA~3UZ;

Great Britain—GAA~GZZ, 2AA~2ZZ;

JAPAN—JAA~JSZ, 8JA~8HZ;

Republic of PANAMA—HOA~HPA, 3EA~3FZ;

Republic of LIBERIA—ELA~ELZ, 5LA~5MZ

Call sign of shore station consists of three letters or combination of letter and numeral such as the call sign of Shanghai port radio is XSG.

2.2 Purposes of call sign

Identity signal may be used in plain language or code message communication for two purposes:

(1) To speak to, or call a station

Examples:

① Juliet—Ok to eight—Foxtrot—Romeo—Bissotwo, this is pilot station, over.

② YP3LABC= I wish to communicate with vessel LABC by Morse signaling lamp.

（2）To speak of, or indicate a station

Examples：

① HY1LABC=The vessel LABC with which I have been in collision has resumed her voyage.

② Inward passage ship, this is Shanghai VTS, there is a LNG ship.

Lima—Alfa—Bravo—Charlie, ahead of you, navigate with caution, over.

3. Identity code

For convenience of identifying each other in radio communication, each ship is given a series of numerals which are different respectively—Maritime Mobile Service Identity Code （MMSI）. It consists of nine digits, i.e. MID×××××. Where MID（ maritime identification digits）is country code which has been allocated to each country by ITU. The MID for China is 412/413. × is any figure from 0 to 9.

A ship equipped with an INMARSAT mobile terminal ship earth station has also a relative MMSI. Because of the different kinds of ship earth station being fitted with an board ships have different MMSI numbers.

For a ship equipped with an INMARSAT C ship earth station, her MMSI is as follows： 4MID×××××, in which "4" represents the standard C ship earth station, "MID" is country code, China's MID is 412/413, "×××××" shows the ship earth station number.

For a ship equipped with an INMARSAT M ship earth station, her MMSI is as follows： 6MID×××××, in which "6" represents the standard M ship earth station, "MID" is country code, China's MID is 412/413, "×××××" shows the ship earth station number.

The MMSI is also programmed into the automatic communication system, such as the digital selective calling （DSC）, satellite earth station （SES）and the emergency position identified radio beacon （EPIRB）.

第四课　船舶识别

海上通信中,船舶间互相识别的途径主要有三种:船名、呼号与船舶识别码。

1. 船名

船舶的名称即船名。每一艘船舶都由其所有人赋予一个名字并登记注册。在我国,不存在两个完全相同的船名。

除了船名外,岸站通常按照他们的工作性质来命名。比如:某某无线电台、某某港调、某某代理公司、某某引航站、某某港海事处,等等。

2. 呼号

每一艘船除船名外,还必须具有它自己的呼号。呼号是在国际范围内统一分配的,所以,呼号不但能代表某一特指的船,而且还可以代表它的国籍。

2.1　呼号的组成

船舶呼号是船舶所有国政府指定给该船的一组字母和数字,通常由四个或四个以上的英文字母或字母与数字混合构成。起始的一个或两个字母通常代表船舶所属国籍。

例如:

中华人民共和国——BAA～BZZ,3HA～3UZ;

英国——GAA～GZZ,2AA～2ZZ;

日本——JAA～JSZ,8JA～8HZ;

巴拿马——HOA～HPA,3EA～3FZ;

利比里亚——ELA～ELZ,5LA～5MZ;

岸台呼号由三个字母或字母与数字混合构成。如上海无线电台呼号为:XSG。

2.2　呼号的用途

由于呼号是特指某一船舶的一组符号,它比船名更有可靠性,并且方便简洁,因此在通信中互相识别时经常使用。呼号的作用主要有两个:

(1)与某一船(台)通话或呼叫某一船(台)

例1:某引航站用明语呼叫呼号为J8FR2的船

Juliet—Ok to eight—Foxtrot—Romeo—Bissotwo,this is pilot station,over.

例2:码语信文 YP3LABC=I wish to communicate with vessel LABC by Morse signaling lamp。

(2)通信中讲到或指到某一船(台)

例1:码语信文 HY1LABC=The vessel LABC with which I have been in collision has resumed her voyage.

例 2：明语信文 Inward passenger ship, this is Shanghai VTS. There is a LNG ship. Lima—Alfa—Bravo—Charlie, ahead of you, navigate with caution, over。

3. 船舶识别码

为便于无线电通信中的相互识别,每一船舶都被赋予一组各不相同的字符——海上移动业务识别码（Maritime Mobile Service Identity Code，MMSI）,识别码由九位数字组成 MID ××××××,其中 MID 是分配给每个国家或地区的海上识别字符,又称国家码。我国的 MID 为 412/413。×代表 0~9 的任意数字。

配备海事卫星（INMARSAT）终端设备(船站)的船舶也都有相应的 MMSI,依据船舶所配备的船站种类的不同,MMSI 也有所不同:

配有 C 船站的船舶,识别码由七位组成,首位为数字"4":4MID×××××,其中,"4"表示 C 标准移动业务。"4"后面的 MID 是国家码,我国的 MID 是 412/413,"××××××"代表船舶地面站的号码。

配有 M 船站的船舶,识别码首位为数字"6":6MID×××××,其中,"6"表示 M 标准移动业务。"6"后面的 MID 是国家码,我国的 MID 是 412/413,"××××××"代表船舶地面站的号码。

船舶的海上移动业务识别码通常被编入具有自动通信功能的系统中,比如数字选择性呼叫、卫星地面站或者船舶紧急无线电示位标。

练 习 题
Exercises

🔊 一、单字母信号

1. 给出下列各句所对应的单字母信号。

    (1)我船正在后退。

    (2)你正在接近危险中。

    (3)我需要援助。

    (4)我正在走锚。

    (5)我正在向左转向。

    (6)我船没有染疫,请发进口检疫证。

    (7)请让开我,我正在进行对拖作业。

    (8)请让开我,我操纵困难。

    (9)我船上有引航员。

    (10)我需要医疗援助。

2. 写出下列单字母信号旗的意义。

B	D	N	H
C	M	Z	Y
I	F	X	T

📖 二、通用部分

1. 利用《国际信号规则》,将下列国际信号码译成明语。

    (1) NJ 3EAD 10

    (2) OA 7M

    (3) OM BPCA A008 R10

    (4) UR Hong Kong T1530

    (5) Wv120

    (6) BT1T1300

    (7) VD Lian yun gang

（8）XFL2130NG12230E

（9）FE TO420

（10）FLC120

（11）CP BOBT

（12）PR2 JAPT

（13）DD1T1140

（14）VML1330NG12030EC300S10

（15）AYC085S4

（16）BD2182

（17）BQV100

（18）EQZ1000

（19）DTT0030L2050NG14010E

（20）CG1JABC

（21）VH200

（22）CH KCBA Island A010 R6

（23）ZR Shanghai

（24）ZW1T0830

（25）PUT1530

（26）MGC330

（27）SAT0530

（28）RD12Z0230

（29）SZ29

（30）HW4 3EHP

（31）EBA130R5

（32）IKS10

（33）RV Yokohama

（34）DY JABC L1005N G11510W

（35）NU18F

2. **将下列明语变成国际信号码。**

（1）当地时间 1230,浅滩的水深 2.5 米。

（2）引航船大概在你船方位 135°处。

（3）你是从哪里驶来的?

（4）我在浅水区,请指引我如何航行。

（5）预计我船到达纽约是当地时间 0430。

（6）长江口高潮水深 16 米。

（7）直升机于当地时间 1200 前往你处救你。

（8）我的位置是推算船位。

（9）在你前进的西北方向有渔具。

（10）你应尽力设法拖带"幸运"轮。

（11）损坏能在 24 小时内修理好。

（12）我在北纬 26° 26′,东经 11°20′处,船后部搁浅。

（13）在你前进的西南方向有渔具。

（14）我不能用莫尔斯信号灯通信。

（15）我已用雷达测定你船的方位是 300°,距离 5 海里。

（16）我的机器将在当地时间 1800 准备好。

（17）引航船大概在你船方位 030°处。

（18）我准备用无线电报在 500 kHz 频率上进行通信。

（19）你应铺泊在距我船 2 海里、方位 150°处进行检疫。

（20）预计风暴(风力 10 级或 10 级以上)将从东南方向袭来。

（21）长江口高潮水深是 15 米。

（22）我是从新加坡(Singapore)来的。

（23）我现在的位置是北纬 36° 36′,东经 123° 30′,航速 14 节。

（24）我正把航向改到 002°。

（25）我现在的航速是 8 节。

（26）预计我船到达曼谷的时间是地方时 1530。

（27）在世界时 0800 时该浅滩的水深为 5 英尺。

（28）我在浅水区,请指引我如何航行。

（29）I am in distress and require immediate assistance.

（30）I am proceeding to your assistance.

（31）You should make a lee for the boat/raft.

（32）I cannot proceed to the rescue owing to weather. You should do all you can.

（33）I have received damage to side plate above water.

（34）Can you get the fire under control without assistance?

（35）I require fire-fighting appliances.

（36）A tug with pilot is coming to you.

（37）When can I enter the canal?

（38）You should keep in the center of the channel/fairway.

（39）What course should I steer?

（40）Navigation is possible only with tug assistance.

（41）You should navigate with caution. There are nets with a boy in this area.

（42）What is your ballast draught?

（43）You should extinguish all the lights except the navigation light.

（44）Sea is too rough, and pilot boat cannot get off to you.

（45）You should wait outside the harbour.

（46）What wind direction is expected in my area?

（47）Your signal has been received but not understood.

（48）I am proceeding to the position of accident at full speed. Expected to arrive at time 1330 Local.

（49）What is the forecast visibility in my area?

（50）What is the name or identity signal of your vessel.

（51）You should keep on my starboard side.

（52）My engines are going ahead.

（53）You can enter the canal at time 1500.

（54）What is the course to reach you?

（55）You should maintain your present course.

（56）Navigation is possible only with pilot assistance.

（57）You should change your anchorage/berth. It is not safe.

（58）What is your maximum draft?

（59）You should pass astern of me.

（60）You should come alongside my starboard side.

（61）I am dragging my anchor.

（62）When will your engines be ready?

（63）Keep clear of me. I am manoeuvring with difficult.

（64）Tropical storm is approaching. You should take appropriate precautions.

（65）I am carrying out exercises. Please keep clear of me.

（66）I am fumigating my vessel. No one is allowed on board.

（67）I can only proceed at slow speed.

（68）What is your estimated time of arrival at Shanghai?

（69）Thank you very much for your cooperation. I wish you have a pleasant voyage.

（70）Do you have latest information of the tropical storm?

（71）What are your present position, course and speed?

（72）Vessel ABCD is stopped in thick fog.

（73）I am unable to proceed under my own power.

（74）I am ready to get under way.

（75）You should maintain where you are.

（76）What is the speed of your aircraft in relation to the surface of the earth?

（77）Do not pass too close to me.

（78）Leak is beyond the capacity of my pumps.

三、医疗部分

1. 将下列明语译成三个字母组成的国际信号码。

（1）病人失去知觉。

（2）我正按照处方指导进行治疗。

（3）治疗无效。

（4）我请求你安排住院。

（5）病人总体情况是严重的。

（6）我请求紧急医疗指导。

（7）在半小时内给我回信,如病情恶化请提前报告。

（8）病人脸及胸中部严重烧伤。

（9）到下一港口,病人应请医生诊治。

（10）尽可能给病人多饮水,但不要引起呕吐。

2. 将你收到的下列国际信号码译成明语（中文）

（1）MAK25 MAM2 MBP MCU MCM MBR39 MBX105 MCE30

　　MDFO9 MBGO9 MDQ MIC MIL MAT18 MAU18 MQE68

（2）MQT MRJ MSL MVK18 MUD MUH MVB MVC MVU MVQ

3. 将下列病例编成国际信号码

（1）我有一个女性病人,45 岁,5 天前突然发病,病人昏迷,打寒战,脉搏微弱、不规则,呼吸局促,病人左侧胸部疼痛,呼吸时疼痛加剧。病人有严重咳嗽,痰不带血。已给患者注射青霉素,无效。病人经药物治疗已有 24 小时,我的初步诊断是肺炎。我请求紧急医疗指导。

（2）我有一个男性病人,31 岁,由于从舱盖上坠落受伤,病人左小腿粉碎性骨折,出血不止,现好像处于休克状态。病人脉搏加快,体温上升,总体情况在恶化。我急需一架直升机来接走伤病员。

Chapter 3
Communication of Visual Signaling and Sound Signaling

第三章
视觉信号与声响信号通信

Lesson 1
Flag Signaling

Flag signaling is a slow method of communication over short distances in clear weather during the daylight hours, whereby various combination of brightly coloured flags and pennants are hoisted to send message, so it is also called flag hoist signaling.

1. International signal flag

A full set of international signal flags consists of 26 alphabetical flags from A to Z, ten numeral pendants from 0 to 9, plus three substitutes (the first substitute, the second substitute, the third substitute) and one answering pendant, 40 pieces in total.

1.1 Specifications of international signal flags

No.	Rectangular		Burgee		Triangular		Pendants		
	Long (cm)	Width (cm)	Long (cm)	Width (cm)	Long (cm)	Width (cm)	Long (cm)	Width (cm)	
1	210	180	240	180	270	180	450	130	30
2	135	115	160	115	180	115	250	90	20
S2	103	90	120	90	135	90	190	60	15
3	70	60	80	60	90	60	120	38	10
4	50	35	63	35	70	35	75	25	6

1.2 Usage of international signal flags

(1) The use of letter flags

Each piece of letter flag is a single-letter signal. It may be used separately or by combination with other letter or numeral flags, and forming variable signal code groups.

(2) The use of numeral flags

Each piece of numeral flag denotes a figure. The decimal point in numerals is indicated by answering pendant.

(3) The use of answering pendant

① To indicate "understanding";

On the first seeing a signal, the receiving station should hoist the Answering Pendant at the dip as an indication to the transmitting station that she has noticed the signal. The receiving station then reads the flags and when understood the meanings of signal, hoists the Answering

Pendant close up as an acknowledgement.

② To indicate that the signal is completed;

③ To indicate a decimal point in numbers, the answering pendant when used as a decimal point is to be disregarded in determining which substitute to use;

④ When a ship of war wishes to communicate with a merchant vessel, she will hoist the Answering Pendant in a conspicuous position, and keep it flying during the whole of the time the signal is being made.

（4）The use of substitutes

Among the international signal flags there are three substitute flags. They are the First Substitute and the Second Substitute, the Third Substitute.

The use of substitutes is to enable the same signal flag, either alphabetical flag or numeral pennant, to be repeated one or more times in the same group, in case only one set of flags are carried on board.

The First Substitute always repeats the uppermost signal flag of that class of flags which immediately precedes the substitute. The Second Substitute always repeats the second and the Third Substitute repeats the third signal flag, counting from the top of that class of flags which immediately precedes them. No substitute can ever be used more than once in the same group. The Answering Pennant when used as a decimal point is to be disregarded in determining which substitute to use. Class is defined as either an alphabetical flag or a numeral pennant; in other words a letter or a figure.

The following examples will explain the use of substitutes:

Code	V H V	1100
Usage	V H First substitute	1 First substitute 0 Third substitute
Code	L2330	1.33
Usage	L 2 3 Second substitute 0	1 Answering pendant 3 Second substitute

2. Some terms associated with flag hoist signaling

The following are some general terms associated with flag hoist signaling.

（1）Group

Group denotes one or more continuous letter and/or numeral which together compose a signal.

（2）A hoist

A hoist consists of one or more groups displayed from a single halyard.

（3）At the dip

A hoist or signal is said to be at the dip when it is hoisted about half of the full extent of the halyards.

（4）Close up

A hoist or signal is said to be close up when it is hoisted to the full extent of the halyards.

（5）Tackline

Tackline is a length of halyard about 2 m（6 ft.）long, used to separate each group flags.

3. Methods of flag signaling

3.1　Order of displaying and reading for signal flags（See Fig. 3-1）

（1）As a general rule only one hoist should be shown at a time. Each hoist or group of hoists should be kept flying until it has been answered by receiving station. When more groups than one are shown on the same halyard, they must be separated by a tackline. The transmitting station should always hoist the signal where it can be most easily seen by the receiving station, that is, in such a position that the flags will blow out clear and be free from smoke.

（2）When two or more flag hoists are shown at a time, they should be read in the following orders accordingly.

① From starboard to port: When more hoists than one are shown at the port and starboard masthead yardarms of transmitting ship at a time, the order to transmit and read them is first starboard yardarm and then port yardarm.

② From outboard to inboard: When more hoists than one are displayed at the same yardarm, they should be read from outboard to inboard.

③ From top to bottom: When more groups than one are shown at the same hoist, they should be read from top to bottom.

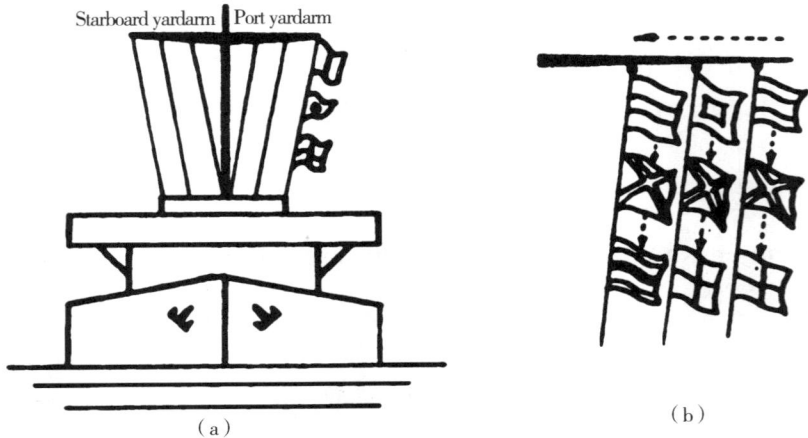

Fig. 3-1　Displaying and reading sequence of signal flags

3.2 Procedure of flag signaling

（1）Calling

① When addressing all stations within visual signaling distances, the transmitting station may directly display the signal which denotes the message. It is not necessary for the dentity signal of receiving station(s) to be hoisted, but the group CQ [Procedure signal means call for unknown station(s) or general call to all stations.] may be hoisted at the position of the first hoist.

② When addressing an indicated station, first the identity signal of the station addressed is to be hoisted and then the message successively. The identity signal of the station addressed can also be hoisted with the message, such as YP2LABC (I wish to communicate with LABC by loud hailer can be shown at the same time), the first hoist is LABC and the second one is YP2.

③ When addressing an unknown station, the group VF (You should hoist your identity signal) or CS [What is the name or identity signal of your vessel (or station)] should be hoisted first; at the same time the station will hoist its own identity signal.

④ When more than two ships are nearby and the above-said signals fail, the group YQ (I wish to communicate by… with vessel bearing… from me) may be used.

（2）Sending and answering signals

The transmitting station may display one hoist or more hoists than one at a time. All stations to which signals are addressed or which are indicated in signals are to hoist the Answering Pennant at the dip as soon as they see each hoist and close up immediately when they understand it; it is to be lowered to the dip position as soon as the hoist is hauled down by the transmitting station, being hoisted close up again as soon as the next hoist is understood.

If the receiving station cannot clearly distinguish the signal made to it, it is to keep the Answering Pennant at the dip. If it can distinguish the signal but cannot understand the meaning of it, it can hoist the following signals:

ZQ = Your signal appears incorrectly coded, you should check and repeat the whole.

ZL = Your signal has been received, but not understood.

When the signal being hoisted by the transmitting station is incorrect and the receiving station has answered it, the following signal should be hoisted:

ZP = My last signal was incorrect. I will repeat it correctly. If the receiving station has not yet answered it, the transmitting station hauls down the incorrect signal and repeat it correctly.

If any signal contains names or names of places in the text, they should be spelt out by alphabetical flags. If necessary, the following signal may be used for clarification before signaling:

YZ = The words which follow are in plain language.

（3）Ending of signaling

The transmitting station is to hoist the Answering Pendant singly after the last hoist of the signal to indicate that the signaling is completed. The receiving station is to answer this in a similar manner to all other hoists.

3.3 General notes on transmission

Clarity and exactness in the transmission of a message are essential. Too rapid sending as

well as too slow sending must be avoided. Choose the best background for transmitting to fly the flag clear of obstructions to eliminate the necessity for repetition. Avoid the use of the system when the wind and weather make it unsatisfactory.

4. Flag etiquette

4.1　Flag hoisting when entering and leaving harbour

（1）When entering or leaving harbour if there is enough light for the ensign to be recognized, the vessel should hoist the national ensign at the ensign staff on the taffrail. When aboard it is required to hoist the ensign of the country visited at the masthead. Particular attention should be devoted to exhibiting the flag correctly. Avoid the ensign being upside down. Nowadays the courtesy ensign is flown from the starboard yardarm out of respect for the host nation.

（2）Hoist ship's signal letters （call sign flag） in harbour.

（3）When entering a foreign country or when entering your own country after visiting a foreign country, quarantine flag "Q" is to be displayed to indicate, "My vessel is healthy and I request free pratique". When passing the quarantining, lower the flag "Q".

（4）If the pilot will be required to guide the vessel into harbour, hoist the flag "G". When the pilot comes aboard, the flag "G" should be replaced by the flag "H".

（5）Hoist other flags according to the other international or local regulations; e.g. if ship is carrying dangerous cargoes, the flag "B" should be exhibited at the masthead.

4.2　Dressing vessel

Sometimes it is required to dress a vessel on ceremonial occasions when in port or in harbour; e.g. on a national day. This is carried out by hoisting masthead flags or by running flags "rainbow fashion". In the latter case, on board a two-masted vessel, the line should run from stem to foremast head, then to mainmast head and down to taffrail. On a single-masted vessel, the line should run from stem to mainmast, then to taffrail.

Attention should be paid particularly to the arrangement of flags so that when flying they will have a symmetrical appearance. The flags should be evenly spaced with the same number of square flags between pendants. Because there are only two burgees （letter flag "A" and "B"） in the International Code, the best position for them is at each end of the line.

Since the appearance of a string of flags is often spoilt by sagging in the middle, the fitting dressing lines may be used to prevent such sagging. These lines may be made of manila, nylon.

The ensign should be hoisted in its proper place. Ensigns are not to be used in dressing lines. When in foreign ports, and it is required to dress ship on a single-masted vessel, the ensign of the country visited should be placed on the top of the masthead. On a two-masted vessel the ensign of the country visited is to be flown at the fore masthead and the owners ensign is to be flown at the main masthead.

When underway, one need not dress "rainbow fashion", but fly a masthead ensign instead.

4.3   Salute by dipping of ensign

In order to salute to your own warships, foreign friendly warships and merchant vessels when meeting, dipping of ensign may be carried out as follows:

(1) Lower the ensign from the "close up" to the "dip" slowly;

(2) Keep the halyards taut;

(3) Hoist the ensign to the "close up" slowly when the salute has been acknowledged.

When the ensign is at half-mast (e. g. on days of national mourning), and if it is necessary to use the ensign for saluting or returning a salute, first hoist the flag to the "close up" position, and keep it at this position for a moment, and then lower to half-mast.

4.4   Mourning by flying ensign at half-mast

At the time of national mourning, the ensign should be flown at half-mast.

(1) To half-mast a flag

Hoist the ensign to "close up" position, if not previously hoisted; and then lower it to half-mast slowly.

(2) To lower a flag from half-mast

Hoist to the "close up" and then lower the ensign slowly.

第一课　旗号通信

旗号通信是指在能见度良好的白天,在视觉范围内使用信号旗传递信息的通信方式。

1. 国际信号旗

一套国际信号旗(International Signal Flag)共40面(见封底)。其中:

字母旗（Alphabetical Flag）A~Z 共26面;

数字旗（Numeral Pendant）0~9 共10面;

代替旗（Substitutes）代一、代二、代三共三面。

回答旗（Answering Pendent）1面;

1.1　国际信号旗的规格

国际信号旗的规格共5种,见下表:

号数	长方旗		燕尾旗		三角旗		梯形旗		
	长（cm）	宽（cm）	长（cm）	宽（cm）	长（cm）	宽（cm）	长（cm）	宽（cm）	
								大	小
1	210	180	240	180	270	180	450	130	30
2	135	115	160	115	180	115	250	90	20
小2	103	90	120	90	135	90	190	60	15
3	70	60	80	60	90	60	120	38	10
4	50	35	63	35	70	35	75	25	6

1.2　国际信号旗的用法

（1）字母旗

每面字母旗是一个单字母信号旗,既可单独使用,也可与其他字母旗或数字旗联合使用,组成各种信号码。

（2）数字旗

每面表示一个数字,数字中的小数点由"回答旗"表示。

（3）回答旗

①在旗号通信过程中,其表示理解的信号。当受信台看见发信台的每一挂信号挂出时,应把回答旗悬挂在拉一半的位置,并在了解其意义时,立即拉到顶;

②可用作整个通信结束的信号;

③在数字组中,可作为小数点,但不作为一面旗计算,与决定使用那一面代旗无关;

④军用船舶如果希望与商船通信,应当在明显的位置悬挂回答旗,并在整个通信期间,该旗始终悬挂。

（4）代替旗

当船上只有一套信号旗时，代替旗可以使一面旗在同一组旗号中重复一次或多次。但在同一组旗号中任何一面代替旗的使用不得超过一次。其中：

①代一旗是代替在同一组中，在它前面的同类旗中第一面旗；

②代二旗是代替在同一组中，在它前面的同类旗中第二面旗；

③代三旗是代替在同一组中，在它前面的同类旗中第三面旗；

④回答旗用作小数点时与决定使用哪一面代替旗无关。

代替旗的用法如下：

信号码	V H V	1100	L2330	1.33
旗号的挂法 （由上至下）	V 旗 H 旗 代一旗	1 旗 代一旗 0 旗 代三旗	L 旗 2 旗 3 旗 代二旗 0 旗	1 旗 回答旗 3 旗 代二旗

2. 旗号通信中的术语

组（group）：由一面或数面字母或数字旗组成的旗号。

挂（hoist）：一组或几组旗号挂在一根旗绳上为一挂。

拉一半（at the dip）：一挂或一面旗悬挂在桅杆旗绳全长一半左右的位置，称为"拉一半"，也称"半扬"。

拉到顶（close up）：一挂或一面旗悬挂在桅杆旗绳顶端，称为"拉到顶"，也称"全扬"。

隔绳（tackline）：旗绳中约 2 米长的一段距离，用来隔开同一挂旗号中不同的组。

3. 旗号通信方法

3.1 旗号的悬挂与收读顺序（见图 3-1）

（1）发信船一次只升一挂旗号时，按信文内容的信号码组先后顺序，逐次悬挂，每一挂旗号一定要待收信船以"回答旗"表示信文收到后才能降下，直至通信完毕。

（2）发信船一次将信文内容所含的多挂旗号全部挂出时，收信船应按下列次序收读，待全部收读后再予以回答。

①先右后左：当多挂旗号悬挂在发信船信号的左、右横桁时，悬挂及收读的顺序为先右横桁、后左横桁；

②先外后内：对同一横桁上的多挂旗号应先读外侧、后读内侧；

③先上后下：对同一挂上的多组旗号，应从上面的旗号读起。

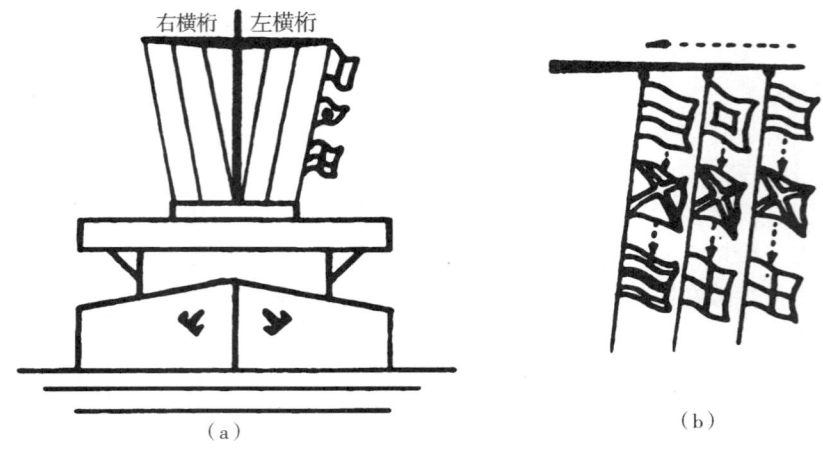

图 3-1 旗号的悬挂与收读顺序

3.2 旗号通信程序

（1）呼叫

当呼叫附近所有可以看到信号的船时，发信船可直接挂出表示信文内容的旗号，无需悬挂收信船的呼号，亦可在第一挂旗的位置挂出 CQ。

当呼叫某一指明的船（台）时，应先挂出收信船（台）的呼号，然后依次悬挂信文内容，也可将呼号与信文内容一起悬挂。例如发送信文：YP2LABC（我希望用扬声器与 LABC 船通信）时，可同时显示：第一挂 LABC 旗，第二挂 YP2 旗。

呼叫某一不知名的船（台）时，应显示下列旗号之一并同时挂出本船的呼号。

VF＝你应该挂出你的呼号。（You should hoist your identity signal.）

CS＝你船的名称或呼号是什么？（What is the name or identity signal of your vessel?）

（2）信文发送与回答

当发信船（台）一次一挂发送信文时，收信船（台）应按顺序对每一挂旗号逐次予以回答：将回答旗置于拉一半的位置，表示已"看到对方旗号"。待了解其意义时，将回答旗拉到顶，表示这一挂已"收到"。如此反复，直至全部收妥。

当发信船（台）一次多挂发送信文时，收信船（台）应将回答旗置于拉一半的位置，表示已"看到信号"。待了解全部旗号的意义后，将回答旗拉到顶，表示全部已"收妥"。

如果收信船（台）不能清楚辨认发送给它的信号，则应将回答旗保持在拉一半的位置。

如果能辨认信号但不明白其意义，可挂出下列旗号：

ZQ＝你的信文似乎有错，你应全部核对并重发。（Your signal appears incorrectly coded, you should check and repeat the whole.）

ZL＝你的信文已收到，但不明白。（Your signal has bean received, but not understood.）

当发信船（台）发现挂出的信号有错误且对方已回答表示看到了信号时，应挂出"ZP"表示"已挂出的最后信号有错误，我将重发"。如果对方尚未回答，则发信船（台）将错误的旗号降下重发即可。

（3）结束通信

发信船（台）降下最后一挂旗号后，单独挂出回答旗，表示通信终结；收信船（台）将回答旗拉到顶,表示全部信文收妥;各自降下回答旗,通信结束。

4. 船舶挂旗常识

船舶所应悬挂的旗类主要有国旗(包括船旗国国旗及各港口国国旗)、信号旗及其他旗类(如公司旗等)。船舶在不同的环境下挂旗应遵循不同的习惯或规定。

4.1　国旗的悬挂

国旗代表国家主权和尊严,各国对国旗的悬挂均有各自的要求。中国籍船舶及进入中国内水、港口、锚地的外国籍船舶都应遵守我国政府的船舶升降国旗管理办法,其中规定:

(1) 悬挂时间

每日日出升、日落降,恶劣天气除外。船舶在航行、锚泊时,由4点至8点值班的水手负责升降;靠泊时则由相应班次水手负责。

(2) 悬挂位置

本国籍船挂于船尾旗杆上。无船尾旗杆的挂于驾驶台信号杆顶部或右横桁。外国籍船悬挂中国国旗时,应悬挂于前桅或驾驶台信号杆顶部或右横桁。当中国国旗与其他旗帜同时悬挂于船舶右横桁时,中国国旗应悬挂于最外侧。

(3) 礼仪

航行中与军舰相遇,需要时,可以使用国旗表示礼仪。其方法是当彼此接近正横时,致敬方将国旗降至一半高度表示敬意;受礼方同样将国旗降至一半高度并随即拉到顶部表示回礼,致敬方将国旗拉到顶,相互致敬结束。

船舶在港停泊时,凡遇到国内重大节日或港口国的节日,根据指示可日间(一般为上午8时至日落)悬挂满旗表示庆祝。满旗悬挂的方法应从船首旗杆经桅顶部直至船尾旗杆,并在桅顶部悬挂国旗。满旗的旗帜应按两面字母旗加一面数字旗(或代旗、回答旗)的顺序连接起来使用。

船舶非经许可不得将中国国旗下半旗。在我国遇有需要下半旗志哀的情况时,海事机构应通知或通过船舶代理人、所有人通知船舶下半旗。外籍船舶根据船旗国的规定需将船旗国国旗下半旗时,应向海事机构报告。

(4) 船舶悬挂的中国旗应当整洁,不得破损、污损、褪色或者不合规格,不得倒挂。

4.2　信号旗类的悬挂

(1) 及时升降

船舶在不同的情况下应及时升降相应的信号旗。例如进行油类作业时,船舶应及时悬挂"B"字旗,表示本船还在装、卸或载运危险物。作业结束时立即降下。悬挂"G"字旗表示本船需要引航员,一旦引航员登轮后立即降下"G"字旗,升起"H"字旗,表示本船上有引航员。

(2) 正确悬挂

不同的港口国或不同的抵达港对船舶应悬挂的信号旗有不同的要求。船舶在进入这些水域之前或当时,应该通过相应航海图书资料或者咨询当地船舶代理公司了解这方面的有关规定以便正确悬挂。例如,船舶进出我国港口时一般应悬挂船名旗,而进靠上海港时还应悬挂泊位旗;通过日本关门海峡的报告线时应悬挂信号旗"KPU"或"KPM"等。

Lesson 2
Flashing Light Signaling

Light signaling is visual communication by flashing light in Morse code. In the Morse code each letter of the alphabet is represented by dot or dash or a combination of them. Letters are produced in Morse signaling by switching the lamp on and off. In practice this is easier to use than sound signals.

At sea, light signaling is the official and the most suitable method for transmitting visual morse messages.

1. Morse code

The Morse code uses dot and dash as basic elements, each of letters or numerals is composed of single dot and dash or a combination of them.

The following ratios are to be observed between dot, dash, letter, word or group when transmitting:

dot = 1 unit;

dash = 3 units;

interval between flashes = 1 unit;

interval between letters = 3 units;

interval between word or group = 7 units.

Naturally the spaces and lengths of dots and dashes vary according to the speed of sending, but they are invariably the same in proportion to the rate. The standard rate of sending in light signaling is 40 letters per minute.

Morse code—letters, numerals:

Letter	Code	Letter	Code	Letter	Code	Numeral	Code
A	• —	K	— • —	U	• • —	0	— — — — —
B	— • • •	L	• — • •	V	• • • —	1	• — — — —
C	— • — •	M	— —	W	• — —	2	• • — — —
D	— • •	N	— •	X	— • • —	3	• • • — —
E	•	O	— — —	Y	— • — —	4	• • • • —
F	• • — •	P	• — — •	Z	— — • •	5	• • • • •
G	— — •	Q	— — • —			6	— • • • •
H	• • • •	R	• — —			7	— — • • •
I	• •	S	• • •			8	— — — • •
J	• — — —	T	—			9	— — — — •

2. Procedure signals

2.1　Procedure signals

Procedure signals	Meaning	Symbol
‾‾‾‾‾ AA AA...	call for unknown station or general call	• — 　 • — 　 • —
‾‾‾‾‾ TTTTT...	answering signal	— 　— 　— 　— 　— 　—
DE	from(— this is)	— • • 　 •
T	word or group received	—
‾‾‾‾‾ EEEEEE...	erase signal	• 　 • 　 • 　 • 　 • 　 •
RPT	repeat signal	• — • 　 • — — • 　 —
RPT AA	repeat all after...	• — • 　 • — — • 　 — 　 • — 　 • —
RPT AS	repeat all before...	• — • 　 • — — • 　 — 　 • — 　— • • •
RPT WA	repeat word or group after...	• — • 　 • — — • 　 — 　 • — 　 • —
RPT WB	repeat word or group before...	• — • 　 • — — • 　 — 　 • — — 　 — • • •
RPT BN	repeat all between... and...	• — • 　 • — — • 　 — 　— • • • 　 — •
‾‾‾ AS	waiting signal or period	• — 　 • • •
‾‾‾ AR	ending signal or end of transmission or signal	• — 　 • — •
R	received or I have received your last signal	• — •
RQ	interrogative signal	• — • 　 — — • —
C	affirmative signal (Yes)	— • — •
N	negative signal (No)	— •

2.2　The use of procedure signals

（1）The General call signal（or call for unknown station）"‾‾‾‾‾‾‾‾‾AA AA AA" etc., is made to attract attention when wishing to signal to all stations within visual signaling distance or to a station whose name or identity signal is not known. The call is continued until the station addressed answers.

（2）The Answering signal "‾‾‾‾‾TTTTTT" etc., is made to answer the call and it is to be continued until the transmitting station ceases to make the call. The transmission starts with the "DE" followed by the name or identity signal of the transmitting station.

(3) The letter "T" is used to indicate the receipt of each word or group.

(4) The Erase signal "EEEEEE" etc., is used to indicate that the last group or word was signaled incorrectly. It is to be answered with the erase signal. When answered, the transmitting station will repeat the last group or word which was correctly signaled and then proceed with the remainder of the transmission.

(5) The Repeat signal "RPT" is to be used as follows:

①by the transmitting station to indicate that it is going to repeat ("I repeat"). If such a repetition does not follow immediately after "RPT", the signal should be interpreted as a request to the receiving station to repeat the signal received ("Repeat what you have received").

②by the receiving station to request for a repetition of the signal transmitted ("Repeat what you have sent").

③The Special Repetition signals "AA", "AB", "WA", "WB" and "BN" are made by the receiving station as appropriate. In each case they are made immediately after the repeat signal "RPT".

Examples:

"RPT AB KL" = "Repeat all before group KL".

"RPT BN 6 'boats' 'survivors' " = "Repeat all between words 'boats' and 'survivors' ".

If a signal is not understood, or, when decoded, it is not intelligible, the repeat signal is not used. The receiving station must then make the appropriate signal from the Code, e. g. "Your signal has been received but not understood".

(6) A correctly received repetition is acknowledged by the signal "OK". The same signal may be used as an affirmative answer to a question ("It is correct").

(7) The Ending signal "AR" is used in all cases to indicate the end of a signal or the end of the transmission. The receiving station answers with the signal "R" = "Received" or "I have received your last signal".

(8) The transmitting station makes the signal "CS" when requesting the name or identity signal of the receiving station.

(9) The Waiting signal or Period signal "AS" is to be used as follows:

The following are some general terms associated with flag hoist signaling.

①When made independently or after the end of a signal it indicates that the other station must wait for further communication (waiting signal).

②When it is inserted between groups it serves to separate them (period signal) to avoid confusion.

(10) The signal "C" should be used to indicate an affirmative statement or an affirmative reply to an interrogative signal; the signal "RQ" should be used to indicate a question. For a negative reply to an interrogative or for a negative statement, the signal "N" should be used in visual or sound signaling and the signal "NO" should be used for voice or radio transmission.

（11）When the signals "N" or "NO", and "RQ" are used to change an affirmative signal into a negative statement or into a question, respectively, they should be transmitted after the main signal.

Examples：

"CY N "（or "NO" as appropriate）= "Boat（s）is（are）not coming to you."

"CW RQ" = "Is boat/raft on board ?"

Notes：

（1）The signals "C", "N "or "NO", and "RQ" cannot be used in conjunction with single-letter signals.

（2）When these signals are used by voice transmission the letters should be pronounced in accordance with the letter-spelling table, with the exception of "NO" which in voice transmission should be pronounced as "NO".

3. Other uses of Morse symbols

Morse symbol can not only be used in light communication, but also widely used in terrestrial navigation. At important turning points or other important marks in busy waterways, in order to facilitate the identification of these marks by naked eyes as well as radar by ship officers, captains and pilots, some lights of aids to navigation in different regions and racons are displayed in Morse symbols. It is very important for navigation safety that ship officers can identify these marks accurately and timely. How to identify these marks accurately and timely depends on whether he/she knows Morse symbols.

For example, HO light buoy in Dalian port is displayed with both light and racon.

As shown in Chinese charts：莫（K）黄 12 s 雷康（C）.

As shown in Admiralty charts：Mo（K）Y 12 s Racon （C）.

The letters in brackets are displayed in Morse symbols. When a ship is navigating within nearby waters, HO light buoy can be identified by the above two means （light and racon）. This light buoy is an important turning point for ships entering and leaving Dalian port.

第二课　灯光通信

灯光通信(Flashing Light Signaling):借助灯光发送莫尔斯码进行的明语或码语信文通信。

1. 莫尔斯符号

莫尔斯符号(Morse symbols)以点(●)和划(——)为基本要素,单独或组合使用,构成字母或数字。

点(●)为1个时间单位;划(——)为3个时间单位;

每两闪之间的间隔为1个时间单位;

字符间的间隔为3个时间单位;

字与字、组与组之间的间隔为7个时间单位。

字母与数字的莫尔斯符号如下:

字母	莫尔斯符号	字母	莫尔斯符号	字母	莫尔斯符号	数字	莫尔斯符号
A	● ——	K	—— ● ——	U	● ● ——	0	—— —— —— —— ——
B	—— ● ● ●	L	● —— ● ●	V	● ● ● ——	1	● —— —— —— ——
C	—— ● —— ●	M	—— ——	W	● —— ——	2	● ● —— —— ——
D	—— ● ●	N	—— ●	X	—— ● ● ——	3	● ● ● —— ——
E	●	O	—— —— ——	Y	—— ● —— ——	4	● ● ● ● ——
F	● ● —— ●	P	● —— —— ●	Z	—— —— ● ●	5	● ● ● ● ●
G	—— —— ●	Q	—— —— ● ——			6	—— ● ● ● ●
H	● ● ● ●	R	● —— ●			7	—— —— ● ● ●
I	● ●	S	● ● ●			8	—— —— —— ● ●
J	● —— —— ——	T	——			9	—— —— —— —— ●

2. 通信程序信号

2.1　程序信号

控制通信程序的莫尔斯符号有以下符号:

程序信号	意　义	符　号
A̅A̅A̅A̅...	呼叫信号	•　—　　•　—　　•　—
T̅T̅T̅T̅T̅...	回答信号	—　　—　　—　　—　　—
DE	识别信号(= This is)	—　•　•　　•
T	收到信号	—
E̅E̅E̅E̅E̅E̅...	撤销信号	•　•　•　•　•　•　•　•
RPT	重发信号	•　—　•　　•　—　•　　•　—
RPT AA	重发某字、组后面的全部	•　—　•　　•　—　•　　•　—　•　—　•
RPT AS	重发某字、组前面的全部	•　—　•　　•　—　•　—　　•　—　•　—　•
RPT WA	重发某字、组后面的一字(组)	•　—　•　　•　—　•　—　　•　—　　•　—
RPT WB	重发某字、组前面的一字(组)	•　—　•　　•　—　•　—　　•　—　　—　•　•　•
RPT BN	重发某字、组与某字、组间的全部	•　—　•　　•　—　•　—　　—　•　•　•　　—　•
A̅S̅	等待信号、句号信号	•　—　　•　•　•
A̅R̅	结束信号	•　—　　•　—　•
R	信文收到信号	•　—　•
RQ	疑问信号	•　—　•　　—　•　—　•
C	肯定信号(Yes)	—　•　—　•
N	否定信号(No)	—　•

2.2　通信信号使用说明

（1）普遍呼叫信号(或者对不知名台的呼叫)"A̅A̅A̅A̅A̅A̅"等,用于发信台希望与在信号视距内的所有台或不知名称或呼号的台通信时引起它们的注意。这种呼叫应不断地发送直到收信台回答时为止。

（2）回答信号"T̅T̅T̅T̅T̅"用于回答呼叫,应不断地发送直到发信台停止呼叫。通信是以信号"DE"开始,后面接着发信台的名称或呼号。

（3）字母"T"是用于表示收到每个字或组。

（4）撤销信号" E̅E̅E̅E̅E̅E̅"用于表示最后一组或字发错。收信台也用撤销信号给以回答。发信台在接到回答后,应重发经过改正的最后一个字或组,然后继续发送下面的报文。

（5）重发信号"RPT"用法如下

①由发信台发出:表示将要重发（"我重发"）。如果发信台在发出"RPT"之后没有紧接

着重发任何信号,这就表示要求收信台复诵收到的信号("复诵你所收到的信号")。

②由收信台发出:表示要求重发已发送的信号("请重发你所发送的信号")。

③专门的重发信号"A""AB""WA""WB"和"BN"都是由收信台发送的,这些信号都应紧接在重发信号"RPT"的后面。

例如:

RPT AB KL="'KL'组以前的全部重发。"

RPT BN "boats" "survivors" =在"boats"和"survivors"之间的全部重发。

④如果信号不明白或译出的信号码不能理解,在此情况下,重发信号是不适用的。收信台应从信号码中找出适当的信号。例如"你的信号已收到,但不明白。"

(6)正确地收到重发的字或组,以信号"OK"表示。这一信号也可以用作肯定地回答一个问题("对的")。

(7)终结信号"$\overline{AR}$"是用于表示信号完结或通信完结。收信台的回答用信号"R"="收到了"或"我已收到你最后的信号"。

(8)发信台在询问收信台的名称或呼号时,应发出信号"CS"。

(9)等候信号或句号信号"$\overline{AS}$"用法如下:

①单独发送或在一个信号末尾发送,表示要求对方台不要终止联系,等待继续通信(等候信号);

②插在组与组之间,是表示隔开它们(句号信号),以免混淆。

(10)信号"C"用于表示肯定的声明或者对询问信号的肯定回答。信号"RQ"用于表示疑问。对询问信号的否定回答或否定声明,在视觉或声号通信中用信号"N"表示,在喊话和无线电通信中应该用信号"NO"表示。

(11)信号"N"或者"NO"和"RQ"分别用于改变肯定的信号成为否定的声明或成为疑问时,应在主体信号后面发出。

例如:

CYN(或 NO)="小艇不能前往你处。"

CWRQ="船上是否有小艇或筏?"

信号"C""N""NO"和"RQ"不能和单字母信号连接使用。

3. 灯光通信法

灯光通信包括下面四个程序——呼叫、识别、信文发送、通信结束。

(1)呼叫

发信船(台)连续发出呼叫信号呼叫周围所有的船(台),或直接发送对方呼号呼叫已知名的船(台),直至对方回答为止。对方应用回答信号"$\overline{TTTTT}$"回答,直至呼叫停止。

(2)识别

发信船(台)发送 DE 并紧接着发送自己的呼号或名称,收信船(台)收到后应全部复诵,并发送自己的呼号或名称,发信船(台)收到后亦应复诵一遍。

(3)信文发送

①码语信文

• 发信船(台)首先发送信号码"YU"表示"我准备用国际信号码与你通信"。

● 收信船(台)回答"T"表示准备接收。之后,发信船(台)方可发送信文。

● 收信船(台)收到每一字或组,均应以"T"回答,表示收到。

● 当信文中有名称、地名时,应使用明语发送。

②明语信文

可将信文逐字发送[中国籍船(台)间可使用汉语拼音],收信船(台)对收到的每一个字均应以"T"回答, 表示收到。

(4)通信结束

发信船(台)将信文全部发送完毕后,以信号"$\overline{\text{AR}}$"表示通信结束。收信船(台)以"R"回答表示信文全部收到。

4. 莫尔斯符号的其他用途

莫尔斯符号不仅能用于灯光通信,而且在地文航海中有广泛的应用。在繁忙水道重要转向点处或其他重要物标处,为便于船舶驾驶员、船长、引航员用肉眼、雷达辨认这些航标,各地区助航标志的一些重要灯标和雷康可用莫尔斯符号进行显示。船舶驾驶人员能否准确及时辨认出这些航标对航行安全非常重要。能否准确及时辨认出这些航标,就取决于是否熟记莫尔斯符号。例如:大连港水域的 HO 号灯浮既有灯光显示又有雷康显示。

在中版海图上显示:莫(K)黄 12 s 雷康(C)

在英版海图上显示:Mo(K)Y 12 s Racon (C)

括号中的字母用莫尔斯符号显示,船舶航行附近水域时,可以通过两种手段辨认 HO 号灯浮。该灯浮是船舶进出大连港的重要转向参照点。

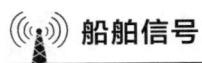

Lesson 3
Hand-flags Signaling and Arms Signaling

1. International flag semaphore system

A	B	C	D	E	F
G	H	I	J	K	L
M	N	O	P	Q	R
S	T	U	V	W	X
Y	Z	ACKNOWLEDGE / CORRECT	CANCEL / ANNUL	NUMERALS	RESET / SPACE
ERROR					

The semaphore signal is made of two-sided signal flag "O" or "P" set on the wooden handle, and uses the two hands holding the flag to change different positions to represent 26 English letters and five symbols, namely "acknowledge/correct"; "cancel/annul"; "numerals"; "reset/space" and "error".

The procedure of hand flag communication is that the transmitting station first sends the signal "K1" to the addressed station by any means, which means "I hope to communicate with you by hand flag", and the addressed station answers the signal "T" in the corresponding way, which means that the message was received or the call was answered. "YS1" should be sent in any way if the addressed station fails to use the hand flag. At the end of the communication, the ending signal "AR" should be sent out, and the signal "R" should also be sent out by the addressed station.

If two ships are at close range, the transmitting station can also send an "attention signal" to the addressed station with the meaning of semaphore signal.

2. Morse signaling by hand-flags or arms

This is one of the visual signals which may be used by the transmitting or receiving station or both when the other methods of signaling are not available or effective.

2.1　Morse signaling by hand-flags or arms

1. Raising both hand-flags or arms 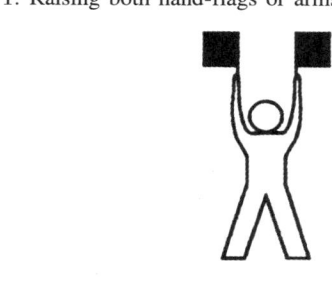 Dot	2. Spreading out both hand-flags or arms at shoulder level  Dash
3. Hand-flags or arms brought before the chest  Separation of dot and/or dashes	4. Hand-flags or arms kept at 45° away from the body downwards  Separation of letter, groups or words
	5.Circular motion of hand-flags or arms over the hand —erase signals, if made by the transmitting station; —request for repetition, if made by the receiving station

Note：The space of time between dots and dashes and between letters, groups or words should be such as to facilitate correct reception

2.2 Procedure

（1）A station which desires to communicate with another station by Morse signaling by hand-flags or arms may indicate the requirement by transmitting to that station the Signal "K1" by any available method. The call signal "$\overline{AA}$ $\overline{AA}$ $\overline{AA}$" may be made instead.

（2）On receipt of the call, the station addressed should make the answering signal, or, if unable to communicate by this means, should reply with the signal "YS1" by any available method.

（3）The call signal "$\overline{AA}$ $\overline{AA}$ $\overline{AA}$" and the signal "T" should be used respectively by the transmitting station and the addressed station.

（4）Normally both arms should be used for this method of transmission but in cases where this is difficult or impossible one arm can be used.

（5）All signals will end with the ending signal "$\overline{AA}$".

第三课   手旗通信和手臂通信

1. 手旗通信

A	B	C	D	E	F
G	H	I	J	K	L
M	N	O	P	Q	R
S	T	U	V	W	X
Y	Z	确认/正确	取消/无效	数字符号	重置/空格
错误					

　　手旗是用两面信号旗"O"或"P"套在木柄上制成的,利用两手握旗变换不同位置来表示 26 个英文字母和 5 个符号(即:确认/正确;取消/无效;数字符号;重置/空格和错误)。

　　手旗通信的程序是,发信方首先用任何方法向收信方发出信号"K1",以此向对方表示"我希望用手旗与你通信",收信方以相应的方法回答"T"信号,表示信文收到或者回答对方的呼叫。如收信方不会使用手旗通信应以任何方式发"YS1"。通信结束时发信船应发送结束信号"AR",收信船发送信号"R"表示结束。

如果两船距离较近,发信方也可以发送"注意信号"表示要求手旗通信。

2. 手旗或手臂发送莫尔斯符号的通信方法

手旗或手臂发送莫尔斯符号的通信方法是用两手握旗或只用两臂变换不同的位置发出点、划组成莫尔斯符号进行通信的方法。手旗是用两面信号旗"O"或"P"套在木柄上制成的。

2.1 手旗或手臂发送莫尔斯符号方法

1. 举起两面旗或双臂  点	2. 双臂平直伸展两面旗或双臂  划
3. 两面旗或者双臂放在胸前  点与点、划与划或者点与划之间的间隔	4. 两面旗或者双臂放下,与身体成45°角  字母与字母、组与组或者字与字之间的间隔
5. 两面旗或者双臂在头上画圈  如果由发信台发送,表示撤销信号; 如果由收信台发送,表示要求重发	
注:点和划之间和字母、组或字之间的间隔时间,应以便于正确收信为准	

2.2　通信程序

（1）如一台想与另一台用手旗或手臂发送莫尔斯符号进行通信，可用任何其他方法向对方发送信号"K1"表示这一要求，也可以用呼叫信号"$\overline{\text{AAAAAA}}$"代替。

（2）受信台在收到呼叫信号后，应发出回答信号。如果受信台不会使用这种方法通信，应用其他方法发送信号"YS1"回答。

（3）呼叫信号"$\overline{\text{AAAAA}}$"、信号"T"应分别由发信台和收信台使用。

（4）这种通信方法通常使用双臂，但在困难或不可能的情况下，也可以用单臂。

（5）所有信号都以完结信号"$\overline{\text{AR}}$"表示完结。

Lesson 4
Sound Signaling and Voice over a Loud Hailer

1. Sound signaling

Sound signaling refers to the sending of Morse signals by whistle, siren, foghorn, bell or other sound apparatus, it is simple and practical. Sound signaling should comply with the related revisions in COLREG and the prescription of coastal port signals in our country. When carrying out sound signaling, the following should be noted:

(1) Owing to the nature of the apparatus used (whistle, siren, foghorn, etc.), sound signaling is necessarily slow. Moreover, the misuse of sound signaling is of a nature to create serious confusion at sea. Sound signaling in fog should therefore be reduced to a minimum. Signals other than the single-letter signals should be used only in extreme emergency and never in frequented navigational waters.

(2) The signals should be made slowly and clearly. They may be repeated, if necessary, but at sufficiently long intervals to ensure that no confusion can arise and that one letter signals cannot be mistaken as two-letter groups.

(3) Masters are reminded that the one letter signals of the Code, which are marked by an asterisk (*), when made by sound, may only be made in compliance with the requirements of the International Regulations for Preventing Collisions at Sea. Reference is also made to the single-letter signals provided for exclusive use between an icebreaker and assisted vessels.

2. Voice over a loud hailer

Voice over a loud hailer refers to the transmitting of information by shouting to the other with a loud speaker over short distances.

Whenever possible plain language should be used, but where a language difficulty exists, groups from the International Code of Signals could be transmitted using the phonetic spelling tables.

第四课   声号通信和扬声器喊话

1. 声号通信法

声号通信法是用声响设备（汽笛、雾角等）发送莫尔斯信号。声号通信应按照《国际海上避碰规则》有关条款和《国际信号规则》及我国沿海港口信号的规定要求进行。进行声号通信时，应注意以下几点：

（1）为避免滥用声号造成混乱，雾中应尽量少用声号。

（2）单字母信号以外的信号只能在非常紧急时使用，并且绝不要在通话繁忙的水域中使用。

（3）由于声响设备的特性，发送信号应缓慢、清楚，必要时可以重发，但应有足够长的间隔以保证不会引起误解，不会使单字母"K"号被误认为双字母信号码。

（4）用声号发送带有单字母信号码时，只能按照《国际海上避碰规则》的规定发送。破冰船和被救助船之间使用专用的单字母信号。

2. 扬声器喊话通信

强力扬声器喊话通信法是利用扬声器在近距离范围内与对方喊话传递信息。在不存在语言隔阂的情况下，通常采用明语通信。使用明语通信时，应力求语言标准化。在语言交流发生困难时，也可用语言拼读表发送信号码语。

练 习 题

Exercises

 一、莫尔斯信号的使用

1.请使用手旗或灯光莫尔斯信号发送以下信息。

MHSIS	QADGY	1DRBC	5LDFR	0MBDX	A3CWK	A2WCV
BHCWF	RVGAZ	MTBFW	FCUI7	DEIN4	LJGDX	ZDRY5
2TGBS	MHT4X	XBMJG	WRYI8	2DXCG	JGRCS	NGDQU
IJFET	F6BIQ	AWDBJ	OIHG7	ABGTJ	XYMFR	MHYXJ
IYBAF	EDF4G	YHN8W	CH1SL	FGHRS	SDVT6	EDJIP
SDFHT	VH4HK	2FGJL	TDV6C	SGYU4	OT8FS	FDYNM

2. 请使用莫尔斯信号码语发送以下信息。

（1）A：到达你处的航向是多少？

B：你驶向我处的航向是东030°。

（2）A：什么时候开始落潮？

B：1830 时开始落潮。

（3）A：你机的地面相对速度是多少？

B：我机相对与地面的速度为200 千米/小时。

（4）A：你需要立即援助吗？

B：我需要立即援助，我船失火。

（5）A：你船的呼号是什么？

B：我船的呼号是 ZAPD。

（6）A：你能提供援助吗？

B：我能援助你。

（7）A：船舶沉没处的水深是多少？

B：船舶沉没处的水深是 30 米。

（8）A：你船受损情况如何？

　　　　B：我船未受任何损坏。

（9）A：你的航向是多少？

　　　　B：我的航向是 090°。

（10）A：你的满载吃水是多少？

　　　　B：我的满载吃水是 8 米。

（11）A：你打算实行何种操纵？

　　　　B：我正在试航。

（12）A：你现在的速度是多少？

　　　　B：我现在的速度是 12 节。

（13）A：你船预计何时到达？

　　　　B：我船预计到达的时间是 1130。

（14）A：你从哪里来？

　　　　B：我从日本来。

（15）A：我请求准许抛锚。

　　　　B：准许你抛锚。

3. 请使用莫尔斯信号明语信文发送以下信息。

（1）I am altering my course to starboard.

（2）I have a pilot on board.

（3）Keep clear of me, I am manoeuvring with difficulty.

（4）My engines are going full speed astern.

（5）You should stop your ship instantly.

（6）Do not pass ahead of me.

（7）My vessel is healthy, I request free pratique.

（8）I am aground, will you tow my off?

（9）Who are your agent?

（10）You should keep ahead of me.

（11）I agree with your suggestion.

（12）Owner orders you to proceed to Nagoya.

（13）Can you indicate a good anchorage for me?

（14）You should try to arrive loading port at the earliest date.

（15）Please allocate a berth for me as soon as possible.

（16）I require fresh water and provisions urgently.

（17）You have to give us 24 hours notice.

（18）You must advise your agent by cable, giving ETA and drafts.

（19）We are passing through a heavy traffic area.

（20）Which berth are we going to take?

（21）We shall be there in one and a half hours.

（22）Give a wide berth to the passing vessel.

（23）Keep straight to the lighthouse.

（24）You should follow the regulations of this port.

（25）How long shall the quarantine last?

（26）When will you be underway?

（27）Maintain the present course without any deviation.

（28）Let's keep contact with one another during sailing.

（29）My destination is Port Said.

（30）What is the weather forecast for this area?

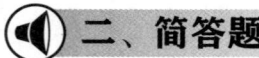 二、简答题

1. 请根据问题简述信号旗使用的相关知识。

（1）简述信号旗的悬挂顺序。

（2）简述代旗的使用方法。

（3）如何使用信号旗建立通信？

（4）船舶遇险信号有哪些？

（5）旗号通信的术语有哪些？

Chapter 4
Special Signals

第四章

特殊信号

Lesson 1
International Distress Signals

(Prescribed by the International Regulations for Preventing Collisions at Sea,1972)

The following signals, used or displayed either together or separately, indicate distress and need of assistance:

(1) A gun or other explosive signal fired at intervals of about a minute;

(2) A continuous sounding with any fog-signaling apparatus;

(3) Rockets or shells, throwing red stars fired are at a time at short intervals;

(4) A signal made by radio telegraphy or by any other signaling method consisting of the group " • • • — — — • • • " (SOS) in the Morse Code;

(5) A signal sent by radio telephony consisting of the spoken word "MAYDAY";

(6) The International Code signal of distress indicated by NC;

(7) A signal consisting of a square flag having above or below it a ball or anything resembling a ball;

(8) Flames on the vessel (as from a burning tar barrel, oil barrel, etc.);

(9) A rocket parachutes flare or a hand flare showing a red light;

(10) A smoke signal giving off orange-colored smoke;

(11) Slowly and repeatedly raising and lowering arms outstretched to each side;

(12) The radiotelegraph alarm signal*;

(13) The radiotelephone alarm signal**;

(14) Signals transmitted by emergency position-indicating radio beacons (EPIRB)***;

(15) Approved signals transmitted by radio communication systems, including survival craft radar transponders.

Note:

* A series of twelve four second dashes at intervals of one second.

* * Two audio tones transmitted alternately at frequency of 2,200 Hz and 1,300 Hz for a duration of 30 seconds to 1 minute.

* * * Either the signal described in * * above or a series of single tones at a frequency of 1,300 Hz.

Search and Rescue Manual (which has being replaced by the IAMSAR Manual) and the following signals:

(1) a piece of orange-colored canvas with either a black square and circle or other appropriate symbol (for identification from the air);

(2) a dye marker.

第一课　国际遇险信号

1.下列信号,不论是一起或分别使用或显示,均表示遇险和需要救助:

(1)每隔约1分钟鸣炮或燃放其他爆炸信号一次;

(2)以任何雾号设备连续发声;

(3)以短的间隔,每次放一个抛射红星光的火箭或信号弹;

(4)无线电报或任何其他通信方法发出莫尔斯码组 SOS(• • • — — — • • •)信号;

(5)无线电话发出"MAYDAY"语音的信号;

(6)悬挂《国际信号规则》中表示遇险的国际信号 NC;

(7)由一面方旗放在一个球体或类似球形物体的上方或下方所组成的信号;

(8)在船上燃起的火焰(如从燃着的柏油桶、油桶等所燃起发出的火焰);

(9)用火箭降落伞式的或手持式的显示红色的火光信号;

(10)用烟雾信号发出橙色的烟雾;

(11)两臂向两边伸展,缓慢并反复地上下挥动;

(12)无线电报报警信号*;

(13)无线电话报警信号**;

(14)由无线电应急示位标(EPIRB)发出的信号***;

(15)由无线电通信系统发出的被认可的报警信号。

2. 除为表示遇险需要救助外,禁止使用或显示上述任何信号以及可能与上述信号相混淆的其他信号。

注:

* 一组12个长音,每一长音历时4秒,长音间的间隔为1秒;

** 在2 200 Hz 和1 300 Hz 频率上,交替发送历时30秒至1分钟的两种音调;

*** 使用注2中规定的信号或是在1 300 Hz 频率上发送一组单音信号均可。

3. 应注意《国际航空和海上搜寻救助手册》第三册——移动设备有关章节以及下列信号:。

(1)一块橙色帆布上带有一黑色正方形和圆圈或其他合适的符号(供空中识别);

(2)海水染色标志。

Lesson 2
International Life-saving Signals

1. Landing signals for the guidance of small boats with crew or person in distress

	Manual signals	Light signals	Other signals	Signification
Day signals	Vertical motion of a white flag or of the arms	Firing of a green star signal	Code letter K given by light or sound-signal apparatus	This is the best place to land
Night signals	Vertical motion of a white light or flare	Firing of a green star signal	Code letter K given by light or sound-signal apparatus	
Day signals	Horizontal motion of a white flag or of the arms extended horizontally	Firing of a red star signal	Code letter S given by light or sound-signal apparatus	Landing here is highly dangerous
Night signals	Horizontal motion of a white light or flare	Firing of a red star signal	Code letter S given by light or sound-signal apparatus	

（to be continued）

	Manual signals	Light signals	Other signals	Signification
Day signals	Horizontal motion of a white flag, followed by the placing of the white flag in the ground and by the carrying of another white flag in the direction to be indicated	1. Firing of a red star signal vertically; 2. A white star signal in direction towards the better landing place	The code letter S (···) followed by the code letter R (· — ·) if a letter landing place for the craft in distress is located more to the right in the direction of approach; The code letter S (···) followed by code letter L (· — · ·) if a better landing place for the craft in distress is located more to left in the direction of approach	Landing here is highly dangerous. A more favourable location for landing is in the direction indication
Night signals	Horizontal motion of a white light or flare, followed by the placing of the white light or flare in the ground and by the carrying of another white light or flare in the direction to be indicated	1. Firing of a red star signal vertically; 2. A white star signal in direction towards the better landing place	The code letter S (...) followed by the code letter R (· — ·) if a letter landing place for the craft in distress is located more to the right in the direction of approach. The code letter S (···) followed by code letter L (· — · ·) if a better landing place for the craft in distress is located more to left in the direction of approach	Landing here is highly dangerous. A more favourable location for landing is in the direction indication

Note：A rang（indication of direction）may be given by placing a steady white light or flare at a lower level and in line with the observer

2. Signals to be employed in connection with the use of shore life-saving apparatus.

	Manual signals	Light signals	Other signals	Signification
Day signals	Vertical motion of a white flag or of the arms	Firing of a green star signal		In general: affirmative; Specifically: —rocket line is held; —tail block is made fast; —hawser is made fast; —haul away
Night signals	Vertical motion of a white light or flare	Firing of a green star signal		
Day signals	Horizontal motion of a white flag or of the arms extended horizontally	Firing of a red star signal		In general: negative Specifically: —slack away; —avast hauling
Night signals	Horizontal motion of a white light or flare	Firing of a red star signal		

3. Answers to distress signals sent by ships or personnel by life-saving stations or maritime rescue units

	Manual signals	Light signals	Other signals	Signification
Day signals		Orange smoke signal	Combined light and sound signal (thunder-light) consisting of 3 single signals which are fired at intervals of approximately one minute	

(to be continued)

	Manual signals	Light signals	Other signals	Signification
Night signals		White star rocket consisting of 3 single signals which are fired at intervals of approximately one minute		You are seen. Assistance will be given as soon as possible (Repetition of such signal shall have the same meaning)
Note: If necessary, the day signals may be given at night or the night signals by day				

4. Air-to-surface visual signals

(1) Signals used by aircraft engaged in search and rescue operations to direct ship towards an aircraft, ship or person in distress.

Procedures performed in sequence by an aircraft			Signification
1.CIRCLE the vessel at lest once	2.CIRCLE the vessel's projected course close AHEAD at a low altitude while ROCKING the wings(see note)	3.HEAD in the direction in which the vessel is to be directed	The aircraft is directing a vessel towards an aircraft or vessel in distress (Repetition of such signal shall have the same meaning)
CROSS the vessel's wake close ASTERN at low altitude while ROCKING the wings. Note: Opening and closing the throttle or changing the propeller pitch may also practiced as an alternative means of attracting attention to that of rocking the wings. However, this form of sound signal may be less affective than the visual signal of rocking the wings owing to high noise level on board the vessel			The assistance of the vessel is no longer required (Repetition of such signal shall have the same meaning)

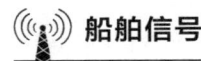

（2）Signals used by a vessel in response to an aircraft engaged in search and rescue operations.

Signals used by a vessel in response to an aircraft			Signification
Hoist "Code and Answering" pendant close up	Change the heading to the required direction	Flash Morse Code signal T by signal lamp	Acknowledge receipt of aircraft's signal
Hoist international flag N (November)		Flash Morse Code signal N by signal lamp	Indicate inability to comply

5. Surface-to-air visual signals

（1）Communication from surface craft or survivors to an aircraft

Use the following surface-to-air signals by displaying the appropriate signal on the deck or on the ground

Message	ICAO/IMO visual signals (see note)
Require assistance	V
Require medical assistance	X
No or negative	N
Yes or affirmative	Y
Proceeding in this direction	↑
Note: IAMSAR Manual Volume Ⅲ —Mobile Facilities	

（2）Reply from an aircraft observing the above signals from surface craft or survivors

Reply from an aircraft				Signification
Drop a message （see note）	Rock the wings （during daylight）	Flash the landing lights or navigation lights on and off twice （during hours of darkness）	or Flash Morse Code signal T or R by light	Message understood
			Use any other suitable signal	
Fly straight and level without rocking wings		Flash Morse Code signal RPT by light	Use any other suitable signal	Message not understood （repeat）
Note: High-visibility coloured streamer				

6. Signals to survivors

（1）Procedures performed by an aircraft

Procedures performed by an aircraft		Signification
Drop a message （see note）	Drop communication equipment suitable for establishing direct contact	The aircraft wishes to inform or instruct survivors
Note: High-visibility coloured streamer		

（2）Signals used by survivors in response to a message dropped by an aircraft

Signals used by survivors		Signification
or Flash Morse code signal T or R by light	Use any other suitable signal	Dropped message is understood by the survivors
Flash Morse code signal RPT by light		Dropped message is not understood by the survivors

第二课　国际救生信号

1. 指引遇险船员或人员的小艇登陆的信号

	手操信号	发光信号	其他信号	意义
白天信号	一面白旗或者双臂上下挥动	发射一颗绿色星光信号	用灯光或声响信号发出字母"K"	这里是最好的登陆地点
夜间信号	一盏白灯或者火焰上下挥动	发射一颗绿色星光信号	用灯光或声响信号发出字母"K"	
白天信号	一面白旗或者双臂平举做水平运动	发射一颗红色星光信号	用灯光或声响信号发出字母"S"	在这里登陆最危险
夜间信号	一盏白灯或者火焰做水平运动	发射一颗红色星光信号	用灯光或声响信号发出字母"S"	

	手操信号	发光信号	其他信号	意义
白天信号	1.一面白旗做水平运动; 2.接着把白旗插在地上; 3.并拿着另一面白旗指示引导的方向	1.垂直地发射一红色星光信号; 2.并向较好的登陆地点方向发射一白色星光信号	如在遇险船艇驶近方向的右边有较好的登陆地点,发出字母"S"(···),接着又发出字母"R"(·—·)。 如在遇险船艇驶近方向的左边有较好的登陆地点,并发出字母"S"(···),接着又发出字母"L"(·—··)	在这里登陆很危险,较好的登陆地点是所指示的方向
夜间信号	1.一盏白灯或者火焰做水平运动; 2.接着把白灯或者火焰放在地上; 3.并拿着另一盏白灯或者火焰指示引导的方向	1.垂直地发射一红色星光信号; 2.并向较好的登陆地点方向发射一白色星光信号	如在遇险船艇驶近方向的右边有较好的登陆地点,发出字母"S"(···),接着又发出字母"R"(·—·)。 如在遇险船艇驶近方向的左边有较好的登陆地点,并发出字母"S"(···),接着又发出字母"L"(·—··)	在这里登陆很危险,较好的登陆地点是所指示的方向

注:可以用一固定的白灯或火焰放在低处并与瞭望者成一直线作示向标(指示方向)

2. 使用岸上救生设备时所用的信号

	手操信号	发光信号	其他信号	意义
白天信号	一面白旗或者双臂上下挥动	发射一颗绿色星光信号		一般情况表示:肯定 特殊情况表示: —火箭绳已握牢; —带尾绳的滑车已系牢; —缆绳已系牢; —拉走
夜间信号	一盏白灯或者火焰上下挥动	发射一颗绿色星光信号		

83

续表

	手操信号	发光信号	其他信号	意义
白天信号	一面白旗或者双臂平举做水平运动	发射一颗红色星光信号		一般情况表示:否定 特殊情况表示: —放松 —停拉
夜间信号	一盏白灯或者火焰做水平运动	发射一颗红色星光信号		

3. 救生站或海事救助单位对船舶或人员发出的遇险信号的回答

	手操信号	发光信号	其他信号	意义
白天信号		橙色烟雾信号	声光混合信号(雷光)三发,每隔一分钟发射一次	已见到你,将尽快给予援助(重复这种信号时,其意义相同)
夜间信号		白色星光火箭三枚,每隔一分钟发射一枚		
注:必要时,白天信号可用于夜间或者夜间信号可用于白天				

4. 空对地视觉信号

（1）飞机在进行搜寻与救助工作中指导船舶驶向遇险飞机、船舶或人员所使用的信号。

飞机先后表演的程序			意义
 1.飞机绕水面船艇转圈,至少一圈	 2.飞机低飞接近水面船艇的船头,环绕船艇的航向,及时摆动机翼(见注)	 3.飞机飞向水面船艇将被指引的方向	飞机正在指引一艘水面船艇驶向遇险的飞机或水面船艇(重复这些信号时,其意义相同)
 飞机摆动机翼低飞,接近船尾,横越水面船艇航迹。 注:也可用开、闭节气阀或者改变螺旋桨螺距作为可供选择的与摇摆机翼一样吸引人注意力的方法。然而,由于船艇上噪声较高,因此,这种声音信号形式比摆动机翼这种视觉信号效果差			已不需要水面船艇发援助(重复这些信号时,其意义相同)

（2）船舶回答执行搜救工作的飞机所使用的信号。

船舶回答所使用的信号			意义
 悬挂"信号旗回答码"到顶	 改航向到所需方向	 用灯光信号发出莫尔斯信号码"T"	认可收到飞机的信号
 悬挂国际信号旗"N"		 用灯光信号发出莫尔斯信号码"N"	表示不能照办

5. 地对空视觉信号

（1）水面船艇或生存者对飞机的通信

在甲板上或地面上，显示下列地对空视觉符号中恰当的符号

信文	国际民航组织/国际海事组织的视觉信号（注释）
需要援助	V
需要医疗援助	X
不或者否定	N
是或者肯定	Y
向此方向前进	↑
注:《国际航空与海上搜寻救助手册》第三册——移动设备

（2）飞机看到从水面船艇或生存者发出的上列信号的回答

飞机回答所演示的程序					意义
投下一书信（见注）	摆动机翼（白天）	着陆灯或者航行灯闪光两次（黑夜）	用灯光发出莫尔斯信号码"T"或"R"	使用其他合适信号	信文收悉
水平直飞不摆动机翼			用灯光发出莫尔斯信号码"RPT"	使用其他合适信号	信文不明白（重复）
注:很远能看到的彩带					

6. 对生存者的信号

(1) 飞机完成的程序

飞机完成的程序		意义
投下一书信(见注)	投下用于建立直接联络的通信设备	飞机希望对生存者发出通知或指示
注:很远能看到的彩带		

(2) 生存者对飞机投下的书信所使用的回答

生存者回答所使用的信号		意义
■■■　或者 ●■■■● 用灯光发出莫尔斯信号码"T"或"R"	使用其他合适信号	生存者对所投信文收悉
●■■■ ●■■■■● ■■■ 用灯光发出莫尔斯信号码"RPT"		生存者对所投信文不明白

Chapter 5
Marine VHF Radiotelephony Communication

第五章
船舶甚高频无线电话通信

Lesson 1
Introduction

1. Types of marine radiotelephony and frequencies

Marine Radiotelephony is one of the marine communication devices which is used between ships or ships and shore. The introduction of radiotelephone(RT), the use of speech on the air, has made communication much more easier for mariners. Nowadays, marine radiotelephony is an important and modern navigational aid through which information can be transferred and exchanged rapidly, conveniently and directly. It has solved many of the earlier commendation problems and made great contributions to the safety of persons and navigation.

Marine radiotelephony may be classified into four types according to the frequency band allocated by international agreement.

Medium frequency (MF) radiotelephony—1,065–4,000 kHz;

High frequency (HF) radiotelephony—4,000–27,500 kHz;

Very high frequency (VHF) radiotelephony—156–174 MHz;

Ultra-high frequency (UHF) radiotelephony—1.5–1.6 GHz.

MF/HF radiotelephones are used in medium distance communication (such as SSB), VHF radiotelephony is used in short distance communication (about 30 miles), and UHF radiotelephony is used in satellite communication (it is not confined by distance).

Medium frequency radiotelephony operates in the bands between 1,605 kHz and 4,000 kHz. Though it is the earliest marine radiotelephony, it is still required on a modern ship. Among these frequencies, the carrier frequency 2,182 kHz is used for distress, safety and calling traffic. The frequency 2,187.5 kHz is used exclusively for distress and safety calling for digital selective calling in GMDSS.

2. Very high frequency radiotelephony

As one of the important marine communication devices over short distances, VHF radiotelephony functions well in marine communication. It may proceed to ship distress, urgency, safety communication and routine services communication, also be the important communication tool of VTS. According to the requirements of SOLAS conventions, all vessels navigating in any NAVAREA should be equipped with VHF radiotelephony after the implementation of the GMDSS.

2.1 Output power

The VHF set has two kinds of output power—25 W and 1 W. The high power is used for the transmission over longer distances, the low one is used for the communication over short distances so as to decrease the signal interference between ships. The output power of VHF radiotelephony on shore is 50 W.

2.2 Working way

There are two types of common working ways for VHF radiotelephony: simplex working and duplex working.

(1) Simplex working

When communicating, the transmission/reception signals use the same frequency, neither station can speak nor listen at the same time. Hold the transmitting switch down when speaking and release it when listening.

(2) Duplex working

When communicating, the transmission/reception signals use the two different frequencies. Either station can speak and listen at the same time. But it should be noted that the duplex working can only be used for ship-to-shore communication and not for ship-to-ship communication.

2.3 VHF radiotelephony channels

According to the international radio rules, there are altogether 57 channels set up at present, channel 01-28 and channel 60-88. Channel spacing is 25 kHz. There are 2 protection channels of channel 16 (channel 75 and channel 76, but not opened). Fifty-five channels have been opened, including 20 simplex channels and 35 duplex channels. At present, as a digital selective calling (DSC), Channel 70 can no longer be used as telephone communication, so there are only 54 channels for voice communication.

There are 2 AIS (Automatic Identification System) channels, that is channel 87 and channel 88 of the shore station.

The allocation of frequencies and standard usage of radio channels so allocated in Maritime VHF Band has been internationally agreed upon, as shown in Table 5-1.

Table 5-1　Transmitting frequencies in the marine VHF band

Channel	Transmitting frequencies(MHz)		Port operation and ship movement	
	Ship station	Coast station	Single frequency	Double frequency
01	156.050	160.650		D
02	156.100	160.700		D
03	156.150	160.750		D
04	156.200	160.800		D
05	156.250	160.850		D
06	156.300	156.300	S	
07	156.350	160.950		D
08	156.400	156.400	S	
09	156.450	156.450	S	

 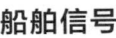
（to be continued）

| Channel | Transmitting frequencies（MHz） | | Port operation and ship movement | |
	Ship station	Coast station	Single frequency	Double frequency
10	156.500	156.500	S	
11	156.550	156.550	S	
12	156.600	156.600	S	
13	156.650	156.650	S	K
14	156.700	156.700	S	
15	156.750	156.750	S	
16	156.800	156.800	S	
17	156.850	156.850	S	
18	156.900	161.500		D
19	156.950	161.550		D
20	157.000	161.600		D
21	157.050	161.650		D
22	157.100	161.700		D
23	157.150	161.750		D
24	157.200	161.800		D
25	157.250	161.850		D
26	157.300	161.900		D
27	157.350	161.950		D
28	157.400	162.000		D
60	156.025	160.625		D
61	156.075	160.675		D
62	156.125	160.725		D
63	156.175	160.775		D
64	156.225	160.825		D
65	156.275	160.875		D
66	156.325	160.925		D
67	156.375	156.375	S	
68	156.425	156.425	S	
69	156.475	156.475	S	
70	156.525	156.525	S	
71	156.575	156.575	S	
72	156.625	156.625	S	

（to be continued）

Channel	Transmitting frequencies（MHz）		Port operation and ship movement	
	Ship station	Coast station	Single frequency	Double frequency
73	156.675	156.675	S	
74	156.725	156.725	S	
75				
76				
77	156.875	156.875	S	
78	156.925	161.525		D
79	156.975	161.575		D
80	157.025	161.625		D
81	157.075	161.675		D
82	157.125	161.725		D
83	157.175	161.775		D
84	157.225	161.825		D
85	157.275	161.875		D
86	157.325	161.925		D
87	157.375	161.975		D
88	157.425	162.025		D
AIS1	161.975	161.975		
AIS2	162.025	162.025		

General notes：

（1）The channels of the present Appendix, with the exception of channels 06, 13, 15, 16, 17, 70, 75 and 76, may also be used for high-speed data and facsimile transmissions, subject to special arrangement between interested and affected administrations.

（2）The channels of the present Appendix, but preferably channel 28 and with exception of channels 06, 13, 15, 16, 17, 70, 75 and 76, may be used for direct-printing telegraphy and data transmission, subject to special arrangement between interested and affected administrations.

（3）The frequencies in this table may also be used for radio communication on inland waterways in accordance with the conditions specified in No. S. 226.

（4）Administrations having an urgent need to reduce local congestion may apply 12.5 kHz channel interleaving on a non-interference basis to 5 kHz channels, provided：

① Recommendation ITU-R M. 1084-2 shall be taken into account when changing to 12.5 kHz channel.

② It shall not affect the 25 kHz channel of the Appendix S18 maritime mobile distress and safety frequencies, especially the channels 6, 13, 15, 16, 17, and 70, nor the technical characteristics mentioned in Recommendation ITU-R M. 489-2 for these channels.

③ Implementation of 12. 5 kHz channel interleaving and consequential national requirements shall be subject to prior agreement between the implementing administrations and administrations whose ship station or services may be affected.

Specific notes:

(5) The frequency 156.300 MHz (channel 06) (see Appendix S13, Appendix S15 and S51. 79) may also be used for communication between ship stations and aircraft stations engaged in coordinated search and rescue operations. Ship stations shall avoid harmful interference to such communication on channel 06 as well as to communication between aircraft stations, ice-breakers and assisted ships during ice seasons.

(6) Channels 15 and 17 may also be used for on-board communication provided the effective radiated power does not exceed 1 W, and subject to the national regulations of the administration concerned when these channels are used in its territorial waters.

(7) Within the European Maritime Area and in Canada these frequencies(channels 10, 67, 73) may also be used. If so required, by the individual administrations concerned, for communication between ship stations, aircraft stations and participating land stations engaged in coordinated search and rescue and antipollution operations in local areas, under the conditions specified in Nos. 551. 69, S51.73, S51.74, S51.75, S51.76, S51.77 and S51.78.

(8) The preferred first three frequencies for the purpose indicated in note are 156. 450 MHz (channel 09). 156. 625 MHz (channel 72) and 156.675 MHz(channel 73).

(9) Channel 70 is to be used exclusively for digital selective calling for distress, safety and calling.

(10) Channel 13 is designated for use on a world-wide basis as a navigation safety communication channel, primarily for inter-ship navigation safety communication. It may also be used for the ship movement and port operations service subject to the national regulations of the administrations concerned.

(11) The channels will be used for an automatic ship identification and surveillance system capable of providing worldwide operation on high seas, unless other frequencies are designated on a regional basis for this purpose, [161. 975 (channel 87B) may only be used for public correspondence in the U. S.].

(12) These channels (18 and 82 to 86) may be operated as a single frequency channels, subject to special arrangement between interested or affected administrations.

(13) The use of these channels should be restricted to navigation-related communication, only and all precautions should be taken to avoid harmful interference to channel 16, e.g. by limiting the output power to 1 W or by means geographical separation.

In the channels of VHF, according to their working nature, they may be divided into as follows:

① Calling channel and working channels

Calling channel—channel 16.

Working channels—all other channels except that channel 16 are the working channel.

② Distress, urgency, safety communication channels

CH16: may only be used for distress, urgency and very brief safety communication and for calling to establish other communication which should then be concluded on a suitable working channel.

CH70: may only be used for Digital Selective Calling for distress not oral communication.

CH06: may also be used for communication between ship stations and aircraft stations engaged in coordinated search and rescue operations. Ship stations shall avoid harmful interference to such communication on channel 06 as well as to communication between aircraft stations, ice breakers and assisted ships during ice seasons.

CH13: is designated for use on a world-wide basis as a navigation safety communication channel, primarily for inter-ship navigation safety communication. It may also be used for the ship movement and port operations service subject to the national regulations of the administrations concerned.

③ ITU and USA channels

In General, all the VHF channels are the ITU channels. When navigating in the Canada and USA territorial waters, the USA channels should be used.

④ Weather channel

It is only used for listening to the weather information by ships.

第一课　概述

1. 海上无线电话种类及其使用频率

海上无线电话是指采用中/高频、高频、甚高频及特高频等海上专用频率进行船舶间或船岸间的无线电话通信。依据其使用的频率可分别称其为：

中频（MF）无线电话——1 065~4 000 kHz；

高频（HF）无线电话——4 000~27 500 kHz；

甚高频（VHF）无线电话——156~174 MHz；

特高频（UHF）无线电话——1.5~1.6 GHz。

中、高频无线电话用于中距离的通信。目前,船舶配备的单边带无线电话（SSB）就工作在这个频率范围内,2 182 kHz 是它的一个重要的遇险呼叫、通信频率。

VHF 无线电话用于近距离的无线电话通信。

特高频无线电话用于卫星通信,凡装备有国际海事卫星（Inmarsat）船站的船舶可进行这类的无线电话通信业务。船与船、船与岸通信不受距离远近的限制,在船上可与南北纬70°之间任何地方的通信单位进行高质量的通话。

2. VHF 无线电话

VHF 无线电话作为水上移动电台的一种近距离通信工具,在海上船舶通信中发挥着巨大的作用。它可以用于船舶遇险、紧急、安全通信和日常业务通信,也是船舶交通管理系统（VTS）中的重要通信工具。按照 SOLAS 公约的要求, GMDSS 实施之后在任何航区航行的船舶均应配有 VHF 无线电话装置。

2.1　输出功率

目前,大多数船载 VHF 无线电话机有两种输出功率供选择——25 W 和 1 W。大功率 VHF 无线电话机用于通信距离较远、需要较强的发射信号,小功率 VHF 无线电话机用于近距离通话。岸台 VHF 无线电话机输出功率为 50 W。

2.2　工作方式

VHF 无线电话的常用工作方式有两种——单工操作与双工操作。

（1）单工操作:电信通路的每一方交替发射/接收信号。通信时,收/发信号都使用同一个频率,每一方讲话与收听都不能同时进行。讲话时,须将话筒上的按钮按下（此时不能收听对方的讲话）。收听时须松开按钮（此时不能向对方讲话）。

（2）双工操作:电信通路的双方可同时发射/接收信号。通信时,收/发信号使用两个不同的频率。每一方讲话与收听都可同时进行。但应注意,此种工作方式只能在船/岸间的通信中使用,船/船间的通信不能使用。这在 VHF 无线电话的通信频道中有所规定。

2.3 VHF 无线电话频道

VHF 无线电话的频道又称信道,按照国际无线电规则的规定,目前共设置 57 个频道,01~28 频道、60~88 频道,频道间隔是 25 kHz,其中 16 频道的保护频道 2 个(75 频道和 76 频道,但未开通,见后面"注释"的"N")。开通了 55 个频道,其中单工频道 20 个,双工频道 35 个。目前,70 频道作为数字选择呼叫通信频道(DSC),该频道已不能进行电话通信,因此,目前能进行话音通信的频道只有 54 个(见表 5-1)。

自动识别系统(AIS)的频道为 2 个,占用岸台的 87 和 88 频道。

2.4 通信距离

VHF 无线电话的通信距离是有限的。理论上通信距离等于视距,因为 VHF 电波不能沿地表弯曲。但大气压力和湿度的增加会在某种程度上增大通信距高,因为大气摩擦导致电波倾向于弯曲传播而不是沿直线传播。

在发射机的发射功率和接收机的灵敏度一定的情况下,另一个影响通信距离的因素是收发信船的 VHF 无线电话天线的高度,通信距离通常情况如下:

(1)岸台与天线高度(距海面)为 90 m 的大型邮轮的通信距离大约为 60 n mile。

(2)岸台与天线高度(距海面)为 9 m 的游艇的通信距离大约为 35 n mile。

(3)岸台与小艇手持 VHF 无线电话的通信距离大约为 15 n mile。

(4)两个小艇用手持 VHF 无线电话的通信距离大约为 5 n mile。

表 5-1 国际通用频道

频道	发射频率(MHz)		港口和船舶移动业务	
	船台	岸台	单频	双频
01	156.050	160.650		√
02	156.100	160.700		√
03	156.150	160.750		√
04	156.200	160.800		√
05	156.250	160.850		√
06	156.300	156.300	√	
07	156.350	160.950		√
08	156.400	156.400	√	
09	156.450	156.450	√	
10	156.500	156.500	√	
11	156.550	156.550	√	
12	156.600	156.600	√	
13	156.650	156.650	√	
14	156.700	156.700	√	
15	156.750	156.750	√	

续表

频道	发射频率（MHz）		港口和船舶移动业务	
	船台	岸台	单频	双频
16	156.800	156.800	√	
17	156.850	156.850	√	
18	156.900	161.500		√
19	156.950	161.550		√
20	157.000	161.600		√
21	157.050	161.650		√
22	157.100	161.700		√
23	157.150	161.750		√
24	157.200	161.800		√
25	157.250	161.850		√
26	157.300	161.900		√
27	157.350	161.950		√
28	157.400	162.000		√
60	156.025	160.625		√
61	156.075	160.675		√
62	156.125	160.725		√
63	156.175	160.775		√
64	156.225	160.825		√
65	156.275	160.875		√
66	156.325	160.925		√
67	156.375	156.375	√	
68	156.425	156.425	√	
69	156.475	156.475	√	
70	156.525	156.525	√	
71	156.575	156.575	√	
72	156.625	156.625	√	
73	156.675	156.675	√	
74	156.725	156.725	√	
75				
76				
77	156.875	156.875	√	
78	156.925	161.525		√

续表

频道	发射频率（MHz）		港口和船舶移动业务	
	船台	岸台	单频	双频
79	156.975	161.575		√
80	157.025	161.625		√
81	157.075	161.675		√
82	157.125	161.725		√
83	157.175	161.775		√
84	157.225	161.825		√
85	157.275	161.875		√
86	157.325	161.925		√
87	157.375	161.975		√
88	157.425	162.025		√
AIS1	161.975	161.975		
AIS2	162.025	162.025		

注释：

（1）06 频道也可以用于船台与从事协调搜索救助的飞机之间通信。

（2）倘若发射功率不超过 1 W,15、17 频道可以用于船内通信,即船舶靠离码头时,驾驶台与船头、船尾通信时使用上述频道之一。

（3）在欧洲和加拿大海域,如果被个别有关主管机关要求,10、67、73 频道可以用于船舶、飞机与从事搜索救助的岸台和地方水域防污染作业的岸台间的通信。

（4）70 频道专门用于遇险、安全、呼叫中的数字选择性呼叫。

（5）13 频道用于全球航行安全通信,主要用于船舶间航行安全通信;也可以用于船舶移动业务和港口业务,服从于国内有关规定。

（6）AIS1、AIS2 用于船舶自动识别和监视业务。

（7）75、76 频道仅局限于与航行有关的通信且采取一切措施避免对 16 频道造成干扰,如采用减小功率到 1 W 和借助地理分隔等。

Lesson 2
Specifications for Use of VHF Radiotelephony

The improper use of VHF channels at sea is very common, especially in distress, safety and calling channels, as well as in ports, ship mobile services and reporting systems. Attention should be paid to this abnormal phenomenon by seafarers and maritime management departments.

Frequent improper use of VHF channels will seriously affect the necessary communications and become a potential danger to maritime safety. Correct use of VHF channels will benefit navigation safety. Therefore, the ITU Radio Rules require:

(1) Channel 16 can only be used for distress, urgency and brief safety communication and for calls to establish contact with other communication, which are immediately transferred to appropriate working channels as soon as they are established.

(2) Channels allocated to port business can only be used for exchange procedures, ship safety, ship movement and other information. In case of urgency, it can be used for personnel safety communication. In congested areas of ports, the use of these channels for ship-to-ship communication may have serious impacts for ship shift and ship safety communication.

In order to maintain the smooth and orderly maritime communication, the crew should observe the following regulations when using VHF radiotelephone on board.

1. General provisions

(1) Preparation

Before transmitting, the communication messages should be well prepared, and if necessary, the drafts should be prepared to avoid unnecessary interruptions so as to ensure that unnecessary time is not taken up on busy channels.

(2) Listening watch

Prior to transmitting, listening watch must be kept to ensure that the channel is not in use, thus avoiding unnecessary and unpleasant distractions.

(3) Precautions for use

VHF shall be used correctly in accordance with radio rules, and in particular the following situations shall be avoided:

① non-distress, non-urgency and non-brief safety communication calls on channel 16 when another calling channel is available.

② communication unrelated to safety and navigation on port working channels.

③ unnecessary transmitting.

④ transmitting that is not correctly identified.

⑤ occupying a specific channel under poor communication conditions.

⑥ use offensive language.

（4）Repetition

Repetition of words should be avoided unless the receiving station has special requirements.

（5）Power reduction

If possible, the minimum power of transmitter is used to ensure satisfactory communication.

（6）Communication with shore station

The ship station shall obey the instructions of the shore station on communication matters. Communication should be conducted on the channel indicated by the shore station. It should be confirmed by the ship station when it is necessary to change the channel. When receiving instructions from shore station to stop transmitting, ship station shall stop communicating until further notice is given (at this time, the shore station may receive the distress, urgency and safety communication and any transmitting will cause disruption to it).

（7）Communication with other ship stations

In ship-to-ship communication, the ship station to be called specifies the working channel for further communication, and the calling ship station shall confirm this working channel before switching channels. Before communicating on the selected working channel, keep listening carefully to ensure that the channel is not in use. If this channel is occupied, please switch to another channel.

（8）Calling

Whenever possible, the working frequency should be used. If there is no working frequency, channel 16 can be used if it is not occupied by distress/calling/communicating.

When it is difficult to establish communication with ship stations or shore stations, repeated calling should be made at sufficient intervals. Instead of unnecessarily occupying the channel, try to use another channel.

（9）Channel switching

If communication on a channel is unsatisfactory, indicate the channel to be switched and wait for confirmation.

（10）Spelling

If spelling is required (e.g., ship name, call sign, confusable words, etc.), use the international signal rules spelling table.

（11）Addressing

Words like "I" and "You" are used with caution. Use names whenever possible.

（12）Watch keeping

At sea, vessels equipped only with VHF should keep listening watch on channel 16; other vessels should keep listening on channel 16 if practicable when they are within the working range of the shore station. Under certain circumstances, the government may request ships to listen on other channels.

（13）Lookout

When communicating with VHF during navigation, do not forget the responsibility of look-out and pay attention to lookout ahead.

2. Specific provisions

（1）Notes on the use of 156.8 MHz（channel 16）: 156.8 MHz（channel 16）is the international distress, urgency, safety communication and public calling frequency of maritime mobile service radio. It can be used for distress signal, distress calling and distress communication, as well as for urgency signals, urgency communication and safety communication. If it is used for urgency and safety communication, the preface should be issued on 156.8 MHz（channel 16）, followed by urgency and safety communication on the working channel.

（2）In order not to interfere with distress calls and distress communication, the frequency and time of other communication on 156.8 MHz（channel 16）should be kept to a minimum of no more than 1 minute.

（3）If other ship is called continuously three times on 156.8 MHz（channel 16）（one calling within 2 minutes）, and still no reply is received from other ship, the calling shall be stopped, and if it is really necessary, the calling shall be made 3 minutes later.

第二课　甚高频无线电话使用规范

在海上不正确使用 VHF 频道现象很普遍,尤其是遇险、安全和呼叫频道及用于港口、船舶移动业务和报告系统的频道被不正确使用现象很普遍。对于这一不正常现象,广大船员和海事管理部门应给予关注。

经常不正确使用 VHF 频道会对必要的通信造成严重影响,且会成为海上安全的潜在危险,正确使用 VHF 频道会对航行安全有所裨益。为此,国际电信联盟的《无线电规则》要求:

(1) 16 频道只能用于遇险、紧急和简短的安全通信及用于与其他通信建立联系,其他通信一经建立,马上转入合适的工作频道。

(2)分配给港口业务的频道只能用于交换业务处理、船舶安全、船舶移动等信息。在紧急情况下,可以用于人员安全通信。在港口拥挤区域,由于这些频道用于船对船之间的通信,可能会对船舶移动业务和船舶安全通信造成严重影响。

为了保持海上通信的畅通与秩序,广大船员在使用船上 VHF 无线电话时应该自觉遵守下列有关规定:

1. 一般规定

(1)准备

在发射之前,准备好通信内容,如果必要的话,准备好草稿以避免不必要的中断,从而保证在繁忙的频道上不占用不必要的时间。

(2)守听

在发射之前,注意守听以确保当前频道没有被使用,这样可以避免不必要的或令人不愉快的干扰。

(3)使用注意事项

VHF 设备应按照无线电规则正确使用,特别应避免下列情况:

①另一呼叫频道可用时,在 16 频道上进行非遇险、紧急、非常简短的安全通信的呼叫。

②在港口工作频道上进行与安全和航行无关的通信。

③非必要的发射。

④没有正确识别的发射。

⑤在通信条件较差的情况下占用某一特定频道。

⑥使用冒犯性语言。

(4)重复

字词的重复应该避免,除非接收台有特殊要求。

(5)功率减低

如可行的话,在保证令人满意的通信情况下使用发射机最小功率。

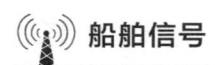

（6）与岸台通信

船台应该服从岸台关于通信事情的指示。通信应该在岸台指示的频道上进行。当需转换频道时应该得到船台的确认。收到岸台对船台停止发射的指示时,船台应该停止通信直至另有通知（此时岸台可能收到遇险、紧急、安全通信且任何发射会对此造成干扰）。

（7）与其他船台通信

在船对船通信时,被叫船台指定进一步通信所用的工作频道,在转换频道前,呼叫船应确认此工作频道。在选定的工作频道进行通信前,注意守听以确保该频道没有正在被使用,方可进行通信。倘若该频道被使用,请转其他频道。

（8）呼叫

无论什么时候只要可行,应该使用工作频率,如果没有工作频率,倘若16频道没有被遇险/呼叫/通信占用,可以使用16频道。

在与船台或岸台建立通信困难的情况下,重复呼叫要有足够的时间间隔,不要不必要地占用该频道而应该试着使用另一频道。

（9）转换频道

如果在某一频道上的通信效果不令人满意时,指明转换频道且等待证实。

（10）拼读

如果必须拼读(如船名、呼号、易混淆的字等)则使用《国际信号规则》拼读表拼读。

（11）称呼

应谨慎使用"我"和"你"这样的字眼。尽量用名称。

（12）值守

在海上,只装备VHF设备的船舶在16频道上保持守听;其他船舶,当其处在岸台工作范围内,如实际可行应守听16频道;在特定情况下,政府可以要求船舶守听其他频道。

（13）瞭望

在航行中使用VHF进行通话时,不要忘记瞭望的责任。应该面向前方,注意瞭望。

2. 特殊规定

（1）关于156.8 MHz（16频道）的使用注意事项:156.8 MHz（16频道）是水上移动业务电台的国际遇险、紧急、安全通信和公共呼叫频率。它用于遇险信号、遇险呼叫和遇险通信,还可以用于紧急信号、紧急通信和安全通信。如果用于紧急、安全通信,应在156.8 MHz（16频道）上发布引语,然后在工作频道上进行紧急通信和安全通信。

（2）为了不影响遇险呼叫和遇险通信,在156.8 MHz（16频道）上的其他所有通信次数和时间应保持在最低限度,不得超过1分钟。

（3）在156.8 MHz（16频道）上连续呼叫他船三次(2分钟内呼叫一次),仍然没有收到他船的回答时,应停止呼叫,若确实需要呼叫,应3分钟后再呼叫。

Lesson 3
Methods of VHF Radiotelephony Communication

Marine VHF radiotelephony communication includes: ship-ship, ship-aircraft, ship-shore station.

1. Basic methods of VHF communication

There are two basic methods for radiotelephony communication: plain language and code message. According to the requirements of the International Code of signals, plain language should be first used when communicating. English is commonly used as the international marine language. Code message communication is used when language difficulties arise.

According to the contents of message, VHF communication will be divided into:

(1) Routine services communication

Routine services include:

● ship's arrival at and departure from port, berthing and unberthing, arrangement of pilot, etc.

● ship manoeuvring and collision avoidance, etc.

● all kinds of ship's agency services and so on.

(2) Distress, urgency and safety communication

Order of priority of VHF communication: distress—urgency—safety—routine.

Distress calls/messages have absolute priority over all other communication, when receiving them all other transmissions should cease and a listening watch should be kept.

According to the different communication procedures, VHF communication will be divided into:

(1) Exchange procedure communication: This applies when two or more stations achieve communication with each other, and an exchange is then said to be taking place.

(2) Broadcast procedure communication: Broadcast procedure applies when a station transmits without expecting a response from any other station or a station transmits without knowing if a response from another station will be received or not.

(3) Distress, urgency and safety procedures communication.

2. Code message communication

In code message communication, the message is composed of figure and letter codes. Its meaning is understood by decoding the message according to the International Code of Signals.

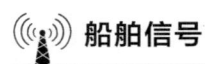
When using radiotelephony and the International Code of Signals in cases of language difficulties, the principles of the Radio Regulations of the International Telecommunication Union in force have to be complied with, and letters and numerals are to be spelt out using the phonetic pronunciations.

When coast and ship stations are called, the identity signals (call signs) or names shall be used.

2.1　Spelling tables of letters and numerals

（1）Spelling of letters

When spelling is necessary, only the Table 5-2 should be used.

Table 5-2　Spelling of letters

Letter	Code word	Pronunciation
A	Alfa	AL FAH
B	Bravo	BRAH VOH
C	Charlie	CHAR LEE
D	Delta	DELL TAH
E	Echo	ECK OH
F	Foxtrot	FOKS TROT
G	Golf	GOLF
H	Hotel	HOH TELL
I	India	IN DEE AH
J	Juliett	JEW LEE ETT
K	Kilo	KEY LOH
L	Lima	LEE MAH
M	Mike	MIKE
N	November	NO VEM BER
O	Oscar	OSS CAH
P	Papa	PAH PAH
Q	Quebec	KEH BECK
R	Romeo	ROW MEOH
S	Sierra	SEE AIR RAH
T	Tango	TANG GO
U	Uniform	YOU NEE FORM
V	Victor	VIK TAH
W	Whiskey	WISS KEY
X	X-ray	ECKS RAY
Y	Yankee	YANG KEY
Z	Zulu	ZOO LOO

Notes：

Spelling of letters may also be used when transmitting plain language. It should be used on following occasions：

①When transmitting ship's call sign.

Example："My ship's call sign is Bravo-Oscar-Lima-Charlie".

②When spelling out ships name or a word, which is not familiar to the receiving station or not understood by others.

Example：I have loaded urea, Uniform-Romeo-Echo-Alfa, urea 25,000 tons. My ship's name is Yu Feng, Yankee-Uniform, Foxtrot-Echo-November-Golf."

③When speaking individual letters.

Example：I am passing Reporting Point Lima Kilo One.

But it is not necessary to spell out some abbreviations with the spelling table of letters, such as GMT, IMO, SAR, AMVER, GMDSS and so on.

（2）Spelling of numerals

Spelling of numerals is shown in as the Table 5-3.

Table 5-3　Spelling of numerals

Numeral	Code word	Pronunciation
0	NADAZERO	NAH DAH ZAY ROH
1	UNAONE	OO NAH WUN
2	BISSOTWO	BEES SOH TOO
3	TERRATHREE	TAY RAH TREE
4	KARTEFOUR	KAR TAY FOUR
5	PANTAFIVE	PAN TAH FIVE
6	SOXISIX	SOK SEE SIX
7	SETTESEVEN	SAY TAY SEVEN
8	OKTOEIGHT	OK TOH AIT
9	NOVENINE	NO VAY NINER
DECIMAL POINT	DECIMAL	DAY SEE MAL
FULL STOP	STOP	STOP

2.2　Communication procedure symbols

（1）"DE"（Delta Echo）= this is.

（2）"CQ"（Charlie Quebec）shall be used for calling all stations in the vicinity, but not more than 3 times at each call.

（3）"INTERCO" or "YU"（Yankee Uniform）indicates that the following message uses code groups of the International Code of Signals.

（4）"YZ"（Yankee Zulu）denotes that the following is in plain language to transmit names of places and stations, etc.

(5) "$\overline{AS}$" (Alfa Sierra) indicates the station called is unable to accept the signal immediately, please awaiting.

(6) "$\overline{AR}$" (Alfa Romeo) indicates end of a transmission or signal.

(7) "R" (Romeo) indicates "received" or "I have received your last signal".

(8) If the transmission is to be repeated in total or in part, the signal "RPT" (Romeo Papa Tango) shall be used, supplemented as necessary by:

"AA" (Alfa Alfa) = all after...

"AB" (Alfa Bravo) = all before...

"BN" (Bravo November) = all between... and...

"WA" (Whiskey Alfa) = word or group after...

"WB" (Whiskey Bravo) = word or group before...

2.3 Communication procedure

VHF code message communication procedure includes: calling, identity, code message and ending.

(1) Calling

① Calling a known station: send the call sign and name of the station being called, not more than three times at each call;

② Calling all stations in the vicinity: the group "CQ" (Charlie Quebec) shall be used, but not more than three times at each call.

(2) Identity

① For the transmitting vessel: send the group "DE" (Delta Echo) and the call sign or name of the transmitting station, not more than three times;

② For the receiving vessel: answer the call in the same procedure as (1) and (2).

(3) Code message

In order to indicate that Code groups of the ICS are to follow, the word "INTERCO" is to be first inserted, then the text. Words of plain language may also be in the text when the signal includes names, places, etc. In this case the group "YZ" (Yankee Zulu) is to be inserted if necessary.

(4) Ending

① For the transmitting vessel: The end of a transmission is indicated by the signal "$\overline{AR}$" (Alfa Romeo) or "over".

② For the receiving vessel: The receipt of a transmission is indicated by the signal "R" (Romeo).

If the station makes a mistake in sending, use the signal "CORRECTION" (cancel my last word or group; the correct word or group follows) to erase the incorrect word or group.

The receiving station thereupon cancels the last word or group received and replaces it with the word or group after correction.

2.4　Examples of code message communication

Example 1：Calling a known station（Table 5-4）

The call sign of transmitting station：BTBM；the call sign of receiving station：S6EI.

The message：You should navigate with caution. Small fishing boats are within 2 miles of me.

The Code message：TH2.

Table 5-4　Example of code message communication（1）

	Transmitting vessel（BTBM）	Receiving vessel（S6EI）
Calling and identity	S6EI　S6EI　S6EI DE BTBM　BTBM	BTEM　BTBM　BTBM DE S6EI　S6EI
Code message	INTERCO TH2	
Ending	$\overline{AR}$（over）	R

Example 2：Calling all stations in the vicinity（Table 5-5）

The call sign of transmitting station：S6EI.

The message：Vessel Sea Star is stopped in thick fog.

The code message：XP Sea Star.

Table 5-5　Example of code message communication（2）

	Transmitting vessel（S6EI）	Receiving vessels （all vessels in the vicinity）
Calling and identity	CQ　CQ　CQ DE S6EI　S6EI　S6EI	No answering
Code message	INTERCO XP YZ Sea Star	
Ending	$\overline{AR}$（over）	No answering

3. Plain language communication

English is seaman's common language of all nations in the world. In order to meet the communication requirements of the STCW Convention 1978 as revised, the IMO SMCP builds on a basic knowledge of the English language. It was drafted intentionally in a simplified version of maritime English in order to reduce grammatical, lexical and idiomatic varieties to a tolerable minimum, using standardized structures for the sake of its function aspects, i. e, reducing misunderstanding in safety-related verbal communication, thereby endeavoring to reflect present mari-

time English language usage on board vessels and in ship-to-shore/ship-to-ship communication.

In plain language communication, the content consists of ordinary words, phrases or sentences, its meaning can be comprehended directly.

3.1 Transmission methods of common communication elements in plain language communication

（1）Number

① In order to avoid mis-listening, the numbers are to be spoken in separate digits, e. g. "One-five-zero"for 150;

② If the number is a whole thousand, e. g. 25,000, the number of thousands is given by separate digits followed by the word "thousand". If it is not a whole thousand, e. g. 2,256, it is given by separate digits without using the word thousand;

③ The decimal point is expressed by the word decimal or point, e. g. "two decimal five" or "two point five" for 2.5.

④ The digit "0" is to be expressed for "zero" or letter "O" (ou).

Notes:

Attention! when rudder angles, e. g. in wheel orders, are given, say: "Fifteen" for 15, etc.

（2）Time

Time should be expressed in the following order:

① The word "time" or a phrase containing the word time like:

Examples: ETA＝Expected (or estimated) Time of Arrival

ETD＝Expected Time of Departure

ETCD＝Expected Time of Completion of Discharging or

Expected Time of Commencing Discharging

ETB＝Expected Time of Berthing

ETS＝Expected Time of Sailing

② The figure

Time should be expressed in the 24-hour notation and in four figures, of which the first two indicate the hour from 00 (midnight) up to 23 (11 p. m.) and the last two indicate the minute (from 00 to 59). The words like "morning ""afternoon""evening", etc. should be avoided using.

It might be confusing if one person says: "half past five" or "five thirty". The recipient will be wondering whether it refers to the morning or afternoon.

③ The unit

The unit of time should be pointed out indicating whether UTC or GMT, or local time or zone time is being used. When at sea, before entry into a harbour or port, time will normally be given in UTC or GMT. While inside a harbour or port, time will normally be given in local time.

Example: My ETA at Shanghai Pilot Station is 0930 hours local time.

④ Owing to usual practice, sometimes the word "hours" is added after the figures

Example: My ETA at quarantine anchorage is 1830 hours local time.

（3）Date

① In normal radiotelephone practice, the date can be expressed in the same way as daily English conversation; i. e, date follows month. If the time and date are expressed at the same time, time is to be put prior to date.

Example: Your ETB is 0500 local time, May 7.

② In order to emphasize the date in communication, the prefix-words "day, month, year" should be spoken in order.

Example: "May 7" is to be read as: day: zero seven; mouth: zero five.

③ The day of the week (Sunday, Monday, etc.) should not be used.

（4）Course

Course is always to be expressed in 360° notation from north (true north otherwise stated). Whether this is To or FROM, a mark can be stated.

Example: "Steer course 005°" is to be read as: Steer course zero zero five degrees.

（5）Speed

Speed is to be expressed in knots.

① without further notation, meaning speed through the water; or

② "ground speed", meaning speed over the ground.

Example: My harbour speed is zero nine knots.

（6）Bearing

① The bearing of a mark or vessel concerned is the bearing in the 360° notation from true north (unless otherwise stated), except in the case of relative bearing. Bearing may be either FROM the mark or FROM the vessel.

Examples: a. Pilot boat is bearing 215° from you.

　　　　　　b. Your bearing is 127° from the signal station.

Note:

Vessels reporting their position should always quote their bearing FROM the mark.

② Relative bearing

Relative bearing can be expressed in degrees relative to the vessel's head. More frequently this is in relation to the port or starboard row.

Example: Buoy 030° on your port bow.

（7）Distance

Distance is preferably to be expressed in nautical miles or cables (tenths of a mile) otherwise in kilometers or meters, the unit always to be stated.

（8）（Ship's）position

Position of a ship may be indicated in the following four methods: latitude and longitude; bearing and distance; reference to a navigational mark: reporting points.

① Latitude and longitude

This method should be used when clear of land, when near a featureless coast, when confusion with geographic names might arise and when giving positions obtained by electronic position

fixing instrument.

When latitude and longitude are used, these shall be expressed in degrees and minutes (and decimals of a minute if necessary), North or South of the Equator and East or West of Greenwich.

Latitude is always spoken before longitude, and latitude and longitude always spoken before numbers. The units to use are degrees and minutes, sometimes with the decimal of a minute or the seconds added if necessary, and the name North or South (of the Equator) and East or West (of Greenwich) is spoken after the units.

Example: WARNING: Dangerous wreck in position 15 degrees 34 minutes north, 061 degrees 29 minutes west.

② Bearing and distance

This method should be used when near land or a conspicuous landmark (e. g. cape lighthouse, light vessel, headlands or other fixed objects, etc., which are well-defined and charted).

The bearing is to be given before distance, and the words "bearing" and "distance" are usually given before the numbers. The bearing to be given is that from the point of reference being used, so the word "FROM" must be spoken before the name of reference point. And the bearing shall be in the 360° notation from true north. The units of distance are nautical miles, cables or meters.

Example: Your position is bearing 137°, distance 2.4 nautical miles from Big Head Lighthouse.

Note:

Vessels reporting their position should always quote their bearing FROM the mark.

③ Reference to a navigational mark

When the position is related to a mark, the mark shall be a well-defined charted object. The bearing shall be in the 360° notation from true north and shall be that of the position FROM the mark.

This method is used in the approaches to harbours and ports. The order of transmission is direction, distance, progress and name of navigation mark. Direction is given from the navigation mark using points of the compass (e. g: North, Southeast, etc.). Progress may be expressed by the words "passing, approaching, leaving, between or near, etc.". In a buoyed fairway, position should be given relative to the buoys lying on the starboard side of the ship.

Example 1: My present position is southeast four cables from the Entrance Buoy.

Example 2: I am now passing Buoy No. 2.

Example 3: My ship's position is between Buoy No. 19 and Buoy No. 21.

④ Reporting points

This method is used in those areas where designated Reporting Points have been marked on the charts, especially in VTS water areas. The ship's name or call sign, name of reporting point and the time will generally be required.

Example: New Harbour VTS Center, this is MV Gold Luck. My position: Point Unaone-alfa, time: one-seven-five-zero hours local time. Over.

（9）Geographical names

Place names used should be those on the Chart or Sailing Directions in use. Should these not be understood, latitude and longitude should be given.

（10）Signal strength

"How do you read（me）？"

"I read you ...

bad/one with signal strength one（i.e. barely perceptible）

poor/two with signal strength two（i.e. weak）

fair/three with signal strength three（i.e. fairly good）

good/four with signal strength four（i.e. good）

excellent/five with signal strength five（i.e. very good）

（11）Corrections

When a mistake is made in a message, say："Mistake..." followed by the word "Correction ... " plus the corrected part of the message.

Example："My present speed is 14 knots—mistake. Correction, my present speed is 12, one-two, knots."

（12）Repetition

If any part of the message are considered sufficiently important to need safeguarding, say "Repeat... "followed by the corresponding part of the message.

Example："My draft is 12.6 repeat one-two decimal 6 meters." "Do not overtake–repeat– do not overtake."

When a message is not properly heard, say："Say again（please）."

Note：

In all cases the radiotelephone procedures as set out in the ITU—Radio Regulations have to be observed.

3.2   General procedure of communication

（1）First call

Except having had an appointment, first call and response to first call are to be made on VHF CH16.

—The name or call sign of the addressed station（ship）（not more than three times at each time）.

—This is ××.

—The name or call sign of the calling station（ship）（not more than three times）.

—On VHF channel ××；

—Over.

Note：

Whenever a transmission is finished and a reply is expected, the word "over" must sent so that it may reduce the unnecessary pause time and improve the communication efficiency. "Over" means that the sender tells the receiver to go ahead and transmit, or "This is the end of my transmission to you and a response is necessary."

Example: Port Radio, Port Radio.

This is Yu Long, Bravo-Oscar-Alfa-Tango.

This is Yu Long, Bravo-Oscar-Alfa-Tango.

On channel one-six, over.

(2) Response to first call

—The name or call sign of the calling station (ship) (not more than three times).

—This is ××.

—The name or call sign of the answering station (ship) (not more than three times).

—Over.

Example: Yulong, Yulong, Bravo-Oscar-Alfa-Tango.

This is Port Radio. Over.

(3) Nominating the working channel

After contact being made, it is necessary that the change-over from the calling channel to the working channel should be made to carry out conversation. If the working channel has been occupied, coming back to the calling channel to renominate the working channel. Usually it is expressed by using the phrase "change to channel ××" or "agree channel ××". If there is inconvenience in the channel chosen, the other station may disagree with the choice by using the phrase "Channel ×× is unable" or "I do not have channel ××."

Example: Yu Long, Yu Long.

This is Port Radio, switch to channel two five, over.

Port Radio, Port Radio.

This is Yulong.

I will change channel two five, over.

(4) The message

The message transmission is the main part of radiotelephone communication. Whatever the message is, it should be expressed as clearly and simply as possible. Important instructions, time, important data, etc. are to be repeated or read back. The receiving station should express the understanding of the message and the receipt condition in time. If a message is not properly received, ask for it to be repeated by "Say again". If a message is received but not understood, "message not understood" can be sent.

(5) Ending

When information has been exchanged and understood, transmission should be terminated. The ending of a transmission will normally be made by the controlling station using the word "out", which means that the sender tells the receiver: "This is the end of my transmission to you and no response is required".

Note:

Before switching back to the appropriate watch keeping channel, both stations should listen to the working channel for a while to ensure that each has said all that he needs to say.

3.3　Message markers

In order to especially facilitate VHF communication or when one of the IMO Standard Marine Communication Phrases will not fit the meaning desired, one of the following eight message markers may be used to increase the probability of the purpose of the message being properly understood. If used, the message marker is to be spoken preceding the message or the corresponding part of the message.

（1）INSTRUCTION

（2）ADVICE

（3）WARNING

（4）INFORMATION

（5）QUESTION

（6）ANSWER

（7）REQUEST

（8）INTENTION

It is easy to acknowledge and give a response after receiving each marked message by using the following reply markers.

（1）INSTRUCTION：　　　INSTRUCTTION RECEIVED

（2）ADVICE：　　　　　ADVICE RECEIVED

（3）WARNING：　　　　WARNING RECEIVED

（4）INFORMATION：　　INFORMATION RECEIVED

（3）QUESTION：　　　　ANSWER

（6）REQUEST：　　　　REQUEST RECEIVED

（7）INTENTION：　　　INTENTION RECEIVEI

If the respondent agrees with the message, use the word "POSITIVE" or "YES". If the addressee disagrees with the message, the word "NEGATIVE" or "NO" should be used. Meanwhile a reason should be given for this inability by the marker word "REASON".

（1）INSTRUCTION

① The word "INSTRUCTION" indicates that the following message implies the intention of the sender to influence others by a regulation.

This means that the sender, e.g. a VTS Station or a naval vessel, must have the full authority to send such a message. The recipient has to follow this legally binding message unless s/he has contradictory safety reasons which then have to be reported to the sender.

② The words "INSTRUCTION RECEIVED" are to indicate the messages in reply to "INSTRUCTION".

Example：INSTRUCTION：Stop your engines.

　　　　　INSTRUCTION RECEIVED：Stop my engines, positive.

　　　　　or INSTRUCTION RECELVED：Stop my engines, negative.

　　　　　REASON：The tide is too strong.

（2）ADVICE

① The word "ADVICE" indicates that the following message implies the intention of the sender to influence others by a recommendation.

The decision whether to follow the ADVICE still stays with the recipient. ADVICE does not necessarily have to be followed but should be considered very carefully.

② The words "ADVICE RECEIVED" are to indicate the a message in reply to "AD-VICE".

Example：ADVICE：Please alter your course to port.

ADVICE RECEIVED：Alter my course to port, positive.

or ADVICE RECEIVED：Alter my course to port, negative.

REASON：Another vessel is approaching me.

（3）WARNING

① The word "WARNING" indicates that the following message implies the intention of the sender to inform others about danger.

This means that any recipient of a WARNING should pay immediate attention to the danger mentioned. Consequences of a WARNING will be up to the recipient.

② The words "WARNING RECEIVED" are to indicate the messages in reply to "WARN-ING".

Example：WARNING：Obstruction in fairway.

WARNING RECEIVED：Obstruction in fairway.

（4）INFORMATION

① The word "INFORMATION" indicates that the following message is restricted to ob-served facts, situations, etc.

This marker is preferably used for navigational and traffic information, etc. Consequences of INFORMATION will be up to the recipient.

② The words "INFORMATION RECEIVED" are to indicate messages in reply to "IN-FORMATION".

Example：INFORMATION：MV Noname will overtake to the west of you.

INFORMATION RECEIVED, MV Noname will overtake to the west of me.

（5）QUESTION and ANSWER

① The word "QUESTION" indicates that the following message is of interrogative character. The word "ANSWER" indicates that the following message is the reply to a previous question.

The use of this marker removes any doubt on whether a question is being asked or statement being made, especially when interrogatives such as what, where, why, who, how are addition-ally used at the beginning of the question. The recipient is expected to return an answer.

Note that an answer should not contain another question.

② Whether the questions beginning with the words "when, what, where, why, who, how, how many" or questions which give alternatives, or questions which require a Yes or No answer, the message-marker "QUESTION" should be spoken before the question sentence, and the message-marker "ANSWER" should be spoken before the answer sentence.

Example 1: QUESTION: (What is) your maximum draft?

ANSWER: My maximum draft is zero seven meters.

Example 2: QUESTION: Do you intend to pass ahead of me?

ANSWER: Yes, I will pass ahead of you.

or ANSWER: No, I will not pass ahead of you.

（6）REQUEST

① The word "REQUEST" indicates that the following message is asking for action from others with respect to the vessel.

The use of this marker is to signal: I want something to be arranged or provided, e. g. ship's stores requirements, tugs, permission, etc.

② The words "REQUEST RECEIVED" are to indicate the messages in reply to "REQUEST".

Example: REQUEST: Please send a boat to me.

REQUEST RECEIVED: Send a boat to you, positive.

or REQUEST RECEIVED: Send a boat to you, negative.

REASON: The sea is too rough.

（7）INTENTION

① The word "INTENTION" indicates that the following message informs others about immediate navigational action intended to be taken.

The use of this message marker is logically restricted to messages announcing navigational actions by the vessel sending this message.

② The words "INTENTION RECEIVED" are to indicate a message in reply to "INTENTION".

Example: INTENTION: I will reduce my speed.

INTENTION RECEIVED: You will reduce your speed.

3.4   Examples for VHF radiotelephony standard communication

（1）Example 1: Ship-to-ship communication

Nippon Maru: Gulf Trader, Gulf Trader, this is Nippon Maru, Juliet-Sierra-Alfa-Alfa; Nippon Maru, Juliet-Sierra-Alfa-Alfa, on VHF channel one six.

Gulf Trader: Nippon Maru, Juliet-Sierra-Alfa-Alfa, this is Gulf Trader, Alfa-Six-Zulu-Zulu. Over.

Nippon Maru: Gulf Trader, this is Nippon Maru, switch to VHF channel zero six. Over.

Gulf Trader: Nippon Maru, this is Gulf Trader, agree VHF channel two six. Over.

Nippon Maru: Gulf Trader, this is Nippon Maru, mistake, switch to VHF channel zero six. I say again, switch to VHF channel zero six. Over.

Gulf Trader: Nippon Maru, this is Gulf Trader, agree VHF channel zero six. Over.

Nippon Maru: Gulf Trader, this is Nippon Maru. QUESTION: What is your destination? Over.

Gulf Trader: Nippon Maru, this is Gulf Trader. ANSWER: My destination is Tokyo. Over.

Nippon Maru: Gulf Trader, this is Nippon Maru, understood, Tokyo. INFORMATION: A vessel is aground. POSITION: near Entrance Light vessel. Over.

Gulf Trader: Nippon Maru, this is Gulf Trader, say again all after position. Over.

Nippon Maru: Gulf Trader, this is Nippon Maru, I say again. POSITION: near Entrance Light Vessel. Over.

Gulf Trader: Nippon Maru. this is Gulf Trader. INFORMATION RECEIVED: A vessel is aground. POSITION: near Entrance Light Vessel. Over.

Nippon Maru: Gulf Trader, this is Nippon Maru. INFORMATION: A delay is expected in the approaches, period four-eight hours. Over.

Gulf Trader: Nippon Maru, this is Gulf Trade. INFORMATION RECEIVED: A delay is expected in the approaches period four-eight hours, thank you. Over.

Nippon Maru: Gulf Trader, this is Nippon Maru, nothing more. Out.

(2) Example 2: Ship-to-shore communication

(Ship station: Western Sky; Shore station: Singapore Port Operations)

Western Sky: Singapore Port Operations. Singapore Port Operations. This is Western sky on VHF channel one-two. Over.

Singapore Port Ops: Western sky, Western Sky, this is Singapore Port Operations. Over.

Western Sky: Singapore Port Operations, this is Western Sky. INFORMATION: My ETA position is East Pilot station. Time is one-three-four-five UTC. Over

Singapore Port Ops: Western Sky, this is Singapore Port Operations, mistake, time is one-four-three-zero UTC now. Over.

Western Sky: Singapore Port Operations, this is Western Sky, correction, my ETA is one-five-four-five UTC. Over.

Singapore Port Ops: Western Sky, this is Singapore Port Operations.

INFORMATION RECEIVED: Your ETA position is East Pilot Station. Time is one-five-four-five UTC.

INSTRUCTION: Anchor in the General Purpose Anchorage. REASON: your berth is occupied. Over.

Western Sky: Singapore Port Operations, this is Western Sky.

INSTRUCTON RECELVED: Anchor in the General Purpose Anchorage, nothing more. Over.

Singapore Port Ops: Western Sky, this is Singapore Port Operations. Out.

Notes:

(1) When ship-to-ship communication, the first calling station is the controlling station; when ship-to-shore communication, the shore station is the controlling station.

(2) Usually, the "OUT" is given by the controlling station to end the communication, the other party does not need answering it.

4. Broadcast communication

VHF Broadcast Communication is a special kind of plain language communication form. It has only one-way information transferring, and no information exchanges. It usually be taken place in ports or VTS waterways.

4.1　Procedure of VHF broadcast communication

（1）First call

This is the transmission that a station uses to start a broadcast.

—The name of listening ship: all ships

all ships in …(water area)…

all ships (type/nationality/company)

—The name of broadcasting station:

Such as: This is Singapore Radio

　　　　　Hong Kong Mardep

　　　　　Kanmon Martis

—Types of broadcast information: navigational warning

　　　　　　　　　　　　　navigational information

　　　　　　　　　　　　　navigational instruction

　　　　　　　　　　　　　weather information and so on

—Designating broadcasting and listening channels:

Except having had an appointment, usually for common broadcast message, the first call should be made on VHF channel 16, and the message should be broadcast and listened to on the working channel. The calling phrase used is: "change to VHF channel ××, over".

Note:

Sometimes the word "attention" may be spoken at the beginning of the first call.

（1）Broadcast message

This is the transmission during which the message will be broadcast. The calling procedure should be first repeated before broadcasting the detailed contents.

（2）Ending

The word "out" is used to indicate the end of broadcast. After saying "out", the broadcasting station should listen for short while to learn whether other stations want a repeat of all or part of the broadcast message. If a repeat is requested, the broadcast becomes an exchange. If no request for a repeat from other stations within a reasonable time, the broadcasting station may change its radio set back to the appropriate watch-keeping channel.

4.2　Examples for broadcast communication

—First call (on VHF channel 16)

Attention all ships in the inner anchorage, attention all ships in the inner anchorage, this is Inchon pilot station, this is Inchon pilot station. Navigational information: change to VHF channel one-four, change to channel one four, change to channel one four, over.

—Broadcast message (on VHF channel 14)

All ships in the inner anchorage, all ships in the inner anchorage, this is Inchon pilot station, information: Inchon pilot service is suspended. Reason: tropical storm, I say again, Inchon pilot service is suspended, reason: tropical storm, out.

Note:

In usual practice, the broadcasting station will transmit the message at regular intervals. Each receiving station should pay particular attention to the message, especially the key words or phrases such as time, position and so on. Write them down, check on your chart and report to the master if necessary.

第三课 甚高频无线电话通信法

1. 概述

按照通信信文的语言形式来分类,VHF 无线电话通信的基本方式有两种:明语通信和码语通信。《国际信号规则》要求,通信时应首先使用明语。当存在语言隔阂时,可以使用码语通信。

按照通信是否有信息交换分类,可以分为交换通信和广播通信。交换通信的通信各方通过交换通话沟通信息。广播通信的各方一般不必交换通话,只由发信台发送信息,收信台只接收即可。比如,岸台向船台发布航行通告、航行警告、气象预报等。

按照信文内容分类,VHF 无线电话通信可以分为日常业务通信、公众业务通信、遇险、紧急与安全通信和搜救作业通信四大类。其中日常业务通信的业务范围很广,是 VHF 无线电话通信的主要业务,包括:

(1)船舶抵离港口、靠离泊位、申请引航员等;

(2)船舶避让;

(3)各种船舶代理业务;

(4)VTS 水域报告。

公众业务通信是船上旅客、船员利用 VHF 通过港口话台与陆地用户通话,此项业务需付费,除此以外利用 VHF 的通信都是免费的。货船不提供公众通信业务,游轮可以提供公众通信业务。

搜救作业通信是负责搜救作业的船舶、飞机、岸台之间或它们与遇险船之间与救助有关的通信。

本节按信文语言形式分别对 VHF 无线电话的码语通信和明语通信这两种方式和广播通信予以介绍。

2. 码语通信方法

码语通信是借助《国际信号规则》,事先将要发送的信文用两字母(通用部分)或三字母(医疗部分)编辑好,用字母拼读的形式发送出去。

2.1 字母和数字拼读表(见表 5-2,5-3)

拼读时应语音清晰,速度稍慢地读给对方,避免造成不必要的重复或通信中断。字母和数字拼读表不仅用于码语通信,在明语通信中也广泛用于拼读船名、呼号、地名和难于听懂的字词等。

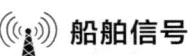

表 5-2　字母拼读表

字母	代号	发音
A	Alfa	AL FAH
B	Bravo	BRAH VOH
C	Charlie	CHAR LEE
D	Delta	DELL TAH
E	Echo	ECK OH
F	Foxtrot	FOKS TROT
G	Golf	GOLF
H	Hotel	HOH TELL
I	India	IN DEE AH
J	Juliett	JEW LEE ETT
K	Kilo	KEY LOH
L	Lima	LEE MAH
M	Mike	MIKE
N	November	NO VEM BER
O	Oscar	OSS CAH
P	Papa	PAH PAH
Q	Quebec	KEH BECK
R	Romeo	ROW MEOH
S	Sierra	SEE AIR RAH
T	Tango	TANG GO
U	Uniform	YOU NEE FORM
V	Victor	VIK TAH
W	Whiskey	WISS KEY
X	X-ray	ECKS RAY
Y	Yankee	YANG KEY
Z	Zulu	ZOO LOO

表 5-3　数字拼读表

数字	代号	发音
0	NADAZERO	NAH DAH ZAY ROH
1	UNAONE	OO NAH WUN
2	BISSOTWO	BEES SOH TOO

续表

数字	代号	发音
3	TERRATHREE	TAY RAH TREE
4	KARTEFOUR	KAR TAY FOUR
5	PANTAFIVE	PAN TAH FIVE
6	SOXISIX	SOK SEE SIX
7	SETTESEVEN	SAY TAY SEVEN
8	OKTOEIGHT	OK TOH AIT
9	NOVENINE	NO VAY NINER
小数点	DECIMAL	DAY SEE MAL
句号	STOP	STOP

2.2 通信程序符号

（1）DE（Delta Echo）= this is。

（2）CQ（Charlie Quebec）表示呼叫在附近的所有船台。

（3）INTERCO 或 YU（Yankee Uniform）表示以下使用国际信号码进行通信。

（4）YZ（Yankee Zulu）表示以下使用明语发送地名、船名等。

（5）$\overline{\text{AS}}$（Alfa Sierra）表示呼叫台不能立即接收信号,请等候。

（6）$\overline{\text{AR}}$（Alfa Romeo）表示信文已发送完毕。

（7）R（Romeo）表示信文已收到。

（8）RPT（Romeo Papa Tango）表示信文重发；

RPT+AA（Ala Alfa）= ……以后全部重发；

RPT+AB（Alfa Bravo）= ……以前全部重发；

RPT+BN（Bravo November）= 在……与……之间的全部重发；

RPT+WA（Whiskey Alfa）= ……以后的一个字（组）重发；

RPT+WB（Whiskey Bravo）= ……以前的一个字（组）重发。

2.3 通信程序

VHF 无线电话码语通信程序包括:呼叫、识别、通信信文、通信结束四个步骤。

（1）呼叫

呼叫指名的船台:发送收信船的呼号或船名,逐字拼读,不超过三次。

呼叫在附近的所有船舶:发送"CQ"不超过三次。

（2）识别

发送"DE"及发信船的呼号或船名,逐字拼读,不超过三次。

收信船按（1）、（2）的相同程序回答。

（3）通信信文

首先发送"INTERCO"；

然后发送信文,所有码组均应拼读发送,信文中的船名、地名用明语发送,但在明语之前应先发送"YZ"。

（4）通信结束

发信船发送"$\overline{AR}$"；

收信船回答"R"。

2.4 码语通信示例

例1 指名呼叫

发信船呼号：BJAA　　收信船呼号：BFQQ

信文内容：你勿进港。

　　　　　　　You must not enter harbour.

码语信文是：UO。

	发信船 BJAA	收信船 BFQQ
呼叫与识别	BFQQ　　BFQQ　　BFQQ DE BJAA　　BJAA　　BJAA	BJAA　　BJAA　　BJAA DE BFQQ　　BFQQ　　BFQQ
信文发送	INTERCO UO	完成接收 R； 没听明白 RPT AA（AB/BN/WA/WB）
结束	$\overline{AR}$	不必回答

例2：呼叫周围所有的船舶

发信船呼号：BJAA

信文内容：预计我船到达钦州的时间是地方时1800。

码语信文是：UR　QINZHOU　1800 LT。

	发信船 BJAA	收信船
呼叫与识别	CQ　　CQ　　CQ DE BJAA　　BJAA　　BJAA	不必回答
信文发送	INTERCO　UR　YZ　QINZHOU 1800 LT	完成接收 R； 没听明白 RPT AA（AB/BN/WA/WB）
结束	$\overline{AR}$	不必回答

3. 明语通信

VHF无线电话通信应首先考虑使用明语通信。明语就是广大船员的母语和英语。标准海事通信用语是国际海员进行通信的日常用语（明语）。

3.1 明语通信中常用通信要素的发送方法

（1）数字

①为了接收方能准确接收，数字应逐位读出。如2 400应读为two four zero zero（2-4-0-0）；150应读作"一五零"，2.5应读作"二点五"。

②整数"千"的数字可将整数逐位读出,然后读"千"。如 12 000 应读为 one two thousand,也可以逐位读出：one two zero zero zero。

③数字中的小数点应用"decimal"一词表示。海员习惯用"point"表示。

④注意,当读舵角及舵令时,应按以下示例：15 读作"十五",20 读作"二十"。

（2）时间

①以 24 小时计时法,用四位数字表示"时"与"分",避免用"上午""下午""早晨""晚上"等字句。

②在数字前应冠以"time"或表示时间的其他习惯用语。如：

　　ETA（Expected Time of Arrival）预计抵达时间

　　ETD（Expected Time of Departure）预计离港时间

　　ETCD（Expected Time of Completion of Discharging）预计完货时间

　　　　　（Expected Time of Commencing of Discharging）预计开始卸货时间

　　ETB（Expected Time of Berthing）预计靠泊时间

　　ETS（Expected Time of Sailing）预计开航时间

③在数字后面加"GMT"或"Local Time"以确认是"世界时"或"地方时"。船舶在海上用"GMT",在港内或其附近用"Local Time"为宜。例如：

Your ETS is 0900 Local Time.

你船预计开航时间是地方时 0900。

④在数字后面加上"hours",表示"钟点"。

Your ETB at quarantine anchorage is 1530 hours.

（3）日期

①一般,按常规的英语习惯表示。如：Your ETB is 0500 Local Time May 7.

②为强调日期时,按日、月、年的次序以"day""month""year"冠在数字之前表示。

　　例如：5 月 7 日应读作 month：zero five；day：zero seven。

（4）航向

航向总是采用由真北起算,以 360°表示。

可说明是驶往物标的航向,还是驶离物标的航向。

航向以"course ×××　degrees"表示。

"×××"表示具体数字,以下相同。

如：航向 005°。应读作：Steer course zero zero five degrees。

（5）航速

航速以"speed ××　knots"表示。例如：

我船对地速度 9 节。应读作：My speed over ground is zero nine knots。

若无其他说明,则表示是相对于水的速度；

"对地速度"表示相对于地（海底）的速度。

（6）方位

方位以"bearing ×××　degrees"表示,并应说明该方位的参照点。

例如：The pilot boat is bearing 215 degrees from you. Your bearing is 127 degrees from signal station.

除相对方位的情况外,物标或船舶的方位是从真北(除非另有说明)起算以 360°表示。方位可以从物标起算,也可以从船舶起算。例如:"Pilot boat is bearing 215 degrees from you." "引航船在你船 215°方位上。"

相对方位可以用相对于船首的度数表示。比较常用的是从船首方向起算向左舷或右舷的度数。例如:"Buoy 030 degrees on your port bow." "浮筒在你船左舷前方 30°。"

(7)距离

距离通常用海里或链(1/10 n mile)、千米或米表示,比如:"distance ×× n mile."

(8)船位

在 VHF 无线电话中,船位的常用表达方法有:经、纬度表示法,方位、距离表示法,以导航标志或船舶报告点为参照的表示法等。

①经、纬度表示法

在无参照物的大海上使用。应读作:

Position:Latitude ××× degrees ×× minutes north(south), Longitude ××× degrees ×× minutes east(west).

当使用纬度、经度时,应以度、分来表示,并应标出北纬或南纬;东经或西经。例如:"WARNING:dangerous wreck in position 15 degrees 34 minutes north 061 degrees 29 minutes west." "警告:在北纬 15°34′,西经 61°29′处有危险沉船。"

②方位、距离表示方法

这种方法应以易于辨认且在海图上明确标示的物标为参照点,按物标的方位+距离+from+参照点名称的顺序来表达。读作:

Position:bearing ××× degrees, distance ×× miles from lighthouse. 如:My anchor position is bearing 128 degrees, distance 6 miles from HUANGBAIZUI lighthouse. 我的船位是距黄白嘴灯塔方位 128°,距离 6 海里。

注意:

作为参照点的物标名称前一定要加"from"。

方位应是由物标起算至船的真方位。

③以船舶报告点(线)为参照点表示法

常用词有:"passing" "approaching" "near" "between… and…" "leaving"。

船舶航行在日本濑户内海和世界各地 VIS 报告水域,有很多报告线。驾驶员可以用"我正通过某某报告线"向日本各交管中心(MARTS=Maritime Traffic Information Service)或 VTS 中心报告船位。

如:I am passing Reporting Line HA.

(9)地理名称

使用的地名必须是《海图》或《航路指南》中所使用的名称。否则,应给出经纬度。

(10)信号强度

How do you read me? 你听我的信号如何?

I read you bad/poor/fair/good/excellent. 极弱/很弱/还好/较好/很好。

(11)改正

当信息出现错误时,说:"……错误",随后说:"改正……"再加上正确信息。

例如："My present speed is 14 knots, mistake. Correction, my present speed is 12, one-two knots.""我现在的速度是 14 节,错误。改正,我现在的速度是 12 节。"

(12)重复

如果你认为某些信息非常重要,为确保无误,可说:"重复……",随后是信文的相应部分。例如："My draft is 12.6, repeat, one-two point six meters.""Do not overtake—repeat—do not overtake.""我的吃水为 12.6,重复,12.6 米。""不得追越——重复——不得追越。"

如果信息没有确切听到,说:"Say again (please).""请再说一遍。"

3.2　明语通信程序

(1)初始呼叫

除已有约定外(VTS 中心、代理和引航站等都有固定工作频道,可以直接在该频道上呼叫并通信),船舶间或船岸间 VHF 无线电话通信的初始呼叫与回答均应在 16 频道上进行,待通信联系建立后转入商定好的工作频道。其格式为:

呼叫:

—被呼叫船名称或呼号不超过 3 次

—This is ×××.

—呼叫船名称或呼号不超过 3 次

—Over

回答:

—呼叫船名称或呼号不超过 3 次

—This is ×××.

—被呼叫船名称或呼号不超 3 次

—Over

(2)商定工作频道

建立通信联系之后,应商定并转换工作频道进行通话。提出转频道一方(被呼叫台)应等待对方(呼叫台)确认所转换的频道后再转换。如果该频道被占用,仍转回呼叫频道重新商定。通常用"请转××频道 change to channel ××"和"同意转到××频道 agree change to channel ××"。

(3)在工作频道上重新识别后进行通信

信文发送是通信的主体,力求简洁,语速稍缓,声音清晰。对于重要的指示、时间、数据等重要内容要复诵。为了保证通信畅通,先按下 VHF 电话机的讲话开关,然后讲话,讲话完毕后,松开讲话开关。通信双方收信发信角色转换时,均以"over"为标志。"over"表示讲话结束,等待对方讲话。

(4)通信结束

在无线电话通信中,以发信船和收信船先后发出"out"为结束标志。

例:

On VHF Channel 16

Yong Yi：　　Yong Xing, Yong Xing. This is Yong Yi, Yong Yi calling over.

Yon Xing：　　Yong Yi, Yong Yi. This is Yong Xing, Yong Xing, please change to channel 12, over.

Yong Yi： Yong Xing, Yong Xing. This is Yong Yi, Yong Yi, agree change to channel 12, over.

On VHF Channel 12

Yong Yi： Yong Xing, Yong Xing. This is Yong Yi, Yong Yi, what is your intention? Over.

Yong Xing： Yong Yi, Yong Yi. This is Yong Xing, Yong Xing, I want to alter my course to port.

Yong Yi： OK, I will alter my course to port. Over.

Yong Xing： What is your last port of call? Over.

Yong Yi： My last port of call is Yokohama. Over.

Yong Xing： What is your destination? Over.

Yong Yi： My destination is Singapore, over. Anything else? Over.

Yong Xing： Nothing more, good bye, out.

Yong Yi： Good-bye, out.

3.3 明语通信中信文标识的使用

信文标识是为了标明其后的语句性质,使收信方便于理解所发送的信文的性质。

信文标识如下：

Question（询问）表示以下信文具有询问性质。

Information（信息）表示以下信文的内容只限于观察到的事实。

Advice(建议) 表示以下信文是发信人向收信人提出建议。

Warning(警告) 表示以下信文是向其他船只通报危险。

Answer（回答）表示以下信文对前面的询问的回答。

Request(请求) 表示以下信文的内容是要求他船对本船采取避让行动。

Intention（意图）表示以下信文是通知他船有关我船要采取的航行措施。

Instruction(指示) 表示以下信文是发信人以某项规则指示收信人。

对信文标识的回答如下：

信文标识	回答
Question	Answer
Information	Information Received
Advice	Advice Received
Warning	Warning Received
Request	Request Received
Intention	Intention Received
Instruction	Instruction Received

3.3.1   询问(**Question**)

表示以下信文是询问性质的。

说明:这一标题用以消除是询问问题还是进行陈述的疑虑。特别是当疑问词诸如"什么""哪里""为什么""谁""如何"等用在问题之首时是期望收话人给予回答的。

(1) Question:What is your ship name and call sign? Spell the name of your vessel.

你的船名和呼号是什么? 拼出你的船名。

(2) Question:What is your GPS position? 你的船位在哪里?

(3) Question:What is your maximum draft and your air draft?

你的最大吃水和净空高度是多少?

(4) Question:What is your present course and speed?

你现在的航向和速度是多少?

(5) Question:What is your pilot boarding time?

你船引航员登船时间?

(6) Question:What is your ETA to Pilot Station/RACON M/Buoy No.15?

你预计到达引航站/RACON M/15 号灯浮的时间?

(7) Question:Are you underway/anchoring/aground/berthing/departing?

你船在航/锚泊/搁浅/靠泊/离泊吗?

(8) Question: What is your cargo? Do you carry any dangerous cargo?

你船装的什么货? 是否装有危险货物?

(9) Question: What is wind direction and force/sea state in your position?

What is visibility in vicinity of your present position?

你船位置的风力和风向/海况怎么样? 你船位置附近的能见度怎么样?

(10) Question：What is your present course/heading?

你船现在的航向/船首向是多少度。

3.3.2   信息(**Information**)

表示以下信文局限于所了解到的事实、情境等。

说明:这一标题适合用于航行和交通信息等,信息的重要程度由收话人决定。

(1) Information：Unknown object(s) in N24°20′, E118°10′.

在 N24°20′, E118°10′处有不明物体。

(2) Information：Wreck/obstruction located in position N24°34′, E118°10′ marked by Emergency Position Indicating Wrecking Beacon.

沉船/碍航物位于 N24°34′, E118°10′处,设有应急沉船示位标。

(3) Information：Uncharted reef/rock/shoal reported in position N23°34′, E117°12′.

据报在 N23°34′, E117°12′处有海图上未标明的暗礁/礁石/浅滩。

(4) Information：Depth of water is not sufficient in position N24°34′, E118°.

在 N24°34′, E118°位置没有足够水深。

(5) Information：Buoy No.15 in position N24°20′, E118°10′ is damaged/off station/missing. Re-established in position N24°20′, E118°10′ .

在 N24°20′，E118°10′处的 15 号灯浮损坏/移位/失踪，在 N24°20′，E118°10′位置重设。

（6）Information：Small fishing boats in area around N24°20′, E118°10′. Navigation with caution.

在 N24°20′，E118°10′区域有小渔船。请谨慎驾驶。

（7）Information：Nets with/without buoys in this area. Navigation with caution.

该区域的渔网上有/没有浮标。谨慎航行。

（8）Information：MV SUN RISE to the 030 degrees on your port bow is turning/anchoring/overtaking you/not under command.

"日升"轮在你船左舷前方 30°转向/抛锚/追越你船/失控。

（9）Information：You will meet crossing traffic vessel in position bearing 080 degrees, 1.6 n mile from you. Navigation with caution.

你船将在距你方位 080°，距离 1.6 海里处遇到穿越船。谨慎驾驶。

（10）Information：Vessel on opposite course is passing to the head of you.

对遇船正在通过你船船首。

（11）Information：You have permission to enter the traffic lane. 你已获准进入航道。

（12）Information：Anchor position N24°18′, E118°01′ allocated to you.

你船被安排 N24°18′，E118°01′锚位。

（13）Information：Collision in position N24°20′, E118°10′.

在 N24°20′，E118°10′处发生碰撞。

（14）Information：Area around JIUJIEJIAO has temporarily been closed for navigation.

在九节礁区域临时封航。

（15）Information：Visibility is reduced by fog. You should proceed with great caution.

由于雾的影响，能见度变差。你船应极其谨慎航行。

（16）Information：VTS don't have your further berthing information. Please contact with your agent.

VTS 没有你船进一步的靠泊信息。请联系你的代理。

（17）Information：Your pilot boarding time is delayed. Please contact with pilot station on channel 06.

你船引航时间延迟。请通过 06 频道联系引航站。

（18）Information：Cable/Pipeline moored in position N24°34′, E118°12′. Wide berth requested.

电缆/管道设置在 N24°34′，E118°12′位置。请注意宽让。

（19）Information：VTS cannot locate you on my radar screen. Please supply your GPS position.

VTS 无法在雷达上发现你船。请提供你船的船位。

（20）Information：Your AIS information is wrong. Please check it again.

你船 AIS 信息发生错误。请重新检查。

3.3.3　建议（Advice）

表示以下信文含有发话人企图通过建议影响他方的意图。

说明:是否遵循这一建议由收话人决定。收话人不必非得执行这一建议,但应非常仔细地加以考虑。

（1）Advice：Please keep clear of the fishing boats/avoid the fishing boats.

保持让清渔船/避开渔船。

（2）Advice：Please do not overtake/cross/leaving the fairway until MV SUN SIRE passing ahead of you.

不要追越/横越/离开航道直到"日升"轮通过你船船头。

（3）Advice：You cannot proceed. Please select position to drop anchor.

你船已不能继续航行。请择地抛锚。

（4）Advice：Area around JIUJIEJIAO temporarily closed for navigation due to poor visibility. Please select position to drop anchor. Waiting for further notice.

由于能见度很差,在九节礁周围区域临时封航。所有船舶必须择地抛锚,等待进一步的消息。

（5）Advice：Please keep your present course/steer a new course of 020 degrees.

保持目前的航向/采用新的航向020°。

（6）Advice：Keep on the starboard side of the channel. 保持航道右侧航行。

（7）Advice：Avoid meeting outbound vessel in vicinity of buoy No.11 area.

避免在11号灯浮附近交会。

（8）Advice：Large vessel is leaving the fairway. Keep clear of the fairway approach.

大型船舶正驶离航道,让清航道的进出口处。

（9）Advice：Maintain/Keep 500 m at least from other anchoring vessels.

请与他船保持至少500米锚泊距离。

（10）Advice：Please contact with MV SUN RISE in position bearing 080 degrees, 1.6 n mile from you as soon as possible and make sure wide berth passing with her.

请尽快联系在距你方位080°,距离1.6海里处位置的"日升"轮,确保宽让。

3.3.4　警告（Warning）

表示以下信文含有发话人企图向其他船舶通报有关危险的情况。

说明:这意味着任何收到警告的收话人应对所提及的危险立即引起警觉。警告的重要程度将由收话人决定。

（1）Warning：You are not keeping to the correct traffic lane. You must keep to port side/starboard side of the fairway.

你船没保持在正确的航道上。你船必须保持在航道左/右侧航行。

（2）Warning：You are proceeding at a dangerous speed. Slow down to your minimum safe speed.

你船正以危险速度航行。降低到最低安全速度通过。

（3）Warning：You present course is too close to inbound/outbound vessel/to the vessel that you are overtaking/to the red buoy/green buoy.

你船目前的航线太靠近进口/出口船/被追越船/红浮筒/绿浮筒。

（4）Warning：You are running into danger. Shallow water/Submerged wreck to the position bearing 080 degrees，1.6 n mile of you. Risk of collision with MV SUN RISE.

你船处于危险中。你船方位 080°,距离 1.6 海里处位置有浅滩/沉船。与他船"日升"轮有碰撞危险。

（5）Warning：You must wait for MV SUN RISE to cross ahead of you before entering the fairway.

你船必须等待"日升"轮横过你船船头后进入航道。

（6）Warning：You must stand by on VHF channel 8 and 16 all the time in this area.

在这个水域你船必须始终保持守听 VHF 08 频道和 16 频道。

（7）Warning：You must report to VTS when you are passing Reporting Line.

当你船驶经报告线时,必须向交管报告。

（8）Warning：You must keep clear of this area，search and rescue in progress.

你船必须让清该区域,搜救作业正在进行。

（9）Warning：It is dangerous to anchor in your present position. You must heave up anchor.

在你船现在的位置抛锚是危险的。你船必须马上起锚。

（10）Warning：Please check your anchor position immediately. I am afraid you are dragging.

请立即检查你船锚位。怀疑你船正在走锚。

3.3.5　回答(Answer)

可以为 Yes,No/Standby/No information/I will/can or I will/can not.

表示以下信文是对前面咨询的答复。

说明:注意一个回答中不应包含另一问题。

例如:"Answer：My present maximum draft is 8 meters."

3.3.6　请求(Request)

表示以下信文是请求他方采取与船舶有关的行动。

说明:这一标题用于示意"我希望有关事项得到安排或提供,如拖轮、引航员、医疗队"。

注意:请求不准用于涉及航行规则也不准用于更改避碰规则。

例如:"Request：I require one pilot and two tugs."

3.3.7　意图(Intention)

这表示以下信文是通知他方关于即将要采取的航行活动。

说明:这一信文标题原则上仅限用于发信船发布航行活动的信文。

例如:"Intention：I will reduce my speed. "

3.3.8　指示 Instruction

这表示以下信文含有发话人企图通过规章制度影响他方的意图。

说明:这意味着发话人诸如 VTS 台或军舰,必须拥有全权发布这样的信文的授权或权限。收话人必须遵循这一合法的约束性的信文,除非他具有悖于安全的理由,并必须报告给发话人。

例如:"Instruction：Do not anchor in the fairway. "

3.4   VHF 无线电话标准通信范例

例1：船舶间通信（初始呼叫一定在 16 频道上）

On VHF channel 16

Sincere Gemini：Ocean Star, Ocean Star, this is Sincere Gemini, Sincere Gemini, calling. Over.

Ocean Star：Sincere Gemini, Sincere Gemini, this is Ocean Star, Ocean Star, please change to channel 12. Over

Sincere Gemini：Ocean Star, this is Sincere Gemini, agree change to channel 12, Over.

On VHF channel 12

Ocean Star. Sincere Gemini, this is Ocean Star. Over

Sincere Gemini：Ocean Star, this is Sincere Gemini, Question：What is your next port of call? Over.

Ocean Star：Answer：My next port of call is New York. Over.

Sincere Gemini：Information：There are some fishing boats ahead of you. You should navigate with caution. Over.

Ocean Star：Information-received（Roger）, Intention：I will alter my course to starboard. Over.

Sincere Gemini：Intention-received, Warning：Tropical Storm Sangmei position latitude 22 degrees 22 minutes north, longitude 122 degrees 21 minutes east, over.

Ocean Star：Waring-received, anything else? Over.

Sincere Gemini：Nothing more, good-bye, out.

Ocean Star：good-bye, out.

例2：船—岸台间通信（如果岸台公告其工作频道，可直接在工作频道呼叫并通信）

On VHF channel 16 calling

Ocean Star：Kanmon Martis, Kanmon Martis, this is Ocean Star, Ocean Star calling. Over.

Kanmon Martis：Ocean Star, Ocean Star, this is Kanmon Martis, Kanmon Martis. Please change to channel 12. Over.

Ocean Star：Agree to change to channel 12. Over.

Kanmon Martis：Ocean Star, Ocean Star, this is Kanmon Martis, Kanmon Martis. What is your call sign? Over

Ocean Star：My call sign is Gast, Golf Alfa Sierra Tango. Over.

Kanmom Martis：Roger, what is last port of call? Over.

Ocean Star：My last port of call is Kobe. Over.

Kanmon Martis：Roger, please report your position. Over.

Ocean Star：Wilco, I am passing Reporting Line MN. Over.

Kanmon Martis：Instruction：You must navigate on traffic lane. Over

Ocean Star：Wilco, What time should I report to you again? Over.

Kanmon Martis：When you passing Reporting Line BG, report to me. Over.

Ocean Star：Wilco, anything else? Over.

Kanmon Marits：Nothing more, good-bye. Out.

Ocean Star：Good bye. Out.

4. 广播通信

广播通信由 VTS 机构对其管辖水域内的船舶用明语播发有关信息,如气象、航行警报等一些与船舶航行安全有关的信息。各播发台在播发信息前,都会在 16 频道上发布引语,即他有什么信息要在哪个频道播发。驾驶员要认真收听引语,然后转到其指定的工作频道(工作频道因信息播发台不同而有所不同)认真收听这些信息。广播通信主要是单向通信,即播发台播发信息,船台接收信息,船台不必做出回答,除非没听清楚所发的信息,可以要求播发台重发全部或部分信息,这时就变成双向通信了。

广播通信程序：

(1)初始呼叫

①首先呼叫该信息的接收对象,如：

all ships 所有船舶

all ships in position... 在……位置的所有船舶

all oil tankers 所有油船

②播发信息的船舶的名称,如：

This is ××× 这是×××

③播发信息台的名称和要转换的工作频道,如：

Hong Kong Mardep 香港海事处

Kanmon Martis 关门交管中心

④信息种类,如：

navigational warning 航行警告

navigational information 航行通告

navigational instruction 航行指示

weather forecast 天气预报

⑤指定播发信息频道。

(2)播发信息

(3)广播结束

广播通信实例：

初始呼叫（在 16 频道上）

Attention all ships in the inner anchorage, attention all ships in the inner anchorage, this is Dalian pilot station, navigational information, change to channel 12, over.

广播信文（在 12 频道上）

All ships in the inner anchorage, all ships in the inner anchorage, this is Dalian pilot station, information：Dalian pilot service is suspended, reason：tropical storm. I say again：Dalian pilot service is suspended, reason：tropical storm. Out.

5. VTS 常见规范处罚条款

5.1 超速行驶

信文原文实例：

MSC HANJIN, this is Beihai VTS calling, over.

INFORMATION：MAIN FAIRWAY OF BEIHAI PORT speed limit is 15 knots. You are over-speed now.

This is first warning. Please slow down. If you refuse to do so, you may get fine(punished) according to local regulation.

译文：

"地中海韩进"，这是北海交管呼叫，听到请回答。

信息提醒：北海港主航道限速 15 节，你现在已经超速。

这是第一次警告，请降速。否则根据相关法规规定，你可能会面临罚款或其他相应处罚。

超速行为：违反《中华人民共和国海上交通安全法》第 9 条，根据《中华人民共和国海上海事处罚法》第 24 条第 3 款和第 2 款第 5 项和《中华人民共和国海上海事处罚法》第 8 条第 1 款和第 9 条，可以处以 1 000 到 10 000 元人民币罚款，并可视情况扣留和吊销船员证书。

5.2 08 值守

信文原文实例：

MSC HANJIN, this is Beihai VTS calling, over.

INFORMATION：keeping watch on channel 08 is come into force.

This is first warning. When you entering BEIHAI water, please standby on channel 08 all the time. Or, you may get fine(punish) according to local regulation.

译文：

"地中海韩进"，这是北海交管呼叫，听到请回答。

信息提醒：请保持在 08 频道值守。

这是第一次警告。当你进入北海水域，请保持在 08 频道值守。否则，根据相关法规规定，你可能会面临罚款或其他处罚。

未有效值守 VHF：违反《中华人民共和国海上交通安全法》第 9 条，根据《中华人民共和国海上海事处罚法》第 24 条第 1 款和第 2 款第 11 项和《中华人民共和国海上海事处罚法》第 8 条第 1 款和第 9 条，可以处以 1 000 到 10 000 元人民币罚款，并可视情况扣留和吊销证书。

5.3 过报告线报告

信文原文实例：

MSC HANJIN, this is Beihai VTS calling, over.

INFORMATION：please call back VTS when you passing JIUJIEJIAO REKON.

This is first warning. If you don't following the regulation, you may get fine (punished) according to local regulation.

译文：

"地中海韩进"，这是北海交管呼叫，听到请回答。

信息提醒:当你船经过九节礁时请向北海交管报告。

这是第一次警告。如你不遵守相关规定,根据相关法规规定,你可能会面临罚款或其他处罚。

靠离泊、过报告线未报的:违反《中华人民共和国海上交通安全法》第 10 条,根据《中华人民共和国海上海事处罚法》第 26 条第 1 款和第 2 款第 26 项和《中华人民共和国海上海事处罚法》第 8 条第 1 款和第 9 条,可以处以 2 000 到 10 000 元人民币罚款,并可视情况扣留和吊销证书。

5.4　遵守避碰规则

信文原文实例:

MSC HANJIN, this is Beihai VTS calling, over.

INFORMATION：Please following the regulation of COLREGs 1972

This if first warning. YOU ARE REQUESTED TO GIVE-WAY FOR THE STAND-ON VESSEL. IF YOU REFUSE TO DO SO, YOU MAY get fine（punished）according to local regulation.

译文:

"地中海韩进",这是北海交管呼叫,听到请回答。

信息提醒:请切实遵守《1972 年海上避碰规则》。

这是第一次警告,你是让路船,请按规定给直航船让路,如果你不遵守相关法规规定,你可能会面临罚款或其他处罚。

不遵守避碰规则:违反《中华人民共和国海上交通安全法》第 9 条,根据《中华人民共和国海上海事处罚法》第 24 条第 1 款和第 2 款第 8 项和《中华人民共和国海上海事处罚法》第 8 条第 1 款和第 9 条,可以处以 1 000 到 10 000 元人民币罚款,并可视情况扣留和吊销证书。

5.5　不开启 AIS,或者 AIS 故障未及时报备的和未按照规定输入信息

违反《中华人民共和国海上交通安全法》第 9 条,根据《中华人民共和国海上海事处罚法》第 14 条第 1 款和第 2 款第 12 项和《中华人民共和国海上海事处罚法》第 8 条第 1 款和第 9 条,可以处以 1 000 到 10 000 元人民币罚款,并可视情况扣留和吊销证书。

5.6　猴屿西航道进口

违反《中华人民共和国海上交通安全法》第 9 条,根据《中华人民共和国海上海事处罚法》第 24 条第 1 款和第 2 款第 6 项和《中华人民共和国海上海事处罚法》第 8 条第 1 款和第 9 条,可以处以 1 000 到 10 000 元人民币罚款,并可视情况扣留和吊销证书。

5.7　违规掉头、追越、停泊和倒车

违反《中华人民共和国海上交通安全法》第 10 条,根据《中华人民共和国海上海事处罚法》第 26 条第 1 款和第 2 款第 9 项和《中华人民共和国海上海事处罚法》第 8 条第 1 款和第 9 条,可以处以 1 000 到 10 000 元人民币罚款,并可视情况扣留和吊销证书。

5.8　未按规定拖带或者非拖带船从事拖带作业

违反《中华人民共和国海上交通安全法》第 10 条,根据《中华人民共和国海上海事处罚法》第 26 条第 1 款和第 2 款第 23 项和《中华人民共和国海上海事处罚法》第 8 条第 1 款和第

9 条,可以处以 2 000 到 10 000 元人民币罚款,并可视情况扣留和吊销证书。

5.9　未取得施工许可证和许可证过期而擅自施工的

违反《中华人民共和国海上交通安全法》第 20 条和《中华人民共和国水上水下活动通航安全管理规定》第 5 条,根据《中华人民共和国水上水下安全管理规定》第 33 条第 2 款和《中华人民共和国海上海事处罚法》第 8 条第 1 款和第 9 条,可以处以 5 000 到 30 000 元人民币罚款。

5.10　发生险情事故和发生碍航事故未向海事机构报告的

违反《中华人民共和国船员条例》第 20 条第 5 项,根据《中华人民共和国船员条例》第 57 条第 3 项和《中华人民共和国海上海事处罚法》第 8 条第 1 款和第 9 条,可以处以 1 000 到 10 000 元人民币罚款,并可视情况扣留和吊销证书。

5.11　交通事故逃逸的

违反《中华人民共和国海上交通安全法》第 37 条,根据《中华人民共和国海上海事处罚法》第 48 条第 1 款第 3 项和《中华人民共和国海上海事处罚法》第 8 条第 1 款和第 9 条,可以处以 1 000 到 10 000 元人民币罚款并可视情况扣留和吊销证书。

5.12　无正当理由拒绝救助遇险船的

违反《福建省海上搜寻救助规定》第 36 条第 2 款,由海事管理机构责令立即改正,并给予警告。拒不改正的,可处 1 万元以上 3 万元以下的罚款。

5.13　其他

船舶进出港、靠离泊、通过交通密集区、危险航区等区域,或遇到恶劣天气和海况,或发生水上交通或者污染事故、船舶保安事件以及其他紧急情况时,船长未在驾驶台值班的:违反《中华人民共和国船员条例》第 22 条第 6 项,根据《中华人民共和国船员条例》第 58 条第 4 项规定,可以处以 2 000 元以上 2 万元以下罚款;情节严重的,给以暂扣船员适任证书 6 个月以上 2 年以下直至吊销船员适任证书的处罚。

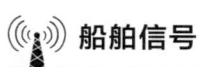

Lesson 4
Distress, Urgency and Safety Communication

1. General

Any message prefixed by one of the following words MAYDAY, PAN-PAN or SECURITE is about the safety. If you hear these words, pay particular attention to them and call the master or the officer on watch.

1.1 Distress communication

The distress signal MAYDAY: to be used to announce a distress message, distress communication applies when a ship or aircraft is threatened by grave and imminent danger, and requires immediate assistance.

1.2 Urgency communication

The urgency signal PAN-PAN: to be used to announce an urgency message. Urgency communication applies when the calling station has a very urgent message to transmit concerning the safety of a mobile unit or a person.

1.3 Safety communication

The safety signal SECURITE: to be used to announce a safety message. Safety communication applies when the station sending it has a message to transmit containing an important navigational or meteorological warning.

Note:

MAYDAY comes from the French "maider" meaning "help me". PAN-PAN is derived from French word "panne" meaning "breakdown". Securite is a French word meaning safety.

2. Distress communication procedure

Distress communication will be conducted primarily on VHF CH16. It has absolute priority over all other radio transmissions. No station is permitted to make transmissions which are unrelated to the resolution. To stop a station, which is interfering with distress communication, the Controlling Station will transmit "Silence MAYDAY" to terminate their communication.

2.1 Distress call

—MAYDAY   MAYDAY   MAYDAY

—This is ×××

—Name or call sign or other identification of the distressed vessel (three times)

—MAYDAY（one time）

—Name or call sign or other identification of the distressed vessel（one time）

—Position of the distressed vessel

—Nature of distress（or danger）

—Type of the assistance required and any other useful information to assistance

—Over

Example：MAYDAY MAYDAY MAYDAY

This is Asia Express, Asia Express, Asia Express

MAYDAY Asia Express

Position：Latitude one three degrees five minutes north, longitude one two four degrees one five minutes east

I am on fire after explosion in hold, I require fire fighting assistance, smoke not toxic, over.

In the GMDSS, the standard procedure of distress message：

—MAYDAY

—This is ×××

—9-digit maritime mobile service identity-code（MMSI）+ ship's name or call sign or any other identification

—Position of the vessel

—Nature of distress

—Type of the assistance required and any other useful information to assistance

—Over

Example：MAYDAY

This is Two-one-one-two-three-nine-six-eight-zero

motor vessel Birte, call sign Delta-Alfa-Mike-Kilo

Position：Six two degrees one one decimal eight minutes north, zero zero seven degrees four four minutes east

I am on fire after explosion. I require fire fighting assistance, smoke not toxic, over.

2.2 Acknowledgement

On receipt of a distress message, any ship in the vicinity should immediately transmit a MAYDAY received（acknowledging receipt of the distress transmission）to the distressed vessel.

The procedure is as follows：

—MAYDAY（one time）

—Name or call sign or any other identification of the distressed vessel（three times）

—This is ×××

—Name or call sign of the ship acknowledging a distress message（three times）

—MAYDAY received（may use Romeo, Romeo, Romeo if language difficulties exist）

Example：MAYDAY Asia Express, Asia Express, Asia Express

This is Asia Angle, Asia Angle, Asia Angle

MAYDAY received.

2.3 MAYDAY relay

If any ship or shore station receiving a distress message is unable to render assistance to the distressed vessel herself, she may transmit a distress relay so that ships or authorities that having ability to render assistance can obtain the information.

The procedure is as follows:

—MAYDAY RELAY (three times)

—This is ×××

—Name or call sign of the relay station (three times)

—Following received from "×××"

—Time of receipt(UTC or GMT)

—Distress message

—Over.

Example: MAYDAY relay, MAYDAY relay, MAYDAY relay

This is Singapore Radio, Singapore Radio, Singapore Radio

following received from motor vessel Asia express at time 1700 GMT

Position: Latitude one three degrees five zero minutes north, longitude one two four degrees one five minutes east, I am on fire after explosion in hold, I require fire fighting assistance, smoke not toxic, over.

3. Urgency communication procedure

When the calling station has an urgent message concerning the safety of a ship, aircraft or other vehicle, or the safety of a person, such as ship aground, engine seriously damaged, man overboard, crew or passenger ill and so on, an urgency message shall be transmitted.

Urgency transmission has priority over all other transmissions except those connected with distress situations. All ships receiving urgency signal do not interfere with the transmission of urgency message and keep listening for at least 5 minutes.

3.1 Urgency Call

—PAN-PAN (three times)

—This is ×××

—Name or call sign or any other identification of the ship station transmitting urgency signal (three times)

—PAN-PAN (one time)

—Name or call sign or any other identification of the ship station transmitting urgency signal (one time)

—Urgency message

—Assistance required

—Over.

Example：PAN-PAN, PAN-PAN, PAN-PAN

      This is Trans Bridge, Trans Bridge, Trans bridge

      PAN-PAN, Trans Bridge.

      I am dragging my anchor, I have problems with main engine,

      I require tug assistance, over.

In the GMDSS, the standard procedure of urgency message：

—PAN-PAN (3 times)

—ALL STATIONS or called station (3 times)

—This is ×××

—9-digit maritime mobile service identity-code (MMSI) + ship's name/call sign or any other identification

—Ship's position

—Urgency message

—Assistance required

—Over

Example：PAN-PAN, PAN-PAN, PAN-PAN

      ALL STATIONS, ALL STATIONS, ALL STATIONS

      This is Two-one-one-two-three-nine-six-eight-zero

      motor vessel "Birte", call sign Delta-Alfa-Mike-Kilo

      Position：Six two degrees one one decimal eight minutes north, zero zero seven degrees tour four minutes east

      I have problems with engines, I require tug assistance, out.

3.2 Answer to urgency (message) call

—PAN-PAN (one time)

—Name or call sign of ship transmitting urgency call

—This is ×××

—Name or call sign of answering ship

—PAN-PAN received

—Over

Example：PAN-PAN

      Trans Bridge

      This is Hong Kong Mardep

      PAN-PAN received, over.

During urgency medical communication, it may become necessary to use medical terms (e.g. drugs, symptoms, physiology). If language difficulties exist, the medical section of the International Code of Signals is to be used as follows：

(a) Prefix any code used with the phrase "Interco medical"；

(b) Spell the code groups using the phonetic alphabet；

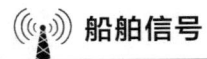

(c) Suffix the code groups with "End of Interco".

Example: PAN-PAN, PAN-PAN, PAN-PAN

        This is Panama vessel Asia Express, Asia Express, Asia Express

        PAN-PAN, Asia Express

        Interco medical

        Mike Alfa Juliet two five, Mike Charlie Whiskey

        End of Interco

        I require immediate medical assistance, over.

4. Safety communication procedure

Safety message usually contains important navigational and meteorological warning: e. g. navigational aids damaged, all kinds of obstructions and derelicts found, abnormal weather and visibility conditions, etc.

Calling of safety communication will be first conducted on CH16, then the safety message should be transmitted on working channel. Safety transmissions have priority over all other transmissions except those connected with distress and urgency situations. Generally, safety message should be transmitted to all stations, and may also to a group of ships or a particular ship. Its communication procedure is the same as a broadcast procedure, in the GMDSS, receipt of safety message is automatically completed by NAVTEX.

Safety Communication is composed of two procedures: safety call transmission and safety message.

4.1　Safety call transmission

—SECURITE (3 times)

—All stations or nominated ship (station)

—This is ×××

—Name or call sign of ship (station) transmitting safety (message) information (3 times)

—SECURITE (one time)

—Name or call sign of ship (station) transmitting safety (message) information (one time)

—Type of message

—Channel of transmitting and listening to the message (switch to channel)

—Over

4.2　Safety message

The procedure is the same as the safety call transmission. The detailed contents of safety message are sent after the "type of message".

Example: SECURITE, SECURITE, SECURITE

        Attention all vessels, attention all vessels, attention all vessels

        This is Singapore Radio, Singapore Radio, Singapore Radio

SECURITE, Singapore Radio

Navigational warning

Switch to channel two five. Over.

···

SECURITE, SECURITE, SECURITE

Attention all vessels, attention all vessels, attention all vessels

This is Singapore Radio, Singapore Radio, Singapore Radio

SECURITE, Singapore Radio

Navigational warning:

Vessel Asia Express is aground in position two cables from Entrance Buoy of east fairway, please navigate with caution, out.

In the GMDSS, the standard procedure of safety message:

—SECURITE (3 times)

—ALL STATIONS (3 times)

—This is ×××

—9-digit maritime mobile service identity-code (MMSI) + ship's name/call sign or any other identification

—Safety message

—Over.

Example: SECURITE SECURITE SECURITE

ALL SHIPS ALL SHIPS ALL SHIPS in area Peter Reef

This is two-one-one-two-three-nine-six-eight-zero

motor vessel "Birte", call sign Delta-Alfa-Mike-Kilo

Dangerous wreck located in position two nautical tiles south of Peter Reef, over.

第四课　遇险、紧急、安全通信

1. 海上遇险报警(呼叫)方法

船舶遇险后,根据船本身配备的通信设备选择正确的报警方法非常重要,它关系到船舶、货物和人员能否及时获得救助。因此 IMO 海安会为使遇险船的船长正确、及时报警,给出下面遇险报警操作指南,如下图所示。

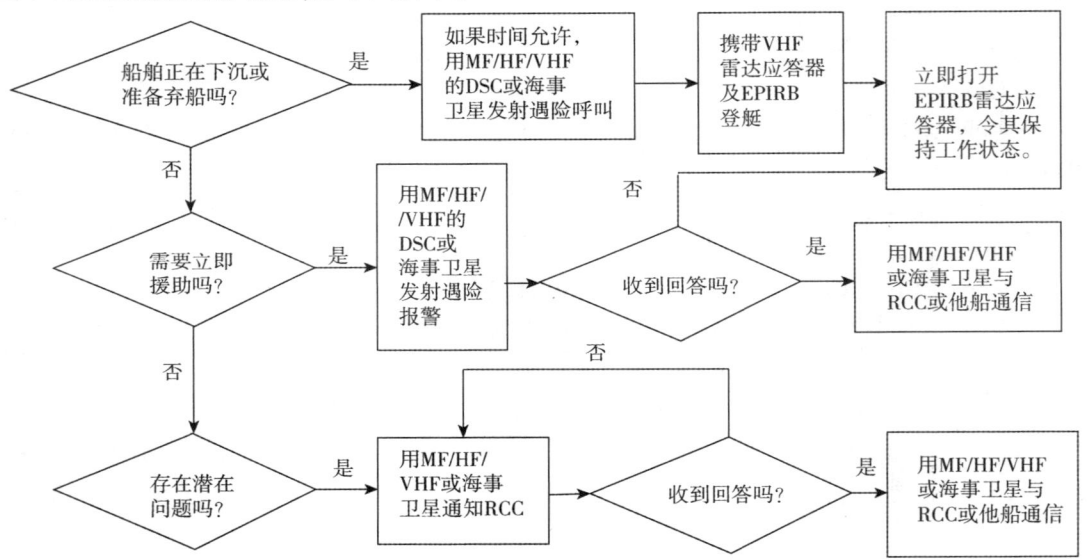

RCC：Rescue Coordinating Center 救助协调中心,负责协调救助任务
MF：Medium Frequency 中频
HF：High Frequency 高频
VHF：Very High Frequency 甚高频
DSC：Digital Selective Calling 数字选择性呼叫

遇险、紧急、安全呼叫手段有很多种类,GMDSS（全球海上遇险与安全系统）1999 年 2 月 1 日开始实施,该系统推荐首选上述通信手段报警,但并不排除话音报警。用 DSC 报警的目的是提高遇险报警成功率因而遇险能获得及时救助,随后的遇险通信则主要依赖于无线电话。国际电信联盟建议:用 DSC 通信手段报警成功后,用与 DSC 报警同频带的电话（电传）进行遇险通信,如在 VHF 70 频道上进行 DSC 报警,则用 VHF16 频道进行遇险通信;用 MF 的 DSC 2 187.5 kHz 报警,则用 MF 单边带（SSB）电话 2 182 kHz 进行遇险通信。用上述 DSC 通信手段进行紧急、安全呼叫后,用与紧急、安全呼叫同频带的电话（16 频道或 SSB

电话的 2 182 kHz）进行紧急、安全通信。也可以直接用 VHF 无线电话和单边带无线电话进行报警，不论是用 VHF 电话的 16 频道还是 SSB 电话的 2 182 kHz 报警或进行遇险、紧急和安全通信，其程序都是相同的。本节主要讲述利用 VHF 无线电话和 DSC 进行遇险、紧急、安全呼叫和利用 VHF 无线电话进行遇险、紧急、安全通信的方法及有关规定。

2. 遇险、紧急、安全呼叫

如果可行的话，遇险、紧急、安全呼叫首先使用明语，明语有困难，再使用码语。在使用码语之前，先发送 INTERCO 标明以下用码语发送。用码语发送时，一定使用字母和数字拼读方式发送信文。遇险呼叫（通信）优先于紧急呼叫（通信），紧急呼叫（通信）优先于安全呼叫（通信）。只有在船长或船舶负责人批准后才能进行遇险呼叫（通信）、紧急呼叫（通信）。安全呼叫（通信）可以不经过船长或船舶负责人批准，由当班驾驶员直接发出。

2.1 遇险呼叫
2.1.1 VHF 无线电话呼叫

呼叫以"MAYDAY"开始，"MAYDAY"表示遇险，即一艘船舶、飞机或其他交通工具受到重大而紧迫的危险，需要立即救助。遇险呼叫应该是普遍呼叫，不能针对某一个船台或岸台。当听到来自某船的遇险呼叫后，应当在其通信频率上认真守听，遇险呼叫和遇险通信都在 16 频道上进行。

（1）呼叫格式

—MAYDAY　MAYDAY　MAYDAY（三次）

—This is（语言困难时可用 DE 的拼读）×××

—遇险船名或呼号（三次）

—MAYDAY

—船位

—遇险性质

—需要救助的种类及其他与救助有关的信息

—Over

例：

MAYDAY　MAYDAY　MAYDAY

This is Trans-wind Trans-wind Trans-wind

MAYDAY，Trans-wind

Position：Latitude 34 degrees 45 minutes north，longitude 126 degrees 42 minutes east.

The hull is broken and sinking. I require immediate assistance，over.

（2）遇险呼叫的承认收妥

遇险呼叫绝对优先于任何其他通信。当听到遇险呼叫时，所有其他发射必须停止且保持守听。任何遇险呼叫必须记录在船舶日志上且呈送船长。收到遇险呼叫时，如果本船在其附近的话，马上确认收妥；如果不在附近，为了使距离遇险船更近的船舶给收妥通知，应间隔较短时间间隔且无他船给收妥通知后再给收妥通知。

（3）承认收妥格式

—MAYDAY（一次）

—遇险船名或呼号（三次）

—this is（语言困难时可用 DE 的拼读）×××

—承认收妥的船台名称或呼号（三次）

—Received MAYDAY

例：

MAYDAY

Trans-wind　　Trans-wind　　Trans-wind

this is Merry-trans　　Merry-trans　　Merry-trans

Received MAYDAY

随后向遇险船发出本船的船舶种类、船位、航速、ETA 等信息，供遇险船决定是否由本船承担救助任务。

例：

—MAYDAY

—Trans-wind　　Trans-wind　　Trans-wind

—this is Merry-trans　　Merry-trans　　Merry-trans

—Received MAYDAY

—My position is latitude 32 degrees 15 minutes north，longitude 125 degrees 40 minutes east. Speed 15 knots. ETA one five zero zero GMT 1 May，I am coming to your assistance，over.

（4）终止遇险通信

当遇险通信结束后，管制此项通信的电台应在遇险通信上发送对所有电台的通告，以表示恢复正常通信。遇险通信频率通常为遇险呼叫频率或遇险船指定的频率。

终止遇险通信通知格式：

—MAYDAY

—Hello all ships（或 CQ），呼叫三次

—This is（如语言困难时，用 DE，读作 Delta-Echo）×××

—发送该通知的电台呼号或其他识别

—该通知的交发时间

—曾经遇险的移动电台的名称或呼号

—SEEIONCE FEENEE

例：

—MAYDAY

—Hello all ships，hello all ships，hello all ships

—This is sea star，sea star，sea star

—Time one three zero zero GMT

—Trans-wind

—SEELONCE FEENEE

（5）遇险通信管制

通信管制是管制台对干扰遇险通信的电台进行强制终止干扰通信的通知。遇险通信管制通常是遇险电台或其他被指定的电台。管制用语有 SEELONCE DISTRESS 和 SEELONCE MAYDAY，意思让干扰遇险通信的船舶保持静默，使用情况如下：

SEELONCE DISTRESS：在遇险通信范围内的船，认为如有必要，可以强制其他对遇险通信造成干扰的电台保持静默。

SEELONCE MAYDAY：遇险通信管制台使用。

（6）遇险转发

收到遇险呼叫（或信号）的电台，确认该电台或遇险人员没有获得救助的情况下，应该转发该遇险通信。

格式：

—MAYDAY　RELAY（三次）

—This is ×××

—转发台的名称或呼号（三次）

—遇险信文

—Over.

例：

—MAYDAY RELAY　　MAYDAY RELAY　　MAYDAY RELAY

—this is MV Yu Long　　MV Yu Long　　MV Yu Long

following message received from motor vessel Trans-wind. Position：latitude 34 degrees 45 minutes north，longitude 126 degrees 42 minutes east. The hull is broken and sinking. I require immediate assistance，over.

2.1.2　VHF DSC（CH70）呼叫

实施 GMDSS 后，DSC 是首选的遇险报警方法。发送遇险报警操作简单，遇险船名、MMSI（海上移动业务识别码，9 位数字组成）、遇险时间、船位自动生成（GPS 输入），报警人员只选择遇险性质，按菜单提示进行操作即可。

（1）呼叫格式

—遇险性质

—船位

—时间

—遇险通信种类

（2）遇险呼叫的收妥确认

收到来自另一船舶的 DSC 遇险报警的船舶，不应在 DSC 上承认收妥，因为只有岸台可以用 DSC 方式承认收妥。

没有其他台收到 DSC 遇险报警，而且 DSC 遇险报警持续发送，这时收到 DSC 遇险报警的船舶可以在 DSC 上承认收妥以终止 DSC 呼叫，然后船舶应通知岸台或岸站。

收到来自另一船舶的 DSC 遇险报警的船舶，在一个或多个岸台覆盖区，为了使岸台首先给出遇险承认收妥，应该延缓一段时间用无线电话承认收妥。

收到来自另一船舶的 DSC 险报警的船舶，应：

在遇险 DSC 频道 CH70（156.525 MHz）守听收妥确认。

准备在 VHF 无线电话 CH16（156.8 MHz）收听遇险通信。

在 VHF 无线电话 CH16（156.8 MHz）确认收妥：

—MAYDAY（一次）

—遇险船 9 位数字识别码（重复三次）

—This is（语言困难时可用 DE 的拼读）×××

—承认收妥的船台 9 位数字识别码或呼号（重复三次）

—Received MAYDAY.

2.1.3 关于误报警

误报警是船员误操作导致的报警,如不及时采取正确措施,会影响搜救系统的正常工作,轻则受到主管当局的批评,重则被罚款。一旦误报警,按下述方法操作取消误报警：

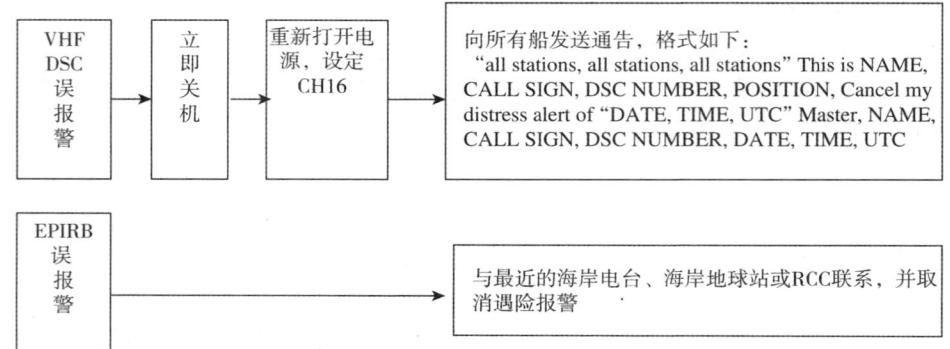

2.2 紧急呼叫

2.2.1 VHF 无线电话呼叫

紧急呼叫是以"PAN-PAN"开头，"PAN-PAN"表示紧急（Urgency），即呼叫台有很紧急的电信要发送,关系到一艘船舶、飞机或其他交通工具的安全或人员的安全。紧急呼可以是普遍呼叫,也可以针对某一个船台或岸台;紧急呼叫和紧急通信同时在 CH16 进行。

紧急呼叫格式：

—PAN-PAN　　 PAN-PAN　　 PAN-PAN

—All stations（三次）

—This is ×××

—发送紧急信号的电台名称或呼号（三次）

—紧急信文

—Over.

例：

—PAN-PAN　 PAN-PAN　 PAN-PAN

—Hello all stations（三次）

—This is Merry-trans　　 Merry-trans　　 Merry-trans.

—I have problem with my main engine，I require tug assistance.

—Over.

2.2.2   **VHF DSC 呼叫**

将 VHF 无线电话机置于 CH70,输入"所有台"或"特定台的 9 位识别码",设定呼叫种类为"紧急",然后发送紧急呼叫。紧急呼叫发送完毕后,在 CH16 发送紧急信息。将 VHF 无线电话机置于 CH16,然后语音发送:

—PAN- PAN   PAN-PAN   PAN-PAN

—All stations   All stations   All stations

—This is ×××

—本船 9 位识别码或呼号

—紧急信文

2.2.3   **接收到紧急信文后的措施**

船舶在 CH70 接收到对所有船的紧急呼叫后,不应对该 DSC 紧急呼叫确认但应该在 CH16 守听紧急信文。

2.3   **安全呼叫**

VHF 无线电话呼叫是以"SECURITE"开头,"SECURITE"表示与安全有关的信文,即呼叫台将要发送有关航行安全的信文或重要的气象警告。安全呼叫(通信)可以是普遍呼叫,即针对周围所有船台,也可以对某一地理区域的船舶呼叫或某一特定的船舶呼叫。

呼叫格式:

—SECURITE   SECURITE   SECURITE

—All station   All station   All station

—This is ×××

—本船船名或呼号

—安全信文

—Over.

例:

—SECURITE   SECURITE   SECURITE

—All station   All station   All station

—This is Sea Star   Sea Star   Sea Star

There is a log drifting, position:latitude 33 degrees 45 minutes north, longitude 123 degrees 32 minutes east. Vessels in vicinity navigate with caution. Over.

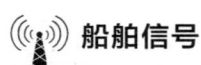

Lesson 5
Radiotelephony Communication in Search and Rescue Operations at Sea

It is a duty-bound obligation to give any possible assistance to ship(s) or person(s) in distress. In Regulation V-10 of the International Convention for the Safety of Life at Sea 1974 (SOLAS), it is regulated:

"The master of a ship at sea, on receiving a signal from any source that a ship or aircraft or survival craft thereof is in distress, is bound to proceed with all speed to the assistance of the persons in distress informing them if possible that he is doing so. If he is unable or, in the special circumstances of the case, considers it unreasonable or unnecessary to proceed to their assistance, he must enter in the logbook the reason for failing to proceed to the assistance of the persons in distress.

The master of a ship in distress, after consultation, so far as may be possible, with the masters of the ships which answer his call for assistance has the right to requisition such one or more of those ships as he considers best able to render assistance, and it shall be the duty of the master or masters of the ship or ships requisitioned to comply with the requisition by continuing to proceed with all speed to the assistance of person in distress."

1. Search and Rescue Organization (SAR Organization)

1.1 Establishment of SAR Organization

The conduct of SAR operations is often a great coordination between ships, air-crafts and shore-based SAR authorities. Perfect organization is the basis of conduct. The efficient, timely search and rescue to ships and persons in distress depends on the perfection and coordination of SAR organization, advanced level of SAR means and cooperation of SAR conduct. For this purpose IMO upheld and drew up "The International Convention on Maritime Search and Rescue" and prescribed the standards of SAR organization, cooperation and procedure of SAR operations in the 13 SAR regions on the globe.

To accomplish a SAR mission, there should be a SAR organization well-established.

1.2 Construction of SAR Organization

A basic SAR organization should include (See Fig. 5-1):

(1) RCC—Rescue Coordination Center

A unit responsible for promoting efficient organization of search and rescue services and for coordinating the conduct of SAR operations within a SAR region.

(2) RSC—Rescue Sub-center

A unit subordinate to a rescue coordination center established to complement the latter according to particular provisions of the responsible authorities.

（3）SMC—SAR Mission Coordinator

Every SAR conduct is carried out under the command and supervision of a SMC. He may be assigned by RCC or directly held by leader of RCC. He may designate OSC or CSS.

（4）OSC—On-scene Commander

A person designated to coordinate SAR operations within a specified search area.

（5）CSS—Coordinator Surface Search

A vessel, other than a rescue unit, designated to coordinate surface SAR operations within a specified search area.

（6）SAR RESOURCES—Search and Rescue Resources

They refer to ships, air-crafts and other units participating in a SAR operation.

Notes：

Other terms concerned：

① Search and Rescue Region (SRR)：An area of defined dimensions associated with a rescue within which SAR services are provided.

② Rescue Unit (RU)：A unit composed of trained personnel and provided with equipment suitable for the expeditious conduct of SAR operations.

③ Search and Rescue Facility：Any mobile resource, including designated search and rescue units, used to conduct search and rescue operations.

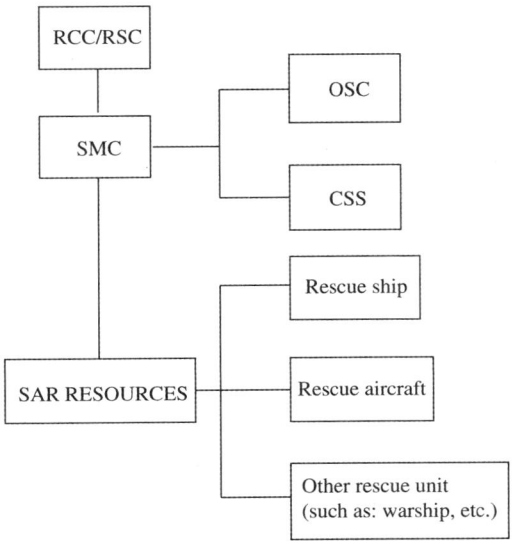

Fig. 5-1   Construction of SAR Organization

2. Search and rescue communication

The unblocked, effective communication is the basic guarantee of SAR conduct. Generally speaking, there are two types of communication in SAR operations：Visual signals and radio

communication. With visual signals set out in chapter 3, here we will only introduce the radio communication.

2.1 SAR coordinating communication

For the coordination and control of SAR operations, RCCs require communication with the ship in distress as well as with units participating in the operation. The methods and modes of communication (terrestrial, satellite, telephone, telex) used will be governed by the capabilities available onboard the ship in distress as well as those onboard assisting units. Where some or all are equipped with satellite terminals the advantage of the Inmarsat system for rapid, reliable communication including receipt of maritime safety information (MSI) can be achieved.

A reliable interlinking of RCCs is important for the GMDSS in which a distress message may be received by an RCC thousands of miles away from where the assistance is needed and may not be the RCC best suited to provide the necessary assistance. In these cases prompt relay of the distress message to the appropriate RCC is essential and any communication means, whether landlines, terrestrial radio networks or satellite links, must be used in such circumstances.

To increase the speed and reliability of RCC-to-RCC communication, some RCCs have installed MES (mobile earth station) providing them with the capability of communicating through the Inmarsat system. This is known as SARNET and these facilities are useful for rapid long-distance interconnection of SAR organizations, especially when dedicated lines or public switched networks are unavailable or unreliable.

2.2 On-scene communication

On-scene communications are those between the ships in distress and assisting vessels and between SAR vessels and the on-scene commander of the coordinator of the surface search. These communications are normally short-range communication which will be made on the VHF or MF distress and safety frequencies in the GMDSS. However, ships fitted with Inmarsat MES could, if necessary, use satellite communication as a supplement to their VHF and MF facilities. Methods of on-scene communication have:

(1) It is preferable to use the distress frequency 2,182 kHz or 156.8 MHz (VHF channel 16) radiotelephony;

(2) NBDP (narrow band direct printing telegraphy) may be used;

(3) Radio communication between ships and aircraft on SAR operations may be made on VHF channel 16 and 06.

The methods and frequencies used of on-scene communication are designated by OSC or CSS. When language difficulties exist, the signal codes or short phrases concerning "search and rescue" in the International Code of Signals and the IAMSAR Manual should be fully used.

Example:

MSA: MV Yu Long, Yu Long, this is Tianjin MSA, vessel Trans-wind is in distress, you should proceed to latitude 37 degrees 45 minutes north, longitude 122 degrees 45 minutes east to pick up survivors and Yongxing will follow you to the position of accident. Over.

Yu Long: Tianjin MSA, this is Yu Long, I am proceeding to the position of accident at full speed, expected to arrive at time 1330 local time. Over.

MSA: Yong Xing, Yong Xing, this is Tianjin MSA, vessel Trans-wind is in distress, you should proceed to latitude 37 degrees 45 minutes north, longitude 122 degrees 45 minutes east to pick up survivors. Over.

Yong Xing: Tianjin MSA, this is Yu Long, I am proceeding to the position of accident at full speed, expected to arrive at time 1530 local time. Over.

MSA: MV Yu Long and Yong Xing are coming to assistance, but from the message which Trans-wind sent before they abandoned, RCC known the crews and master of Trans-wind is on survival craft. RCC noted it to the two vessels, the craft is drifting with wind and far away from the Trans-wind, time is 1530 local time.

Yong Xing: Yu Long, Yu Long, this is Yong Xing, I am near the position which Trans-wind located, but I cannot find the craft. Over.

Yu Long: Yong Xing, Yong Xing, this is Yu Long, I am near the position too, I cannot find the craft yet. Over.

Yong Xing: We should carry out radar search and adjust track spacing to 3 miles, over.

Yu Long: Roger. Over.

(After two hours they found nothing.)

Yong Xing: Tianjin MSA, this is Yong Xing, Yong Xing, we found nothing and what should we do? Over.

MSA: Please go on searching and steer your course to 180 degrees and Yu Long steer course 180 degrees too, the interval between the ships is 2 miles. Over.

Yong Xing: Roger. Over.

Yu Long: Roger. Over.

(Because of strong north-east wind, the craft drifted to the south. After 2 hours they found the craft.)

Yong Xing: Trans-wind, Trans-wind, this is Yong Xing, Yong Xing, I found you and I will steer course 090 degress and keep you on my starboard. Over.

Trans-wind: Roger, thank you very much. Over.

Yu Long: Tianjin MSA, this is Yu Long, Yu Long, we found the craft and we are saving them. Over.

MSA: Yu Long, Yu Long, this is Tianjin MSA, any crew injured? Over.

Yu Long: Yes, one crew injured, it is necessary to take injured crew to hospital by helicopter. Over.

MSA: We send a helicopter to you to pick up the injured crew. Over.

(After half an hour, the helicopter is over the craft.)

Helicopter: Yu Long, Yu Long, this is helicopter, I can not alight but I can lift injured

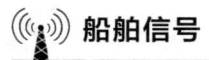

person.

Yu Long: Roger. Over.

(The helicopter took the injured crew to hospital, Yu Long and Yong Xing saved all crew on board. The search and rescue finished.)

Yu Long: Tianjin MSA, this is Yu Long, we have finished the rescue, over.

MSA: Yu Long, Yu Long, this is Tianjin MSA, please take the crews to Tianjin port and Yong Xing go on her voyage, thanks, out.

Yu Long: Good bye, out.

Yong Xing: Good bye, out.

第五课 海上搜救作业通信

随着全球贸易量的增加,从事货物运输和旅客运输的船舶越来越多,尽管造船技术和通信导航设备日益完善,船员水平不断提高,但仍然有船由于各种原因遇险。海上搜救作业及其通信就成为保障海上货物运输和旅客运输安全的最后一道屏障。国际海上人命安全公约(SOLAS)明确规定:船长接收到来自遇险船舶、飞机或救生艇的救生信号时,应全速前往救助遇险人员,如有可能通知他们正在前往救助中。搜救作业通信包括搜救协调通信和现场通信,搜救作业通信是否快速有效,对遇险人员能否及时获救有重大影响,因此,船长和/或驾驶员必须掌握基本的搜救作业通信方法。

1. 搜救组织

1.1 全球搜救区域划分

全球划分 13 个搜救区域,我国负责搜救的区域为:渤海——全部;黄海——124°E 以西;南海——14°N 以北。各区域的救助组织结构、救助程序标准都是相同的。结构如下图所示。

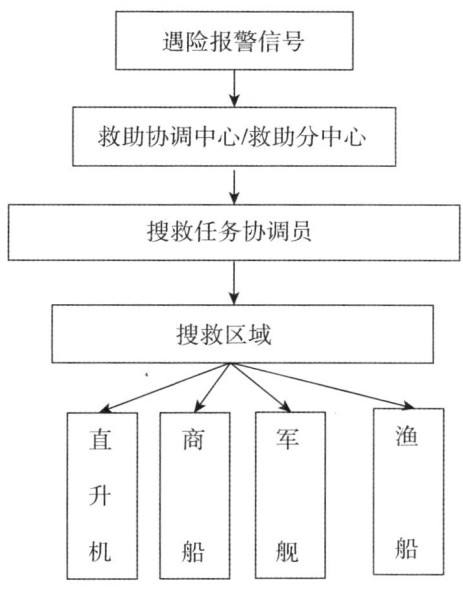

1.2 搜救组织

我国负责搜救指挥的是交通运输部中国海上搜救中心和各地方海事局。

美国、加拿大等负责搜救指挥的是海岸警卫队;日本的是海上保安厅;澳大利亚的是海上安全局。

2. 搜救作业

各种搜救力量接到遇险报警信号或搜救任务协调员的指令后应全速驶向出事地点。但往往由于船员在某些情况下必须弃船登上救生艇,而救生艇又会随风流漂移,结果就是搜救力量不易及时发现救生艇或水面漂浮的船员,此种情况下就要进行搜救作业。搜救作业需要注意以下几点:

(1)船舶在到达出事地点附近时开启 9 GHz 雷达以搜寻救生艇 SART 信号,SART 信号能大大提高搜救成功率,即不至于因为天气原因而不能发现救生艇。

(2)SART 信号在雷达上显示距离大约 6.6 海里。为能够及时发现和正确识别 SART 信号,请选用雷达 6~12 海里量程,同时注意以下三点。

①当搜救单元距 SART 1 海里以外时,SART 信号在搜救单元雷达上沿直线显示等间距的 12 个点,距雷达中心最近的点代表 SART 距搜救单元的方位和距离。

②当搜救单元距 SART 1 海里以内时,SART 信号在搜救单元雷达上显示等间距的 12 个弧形。

③当搜救单元接近 SART 时,SART 信号在搜救单元雷达上显示等间距的 12 个同心圆。

(3)SART 的发射距离:IMO 要求是 SART 水面 1 米,搜救雷达天线高度 15 米,此时 SART 发射距离最少 5 海里,但与 SART 在救生艇上的位置和高度有关。

①SART 平躺在地板上,通信距离大约是 1.8 海里。

②SART 直立在地板上,通信距离大约是 2.5 海里。

③SART 漂浮在水面上,通信距离大约是 2.0 海里。

因此,SART 在救生艇上保持 1 米高度是很重要的。

(4)向下风、向流处搜寻。

(5)开启 VHF CH16,频率守听救生艇手提 VHF 信号。

3. 搜救通信

3.1 搜救协调通信

当出动多种搜救力量进行搜救时,为了协调各方搜救行动,就需要通信来互换信息。通常是搜救协调中心协调与各种搜救力量之间的通信。可以使用近、中、远距离通信工具。

3.2 现场通信

是指遇险船舶与前来搜救的船舶、飞机之间(包括现场指挥员或搜寻协调员)的通信。通信方法有:

(1)使用 VHF CH16 和遇险频率 2 182 kHz 单边带无线电话,与救生艇通信只能使用 VHF CH16。

(2)使用无线电传(NBDP)

(3)船舶与航空器之间可使用 VHF CH06 频率进行通信。

若船员没有弃船,在遇险船的通信工具可用的情况下,应由遇险船指定通信工具。若是与救生艇通信,则只能用 VHF,因为救生艇上的唯一通信工具就是 VHF。负责协调搜索救助的船舶白天应悬挂"FR"旗。

Lesson 6
VHF Communication for Preventing Collisions

When handling a ship at sea, in narrow waters or in limited visibility, it is a major task for the navigating officer to keep a proper lookout and to prevent the collision. He should make a full appraisal of the situation and the risk of collision. To do this work well, the officer on duty should use all available means appropriately in the circumstances, including VHF radiotelephony communication, radar plotting and others to learn the other ship's actions and intentions. He should decide, when and what action shall be taken to avoid the collision. One of the best ways to get such information and to reach the manoeuvring agreement is to use the VHF radiotelephony.

1. Make positive identification

When the other ship's manoeuvring intentions must be known or something must be told to the other vessel to prevent collision, it is better to use the VHF radiotelephony if time permits. But in most of cases the other ship's name or call sign is not usually known at first, since the distance between ships is too great to recognize the ship's name or for other reasons. So, the first problem to be solved is how to make an effective first call to the unknown vessel, and the key in the first call is how to make positive identification each other. In normal practice, the following methods may be utilized for such a first call.

1.1　Making the call by other ship's position

According to the methods of fixing ship's position, use the latitude and longitude to call the other ship directly, or if there are conspicuous landmarks nearby, such as a cape, lighthouse, etc., take these landmarks as reference points and use the bearings and distances to call the other ship.

Example 1:

The vessel in latitude 35 degrees 38 minutes north, longitude 122 degrees 15 minutes east, this is north-bound vessel Chang Liu, Chang Liu, on channel one three, over.

Example 2:

Unknown vessel, in position bearing 270 degrees distance 3.5 miles from Light House, this is north-bound passenger vessel Chang Liu calling you on channel one six, over.

Note:

In the first call, the own ship's name or call sign must be identified so that the ship being called will be able to give a quick response.

This method of first call is convenient and effective. Even with several ships in the vicinity, the officer on duty can judge that his vessel is being called now by other vessel.

1.2 Making the call by relative position from own ship

In open sea or in areas without conspicuous land objects, make the first call by using the relative position (direction/bearing and distance) from own ship to the vessel whose name or call sign is not known. Meanwhile the other ships present course and speed also be pointed out.

Example:

The vessel on my port bow, distance 1. 8 miles, this is north-bound passenger ship Chang Liu calling on channel 06, over.

Note:

This method is used when only a few ships are in the vicinity. Confusion in ships position will happen if there are many ships nearby.

1.3 Making a call by other ship's heading type and special features

During daytime or in moonlight when visibility is good, the heading, appearance and characteristics of vessels can be identified with the binoculars within about eight miles; e. g., ship's type: container ship, roll on/off ship, oil tanker, passenger ship, etc.; hull or chimney colour: black, red, yellow, gray, white, etc. So the first call may be made beginning with the heading, type and feature of the other ship.

Example 1:

The vessel inward (incoming) near Buoy 101, this is outward (out-going) vessel Chang Liu calling on channel 06, over.

Example 2:

The black container ship crossing ahead of my port bow, this is passenger ship Chang Liu calling you on channel 13, over.

In practice, it is better to combine those methods appropriate to the situation. Of course, the duty officer should be familiar with the names and positions of the important landmarks. Whenever the vessel proceeds, he should always know his ship's relative position to landmarks, to other ships, and present speed and course, so that once his ship is called, he will be able to give a quick response.

2. Matters needing attention

(1) VHF radio has the potential to make a positive contribution to collision avoidance in certain circumstances. But it is not always helpful, and if misused, it may well lead to the collision which it sought to avoid.

(2) It must not be assumed that a message broadcast has been received by all other vessels involved.

(3) When communicating for collision prevention, VHF radiotelephony is only used as an aid to safe navigation. Every ship should strictly carry out the Collision Regulations. It is danger-

ous to make agreements by VHF radio to carry out manoeuvres which contravene the Collision Regulations.

（4）On the high seas, channel 13 can be used for preventing collision. In port, use the appropriate channel as per port regulations. In China coastal areas, channel 06 is the channel for collision avoidance communication. Here, channel 16, may also be used for the first call.

（5）After calling and responding, the positions of both ships should be checked so as to avoid "mis-contacting", which is very dangerous.

（6）If a close-quarters situation is already developing, valuable time may be wasted in trying to make VHF contact. Spend this time taking manoeuvring action to prevent collision.

（7）If positive identification has not been achieved, no discussion of possible manoeuvres should be attempted.

（8）A major danger in the use of VHF for preventing collision is misunderstanding arising from language difficulties. Remember that when serious language difficulties arise, VHF communication may be ineffective.

（9）Use the low power setting to avoid interference.

（10）When the visibility is restricted, own ships name and call sign, position, present speed and course, state of visibility should be broadcast at regular intervals to all vessels nearby.

Example：

SECURITE navigation, SECURITE navigation, SECURITE navigation. This is north-bound ship Chang Liu, Chang Liu, my position at time 0800：bearing 270 degrees distance 5 miles from Light House. Present course and speed 002 degrees and 10 knots, visibility less than 2 cables. Vessels navigate with caution, over.

第六课　船舶间利用甚高频协调避让通信

在繁忙水域船舶越来越多,经常发生多艘船会遇且有碰撞危险的局面,而避碰规则仅规定了两船会遇时有碰撞危险的避让方法。能否协调避让行动对航行安全非常重要。船舶起始避让呼叫应在 CH16 进行,沟通后转到 CH06 通话。但起始呼叫比较困难,原因是不知道对方的船名。目前,所有 300 总吨及以上的国际航行船舶、500 总吨及以上的非国际航行货船以及不论尺度大小的客船都装有船载自动识别系统(AIS, Automatic Identification System),它借助 VHF 时时播发本船船名、呼号、航向、航速、船位、航行状况等信息并在雷达上显示其所发出的信息。协调避让行动的关键就是起始呼叫。根据是否安装 AIS 来说明不同的呼叫方法。

1. 装有 AIS 的船舶

航行中应使 AIS 处于开启状态。AIS 时时播发本船船名、呼号、航向、航速、船位等信息。每一船舶驾驶员应认真分析 AIS 所收到的信息,必要时可以根据 AIS 提供的信息进行呼叫。雷达荧光屏出现多个回波时,应根据 AIS 显示的船舶名称及回波在光屏上的方位、距离选择要协商沟通对象。

2. 没有安装 AIS 的船舶

2.1　能见度不良时

能见度不良是航行安全的大敌。能见度不良时,船舶一定开启雷达,同时开启 VHF。
在海上守听 VHF CH16,在港口附近使用 VHF CH06 守听船舶动态。
(1)播发自己的船舶动态 (船名、呼号、船位、航向、航速等资料),以便他船收听并识别。例如:

SECURITE navigation, SECURITE navigation, SECURITE navigation. This is south-bound container ship Ever Green, Ever Green, my position at time 0900:bearing 180 degrees distance 3 miles from light house, present course 230 degrees speed 8 knots, visibility less than 3 cables. Vessels navigate with caution and if necessary please contact with me.

(2)以他船的船位呼叫。用雷达确定他船的船位进行呼叫,确定船位的方法可以是经纬度或方位、距离表示法。
例如:

The vessel in latitude 34 degrees 36 minutes north, longitude 123 degrees 45 minutes east, this is north-bound vessel Yong Xing, Yong Xing calling, over.

Unknown vessel, position:bearing 090 degrees distance 3 miles from light vessel, this is south-bound vessel Xinlianyungang, Xinlianyungang calling, over.

（3）可以以他船距本船的方位距离呼叫。如果被呼叫船有雷达并且处于开启状态,被呼叫船的驾驶员很容易识别是谁在呼叫自己,通常也能对该呼叫做出回答。在本船雷达显示屏上,他船距本船方位是 A°,则本船在他船雷达显示屏上的方位是 180°+A°,如果超过 360°,则方位是 180°+A°-360°,距离相同。

例如:

Unknown vessel, Unknown vessel, bearing 060 degrees, distance 3 miles from my ship, this is Yong Xing, Yong Xing calling, over.

这时不知名船的驾驶员只要一看雷达便知道:是距他方位 240°,距离 3 海里的"永兴"轮呼叫。

2.2　互见中

除上述能见度不良时的呼叫方法可用外,还可以根据他船的船首向、船舶种类、船壳的颜色等特征呼叫。例如:

The vessel inward near Buoy H0. This is outward vessel Merry-trans, Merry-trans calling. Over.

The white container ship overtaking me from my starboard side. This is Yong Xing, Yong Xing calling. Over.

The black oil tanker bound for south, this is Sincere Gemini calling. Over.

Lesson 7
VHF Communication in VTS Areas

A Vessel Traffic System (VTS), as defined by IMO Resolution A.578 (14) Guidelines for Vessel Traffic Services, 1997, is: "A service implemented by a Competent Authority, designed to improve the safety and to protect the environment. The service should have the capability to interact with the traffic and to respond to traffic situations developing in the VTS area." It has been put into practice in many high-traffic density port areas and other important waters now.

This system is composed of communication unit, shore-based radar chain unit, radar automatic processing unit and central processing unit. It may range from the provision of simple information messages to extensive management of traffic within a port or waterway.

1. Functions of VTS

According to the IMO Guidelines for VTS, VTS system has six functions: data collection, data evaluation, information service, navigational assistance service, traffic organization service, and support of allied activities. But to sum up, it has two main functions: provision of maritime traffic information and implementation of traffic control.

1.1　Provision of maritime traffic information

(1) Broadcasting of routine information, such as: weather report, navigational warning, navigational information, etc.;

(2) Coordination of ship movement;

(3) Single-ship information services: at the request of a ship or when VTC (vessel traffic center) considers it necessary, VTS provides position of the ship and its movement, and intentions of other relevant ships relating to her.

1.2　Implementation of traffic control

(1) Provision of advice and guidance;

(2) Monitoring of compliance with established traffic rules;

(3) Establishment of navigational regulations.

2. VHF communication in VTS areas

The key of VTS system is perfect, efficient communication network. To fulfill all of the functions of VTS, effective communication systems are necessary. These may include land-line telephone, radiotelephony, telex, microwave data link and satellite communication. However, in almost every case it will be found the main method of communication between vessels within the

VTS area and the vessel traffic center（VTC）is speech, using radiotelephony on the marine VHF band. Without reliable VHF radio communication, VTS could not function well. Language used in VTS communication must be clear and simple. If possible the IMO SMCP may be used.

2.1   Type of VHF communication in VTS areas

（1）Broadcast communication

VTC transmits all kinds of safety information to all or some of vessels within its area.

（2）Distress, urgency and safety communication

Being used when all kinds of marine traffic accidents occur.

（3）Exchange procedure communication

Linking up of information between VTC and ships includes all kinds of reports to VTC given by ships and all kinds of instructions, suggestions, orders, etc. to ships given by VTC. It is the principal part of VTC to provide traffic services for ships and implement traffic management.

2.2   VHF communication between VTC and a ship

（1）Name of VTC

Name of VTC is a indispensable element as ships name in communication. It is different with nations and regions. Such as: Hong Kong Mardep, × Information Service, Vessel Traffic Center, etc.

（2）Information required by ship

Before entering a VTS area, the captain and officers concerned should know the local regulations and other information about VTS. The following navigation publications which contain VTS information should be consulted in advance—Guide to Port Entry; Admiralty List of Radio Signals, Vol. VI; Admiralty Notices to Mariners; Annual Summary of Admiralty Notices to Mariners, Charts for the area.

（3）Type and content of reporting to VTC given by ship

All kinds of reports to VTC given by ships form the principal topic of communication between VTC and ships:

① Initial report（Report in advance）

Some time（When VHF call can be received）before entering VTS waters, the following items should be reported to VTC, so that VTC can establish the ship's files, upon which to fix and track the ship.

—Name and call sign of vessel;

—Flags of vessel;

—Particulars of vessel（include gross tonnage, net tonnage, length overall, draught and air draught, etc.）;

—Present position;

—Any other relevant information.

Example:

—Kanmon Martis, Kanmon Martis, this is Panama vessel Sea Master, Terrathree-Echo-Alfa-Charlie on channel 16, over.

—Panama vessel Sea Master. Terrathree-Echo-Alfa-Charlie, this is Kanmon Martis, channel 11 please, over.

—Kanmon Martis, this is Sea Master, roger, change to channel 11, over.

—Kanmon Martis, this is Sea Master on channel 11, my ETA at reporting line "Alfa" is time 1315 local today, GRT (Gross Registered Tonnage) 8786, NRT (Net Registered Tonnage) 6478, no dangerous cargo on board, my present position: Latitude 31 degrees 55 minutes north, longitude 130 degrees 40 minutes east. My destination is Himeji, over.

—Sea Master, this is Kanmon Martis. Understood, thank you. Please report when you passing reporting line "Alfa", over.

—Kanmon Martis, wilco, I will report when I passing reporting line "Alfa", over.

—Sea Master, nothing more, out.

Notes

(a) Roger=I have received all of your last transmission.

(b) Wilco=Your instructions have been received, understood and will be complied with.

②Ship's position report

After entering VTS waters, the following items should be reported to VTC when passing reporting point (or line).

—Name and call sign of vessel;

—The name of reporting point (or line) the vessel is passing;

—ETA at next reporting point (or line).

Example:

—Kanmon Martis, Kanmon Martis, this is Panama vessel Sea Master, over.

—Sea Master, this is Kanmon Martis, come in please, over.

—Kanmon Martis, I am passing reporting line "Alfa" at 1317 local time. Over.

—Sea Master, this is Kanmon Martis, next reporting point is point "Bravo". Over.

—Kanmon Martis, OK, I will report at reporting point "Bravo". Over.

—Sea Master, thank you, out.

③ Ship's movement report in VTS area

Include moving berth/berthing/unberthing, dropping/weighing anchor, etc. Taking the moving berth as an example, the report content may have:

—Name and call sign of vessel;

—Present location;

—Intended next berth;

—ETD from present location;

—Whether or not it is intended to move with pilots advice.

Example:

—Himeji VTS, Himeji VTS, this is Panama vessel Sea Master, Terrathree Echo Alfa Charlie, over.

—Panama vessel Sea Master, Terrathree Echo Alfa Charlie, this is Himeji VTS. Go ahead please, over.

—Himeji VTS, I intend to move to buoy "Bravo Four". ETD from present berth is 1320 local time, over.

—Sea Master, please advise your present location and do you need a pilot? Over.

—Himeji VTS, I am now berthing at bulk carrier pier, I do not need a pilot, over.

—Sea Master. This is VTS, please report after completion of your movement, over.

—Himeji VTS, roger, I will report as soon as the movement operation is completed, over.

—Sea Master, this is Himeji VTS, thank you, out.

④ Final report

It refers to the report to VTC given by vessel when a vessel leaves VTS waters or arrivals at berth, anchorage within VTS area. When leaving the last reporting point or boundary line of VTS area, a vessel should report the following information: passing time, present course and speed, kind and amount of cargo, next port of call and destination, etc.

Example:

—Les Escoumious VTS center, Les Escoumious VTS center, this is Tian Tan Hai, Bravo-Oscar-November-November on channel 14, over.

—Tian Tan Hai, Bravo-Oscar-November-November, this is Les Escoumious VTS center, go ahead please, over.

—Les Escoumious VTS center, this is Tian Tan Hai, I am passing reporting point "Bissotwo". My present course is 108 degrees and speed 12 knots. I have loaded 41,000 tons of wheat. Next port of call is Panama and destination is Shanghai, China, over.

—Tian Tan Hai, this is Les Escoumious VTS center, roger, thank you. Out.

(4) Communication for conduct of navigation

In modern VTS systems, service is provided by broadcasting information at fixed time intervals or at any time if deemed necessary by the VTS center, or at request of a vessel.

This information may include:

—Weather, present or forecast;

—Tidal information;

—Scheduled movements of vessels;

—Actual movements of vessels;

—Navigational warning;

—Information relating to pilotage, tug and other port services.

Among these, information about conduct of navigation is the principal topic. By using VHF radiotelephone and high performance shore-based radar, not only can the qualified staff in VTS center command the ship movement, but also guide and control the ships manoeuvring, reduce the marine accidents to minimum, and increase the traffic flow to the maximum as well.

① Information about ship's position

For the reason of poor visibility or a problem on ships radar, etc., the officer on watch may not be sure of the ship's exact position. Positional data can be obtained from VTS shore station through radiotelephone.

② Information about other ship's activity

Sometimes when a ship is passing a reporting point or steering in a VTS area, she may be given the other ship's activity by shore station; e. g., other ship's position, name, type, size and destination, expected time and place of meeting, so that she will be able to take precautions in advance to keep well clear of the approaching vessel.

Example:

—Rose Maru, this is Tokyo Martis. It is estimated that you may meet Apple Maru, 20.960 gross tons at about 1030 hours local time near the north entry of Urago Suido Traffic Route. Navigate with great caution.

③ Information about manoeuvring and navigating

When navigating in VTS area, a ship may sometimes deviate from its route or navigate in the wrong traffic lane, or sail too fast or slow, then the shore station may give advice or orders. These manoeuvring orders may also be given by the VTS center when marine accidents happen or bad weather occurs.

Example 1:

—Red Star, this is Eastern Coast Guard. You are not keeping to your correct traffic lane. Advise you alter course to starboard to enter correct lane. Fairway speed is eight knots. Do not overtake. Over.

Example 2:

—Ming Hua, this is Eastern Coast Guard. There has been a collision in the center of fairway ahead of you. Advise you to wait at a safe place, keeping away from the traffic route until further notice, over.

④ Other information

Besides the above information, VTS center will transmit other information relating to safety of navigation at regular intervals, such as weather report, navigational warning, order of entering or leaving harbour, movement of very large crude-oil carrier or special ship, etc. A vessel can also request information she needs from VTS at all times.

Sometimes VTS center wants to identify and locate a ship on the radar screen. The following sentence may be used: Please alter your course ××× degrees to starboard/port to assist identification.

When you hear the order you should take manoeuvring actions as requested and report what you have done. If you cannot carry out the order, give the reasons.

第七课　甚高频在 VTS 水域的通信

VTS（Vessel Traffic Service）是船舶交通服务系统，在港口附近、岬角和繁忙水道会设置 VTS，这对减少船舶碰撞和其他交通事故并对已发生的各类事故进行抢险、指挥会起到积极作用。

1. VTS 的功能

1.1　提供海上交通信息服务

（1）播发航行警告、气象警告（预报）、大型船舶动态、助航标志状况、通航时间表等。

（2）提供单船所请求的特殊服务。

1.2　海上交通管理

（1）为通航安全，交管部门（VTS）向船舶提出建议、劝告或警告。

（2）制定通航规则。

（3）监督该区域通航状况。

2. VTS 水域通信

世界上各国家和地区根据本地区水域和通航特点制定了其所管理的水域范围和报告方式方法，报告内容大致相同。各 VTS 中心将其管理的水域范围向外界公告，因此船长与驾驶员应当知道其航经的 VTS 水域并在适当时间、位置向 VTS 报告。有的区域报告线是直线，适用于江河、狭水道区域，两条线确定一段水域；有的区域报告线是圆弧，适用开阔水域；不管哪种报告线，只要一进入或驶出报告线马上报告。

2.1　通信注意事项

各 VTS 水域都规定了其呼叫和工作频道，船舶应严格遵守。在该水域内，在 VTS 规定的呼叫和工作频道上不能进行与航行安全无关的通信；也不能在该水域附近的陆地工作单位的工作频道上进行与这些单位业务无关的通信。有些 VTS 水域规定了船舶间通信频道，船舶之间通信就应该在该频道上。船舶进入某一 VTS 水域前，应首先查阅有关资料，如《无线电信号书》（NP 286）、航海通告、进港指南、相关海图，搞清 VTS 通信的具体要求和注意事项。VTS 水域通常都守听两个频道，16 频道和另一工作频道，如果在 16 频道呼叫，一定转到其指定的工作频道通信。如果在工作频道呼叫，则可直接在该频道通信。

2.2　船舶向 VTC（Vessel Traffic Center 船舶交管中心）报告种类及内容

VTS 水域通信主要是船舶向 VTC 报告，各 VTS 要求的报告种类有所不同，主要报告有：

（1）航行计划报告（Sailing Plan, SP），也叫初始报告或事先报告船舶从适用水域的港口出发前或从海上驶入该水域前提前若干时间向 VTS 所做的报告。报告内容大致如下：

　　—船舶名称和呼号

　　—船旗国

　　—船舶资料

　　—现在船位

　　—其他相关信息（如航向、航速、目的港等）

（2）船位报告（Position Report，PR）

船舶进入 VTS 水域后，航经报告点或报告线时或者离开泊位时向 VTC 所做的报告表明自己的身份，以便 VTC 对该船舶实施全程跟踪辨认和管理。报告内容大致如下：

　　—船舶名称和呼号

　　—船舶通过报告点或报告线的名称或通过报告线时的船位

　　—预计抵达下一报告点的时间

（3）偏航报告或变更报告（Deviation Report，DR）

如有需要则做此变更报告，即改变航行计划时进行此项报告，比如进入或离开锚地时。

（4）事故报告（Incident Report，IR）

当船舶发生或发现交通事故、污染事故或其他紧急情况后向 VTC 所做的报告。报告内容大致如下：

　　—船舶名称和呼号

　　—船舶位置

　　—紧急情况及 VTC 要求的其他信息

注意：并不是船舶航经每个 VTS 水域都要进行上述四个报告，但航行计划报告和船位报告是必须报告的。有些 VTS 水域还有定点报告、到达报告、移泊报告、异常情况报告等，具体情况可查《无线电信号书》NP 286。

2.3　通信范例

2.3.1　以北海港为例

其管辖的水域有北海港、铁山港和涠洲岛水域，北海港和铁山港报告线分别是由 4 个指定点所围成的区域组成，涠洲岛水域报告线范围是以指定点 W 为圆心、半径 10 海里以内水域，在此三个水域的报告区域航行时，船舶需要呼叫"北海交管中心"（Beihai VTS），呼叫频道和工作频道为 CH10，备用频道是 CH65。

（1）初始报告

以 Sincere Gemini 通过涠洲岛水域向"北海交管中心"（Beihai VTS）报告为例。

（B＝Beihai VTS，S＝Sincere Gemini）

On VHF CH16

S：Beihai VTS，Beihai VTS，this is MV Sincere Gemini，Sincere Gemini calling，over.

B：Sincere Gemini，Sincere Gemini，this is Beihai VIS，please change to channel 11，over.

S：Beihai VTS，Beihai VTS，this is MV Sincere Gemini，Sincere Gemini，agree change to channel 11，over.

On VHF CH11

B：Sincere Gemini, Sincere Gemini, this is Beihai VTS, coming please, over.

S：Beihai VTS, this is MV Sincere Gemini, my flag is panama and call sign is H2SD, and my GRT（Gross Register Tonnage）is 14971, NRT（Net Register Tonnage）is 8855. LOA（Length Overall）is 159. 76 meters. Maximum draught is 10.5 meters, last port of call is Rubert Prince, next port is Qinzhou, ETA at Qinzhou is 2030 local time, over.

B：Sincere Gemini, this is Beihai VTS. Roger, good-bye, out.

S：Beihai VTS, this is MV Sincere Gemini, thank you, good-bye, out.

（2）船位报告

On VHF CH16　（B＝Beihai VTS，S＝Sincere Gemini）

S：Beihai VTS, Beihai VTS, this is MV Sincere Gemini, Sincere Gemini calling, over.

B：Sincere Gemini, Sincere Gemini, this is Beihai VTS, please change to channel 10, over.

S：Beihai VTS, Beihai VTS, this is MV Sincere Gemini, Sincere Gemini, agree change to channel 10, over.

On VHF CH10

B：Sincere Gemini, Sincere Gemini, this is Beihai VTS, coming please, over.

S：Dalian VTS, this is MV Sincere Gemini. I am passing Reporting line, position is latitude 109 degrees 12 minutes north, longitude is 21 degrees 09 minutes east, over.

B：Sincere Gemini, this is Beihai VTS, roger, nothing more, good-bye, out.

S：Beihai VTS, this is MV Sincere Gemini, nothing more, good-bye, out.

2.3.2　以德国 Elbe 水域为例

德国 VTS 水域多为长条形,某一个水域分为多个交管区（Traffic Area）,一个交管区分为多个雷达监管站;或者某一个水域就划分一个交管区,该交管区分为多个雷达监管站。在同一个 VTS 水域,交管中心的名称是相同的,只是在不同的交管区或不同的雷达监管区呼叫频道不同,该呼叫频道就是工作频道。

以"永兴"轮从外海进入 Cuxhaven Elbe Traffic 为例。

（1）初始报告

On VHF channel 19

—Cuxhaven Elbe Traffic, Cuxhaven Elbe Traffic, this is Yong Xing, Yong Xing calling, over.

—Yong Xing, Yong Xing, this is Cuxhaven ELBE Traffic, Cuxhaven Elbe Traffic, coming please, over.

—My call sign is J8FR2, Juliett-Oktoeight-Foxtrot-Romeo-Bissotwo, over.

—Roger, Go ahead, over.

—My position is longitude 8 degrees 10 minutes east, latitude 54 degrees 15 minutes north, over.

—Go ahead, over.

—My ship is bulk cargo ship and LOA is 189.9 meters. Beam is 28.8 meters, over.

—Go ahead, over.

—My draught is 16. 4 meters, over.

—My last port of call is Port Said, over.

—Next please, over.

—My destination is Hamburg, over.

—No dangerous goods, over.

—Next please, over.

—My ship is in good condition, over.

—Next please, over.

—My owner is Dalian Vivid Dragon ship company, and agent is Kiel Canal, over.

—Roger, Bon-voyage, good-bye, out.

—Thank you good-bye, out.

（2）船位报告

On VHF CH18

—Cuxhaven Elbe Traffic, Cuxhaven Elbe Traffic, this is Yong Xing, Yong Xing calling,
Over.

—Yong Xing, Yong Xing, this is Cuxhaven Elbe Traffic, Cuxhaven Elbe Traffic, coming
please, over.

—My call sign is J8FR2, Juliett-Oktoeight-Foxtrot-Romeo-Bissotwo, over.

—Roger, go ahead, over.

—1330 local time position: longitude 8 degrees 15 minutes east, latitude 54 degrees 30 minutes north. My speed is 10 knots, over.

—Roger, nothing more, good-bye, out.

—Nothing more, good-bye, out.

Yong Xing went on navigating in the Cuxhaven Elbe Traffic, reported on VHF CH05,
CH12 and CH03 as above till went alongside the wharf.

Lesson 8
Comprehensive Examples of Plain Language Messages for Marine Radiotelephony Communication

1. Establishment of communication contact

1.1　Useful expressions

（1）Calling/Answering.

（2）Who is calling?

（3）Which ship is calling me?

（4）Come in/go ahead/Send your message please.

（5）Wilco/roger/over/out.

（6）Do you read me?

（7）How do you read me?

（8）I read you bad/poor/fair/good/excellent.

（9）Nothing more.

（10）I can not read you.

（11）Change to channel ××/Switch to channel ××.

（12）Agree（VHF）channel ××.

（13）I will switch to channel ××.

（14）Do not use this channel, shift to another channel.

（15）Keep watch（listening）on channel ××/stand by channel ××.

（16）Hold on/read back please.

（17）Say again/repeat it.

（18）I can not follow you.

（19）Speak slowly, please.

（20）I understood/that is correct.

（21）Please spell your ship's name（call sign）.

（22）Motor vessel（MV）/motor tanker（MT）/steam ship（SS）.

（23）Is that correct?

（24）Negative/positive.

（25）Mistake/correction.

（26）Please confirm/advise.

（27）There is a message for you.

1.2 Examples

Example 1

Communication between ship and shore station

—Dalian radio, this is motor vessel Zheng He calling on channel 16, how do you read me? Over.

—Motor vessel Zheng He, Zheng He, this is Dalian radio answering, I read you good, please change to channel 13, over.

—Dalian radio, this is Zheng He, roger, I will change to channel 13, over.

—Dalian radio, this is Zheng He calling on channel 13, over.

—Zheng He, this is Dalian radio, go ahead please, over.

Example 2

Communication between ship and pilot station

—Xiamen pilot station, Xiamen pilo station, this is MV Yu Cai, Yu Cai calling on channel 16, over.

—Motor vessel Yu Cai, this is Xiamen pilot station, please call me on channel 11, I say again, channel 11, over.

—Pilot station, this is Yu Cai, understood, I will call you on channel 11, over.

—Xiamen pilot station., this is motor vessel Yu Cai calling you on channel 11, do you read me? Over.

—Yu Cai, Yu Cai, this is Xiamen pilot station, spell your ship's name please, over.

—Xiamen pilot station, roger, my ship's name is Yu Cai, Yankee-Uniform-Charlie-Alfa-India, over.

—Yu Cai, this is pilot station, sorry, I cannot follow you, please say again slowly, over.

—Pilot station, wilco. I will spell it again slowly, Yankee-Uniform-Charlie-Alfa-India, over.

Example 3

Communication between ships

—Golden Bridge, Golden Bridge, this is steam ship Sea Master, Sea Master, over.

—Who is calling me? This is motor vessel Golden Bridge answering. Over.

—Golden Bridge, this is Sea Master, Sea Master calling you on channel 16, over.

—Sea Master, this is Golden Bridge, switch to channel 72, repeat, channel 72, over.

—Golden Bridge, roger, channel 72, over.

2. Calling for a pilot

2.1 Useful expressions

(1) I require a pilot.

(2) Please send a pilot to meet me.

(3) Please arrange a pilot to board my ship.

（4）No pilot is available at present（The pilot is not available at present），please await.

（5）When（at what time）will the pilot be available?

（6）Pilot can be available at short notice.

（7）Where shall we wait for pilot?

（8）Where can I take（pick up，meet）pilot?

（9）When and Where will the pilot come on board?

（10）Please advise pilot boarding time and position.

（11）Please meet（take，pick up）pilot at...

（12）You can take pilot near...（at... hours）.

（13）Pilot is coming to you.

（14）Pilot is on his way to you.

（15）Pilot boat is approaching your vessel.

（16）Pilot will board your ship at... hours（in half an hour），please get pilot ladder ready.

（17）Owing to（Due to）strong wind and rough sea outside，pilot（pilot boat）cannot get off to you.

（18）Sea is too rough，pilot cannot proceed to you.

（19）Stop where you are and wait for pilot.

（20）What's your ETA at pilot station?

（21）On which side do you want pilot ladder?

（22）On which side is pilot ladder to be rigged?

（23）On which side shall I get pilot ladder ready?

（24）Please rig pilot ladder on your lee（port/starboard）side.

（25）（I want）pilot ladder on port（starboard/lee）side，2 meters above water.

（26）Put on lights at pilot ladder position.

（27）Have a heaving line ready at pilot ladder position.

（28）Make a lee for pilot boat.

（29）Keep pilot boat on your... side.

2.2　Examples

Example 1

—Canal pilot station，this is Chinese vessel Jin Sha calling you on channel 16，over.

—Chinese vessel Jin Sha，this is canal pilot station speaking，please change to channel 11，over.

—Pilot station，OK，change to channel 11，over.

—Pilot station. this is Jin Sha calling on channel 11，do you read me? Over.

—Jin Sha，this is canal pilot station answering，come in please，over.

—Pilot station，this is Jin Sha，my ETA at pilot station is 1500 hours. I require a pilot，please advise pilots boarding time，over.

—Jin Sha，this is pilot station，you can pick up pilot at 1700 hours，near Buoy number 1，please drop anchor there and wait for pilot，over.

—Pilot station, roger, I will drop anchor near Buoy number 1 to wait for pilot. On which side do you want pilot ladder? Over.

—Jin Sha, please stand by pilot ladder on your lee side and put on the lights at pilot ladder position, over.

—Pilot station, this is Jin Sha, understood, I will have pilot ladder ready on my lee side and put on lights at pilot ladder position, over.

—Jin Sha, this is pilot station, thank you, nothing more. Out.

Example 2

—Inchon pilot station, Inchon pilot station, this is Ocean Bright on channel 09, over.

—Ocean Bright, this is Inchon pilot station answering, spell your ship's name please. Over.

—Inchon pilot station, my ship's name is Ocean Bright, Oscar Charlie Echo Alfa November, Bravo Romeo India Golf Hotel Tango, over.

—Ocean Bright, this is Inchon pilot station, what is your ETA at pilot station? Over.

—Inchon pilot station, my ETA at pilot station is 0300 hours, please arrange a pilot to meet me at outer pilot boarding ground, over.

—Ocean Bright, this is Inchon pilot station, sea is too rough today, pilot boat cannot approach to you, please proceed to the inner boarding ground to take pilot, over.

—Inchon pilot station, I cannot proceed to inner pilot boarding ground without the help of pilot, over.

—Ocean Bright, roger, you may anchor where you are and wait for fine weather, please contact with me tomorrow morning, over.

—Inchon pilot station, OK, I will call you again tomorrow morning. Out.

Example 3

—Inchon pilot station, this is Ocean Bright on channel 16, over.

—Ocean Bright, this is Inchon pilot station, channel 09 please. Over.

—Pilot station, this is Ocean Bright, channel 09, over.

—Ocean Bright, this is pilot station, pilot boat is coming to you. Please keep watch on this channel. Over.

—Pilot station, understood, I will keep listening on this channel, over.

—Ocean Bright, this is pilot boat on channel 09 calling you. Do you read me? Over.

—Pilot boat, this is Ocean Bright, go ahead please, over.

—Ocean Bright, this is pilot boat, I am proceeding to you, please advise your present position, over.

—Pilot boat, my present position is 0. 5 mile north of light buoy. Over.

—Ocean Bright, this is pilot boat, roger. There are several ships in the vicinity of light buoy. Please show a green signal light for identification, over.

—Pilot boat, this is Ocean Bright, I will do that, over.

—Ocean Bright, this is pilot boat, I have found your signal light. I will board you in 10 minutes. Please heave up anchor, 3 shackles on deck, over.

—Pilot boat, this is Ocean Bright, wilco, heave up anchor 3 shackles on deck, out.

Example 4

—Shantou pilot station, this is Zheng He, over.

—Zheng He, this is pilot station, come in please, over.

—Pilot station, this is Zheng He, my cargo handling operation have been completed ETD is 2030 today, now it is time for sailing. Please advise when pilot board my vessel, over.

—Zheng He, this is pilot station, your message received, hold on please, let me check, over.

—Zheng He, this is pilot station, your ETD has been changed. Pilot will board your ship in 1 hour, please advise your location, over.

—Pilot station, this is Zheng He, understood, now I am berthing at wharf No. 3, over.

—Zheng He, thank you, nothing more, out.

3. Advising ship's particulars

3.1　Useful expressions

(1) Ship's particulars.

(2) Advise (give) the following ship's particulars: ship's name/call sign/Gross Register Tonnage (GRT)/Net Register Tonnage (NRT)/Length overall (LOA)/breadth.

(3) What is your port of registry/port of destination/port of departure/next port of call/last port of call.

(4) What is your nationality (ship's flag)?

(5) What is your deadweight (DW)/displacement?

(6) What is your drafts fore and aft/max. draft in fresh water/air draft/drafts in ballast?

(7) What is your depth/max. height from bottom?

(8) I am on even keel.

(9) What is your ship's owner/operator?

(10) Advise the type of vessel/cargo quantity.

(11) What is your cargo capacity (grain and bale)?

(12) Please inform the lifting capacity of your cargo gear/derrick/crane.

(13) What is the SWL. (safe working load) of your cargo gear?

(14) The SWL. of derricks in union purchase is ××× tons.

(15) The lifting capacity of heavy derrick/crane is ××× tons.

3.2　Examples

Example 1

—Yokohama pilot station, this is motor vessel Merry Trans on channel 14, over.

—Merry Trans, this is Yokohama pilot station. Please repeat your ship's name, over.

—Pilot station, my ship's name is Merry Trans. I spell it: Mike Echo Romeo Romeo Yankee, Tango Romeo Alfa November Sierra, over.

—Merry Trans, I read you good, thank you. Please give me the following ship's particulars: LOA, GRT, drafts fore and aft, repeat: LOA, GRT, drafts fore and aft, over.

—Pilot station, this is Merry Trans, my LOA 141 meters, GRT 8786, drafts fore 7.52 meters, aft 8.05 meters, over.

—Merry Trans. I see, thank you. What is your port of registry, last port of call? Over.

—Pilot station, my port of registry is Kingstown and the last port of call is Shanghai, China, over.

—Merry Trans, this is pilot station, your message received, nothing more, out.

Example 2

—Port Taufiq, Port Taufiq, this is Chinese ship You Yi on channel 16, over.

—You Yi, You Yi, this is Port Taufiq, change to channel 11 please, over.

—Port Taufiq, OK, channel 11, over.

—Port Taufiq, this is You Yi on channel 11. I am proceeding to Quarantine anchorage and expect to be there in half an hour. I want to join the convoy to transit the canal, over.

—You Yi, roger, what are your ports of departure and destination? Over.

—Port Taufiq, I sailed from Shanghai China and bound for Hamburg Germany, over.

—You Yi, give me your ship's particulars please, over.

—Port Taufiq. This is You Yi, I am 134 meters long, 26.5 meters wide, my GRT 12 thousands, drafts fore 7.5 meters and 8 meters aft, over.

—You Yi, what kind of ship are you? Over.

—Port Taufiq. I am a general cargo ship, I have 11,000 tons of steel products, over.

—You Yi, will you discharge or load any cargo at this port? Over.

—Port Taufiq, I do not load or discharge any cargo at this port. I am a north bound ship. I want to transit the canal only, over.

—You Yi, roger, please drop your anchor at Quarantine anchorage, and keep watch on channel 06, over.

—Port Taufiq, OK. I will drop anchor at Quarantine anchorage and stand by VHF channel 06, out.

Example 3

—Panama ship Ocean Bright, Panama ship Ocean Bright, this is Korean navy, this is Korean navy on channel 16, over.

—Korean navy, this is Panama ship Ocean Bright. What can I do for you? Over.

—Ocean Bright, this is Korean navy. Please advise your call sign, over.

—Korean navy, my call sign is 3HEMM, Terrathree Hotel Echo Mike Mike. I say again, Terrathree Hotel Echo Mike Mike. Over.

—Ocean Bright, roger. What is your last port and destination? Over.

—Korean navy, my last port is Yingkou China, and my destination is Busan Korea. Over.

—Ocean Bright, this is Korean navy. How many crew members do you have? What are their nationalities? Over.

—Korean navy, there are 27 crew members on my vessel including master. All of them are Chinese, over.

—Ocean Bright, roger. What cargo do you carried? What is the cargo quantity? Over.

—Korean navy, 15,000 tons of Chinese coal and 8,000 tons of cement in bulk are carried on board, total cargo 23,000 tons, over.

—Ocean Bright, roger, thank you for your good cooperation, a nice trip, out.

4. Enquiring ship's movement

4.1　Useful expressions

(1) Port control/Port operation.

(2) Any berthing information/schedule/instruction for me?

(3) Port is congested, there is no vacant berth now.

(4) No berth for you these two days.

(5) Your berth will be clear this afternoon (×× hours latter).

(6) The previous berthing time/schedule/instruction was canceled (changed).

(7) When shall we go alongside the wharf/what is the berthing schedule?

(8) You will go to berthing at ×× hours.

(9) What is the berth number?

(10) Which berth are we going to take?

(11) You will moor buoys number 1 and number 2.

(12) Wait for further notice please.

(13) Stand by main engine ×× hours before berthing.

(14) Please give me ×× hours notice to stand by engine.

4.2　Examples

Example 1

—Port control, port control, this is Chinese ship Yu Ying on channel 13, over.

—Yu Ying, this is port control, your ship's name and call sign please, over.

—Port control, my call sign is BTBM, Bravo Tango Brave Mike. Ship's name is Yu Ying, Yankee Uniform, Yankee India November Golf, do you read me? Over.

—Port control, any berthing information for me? Over.

—Yu Ying, sorry, there is no your berthing schedule this week. Port is congested very much due to bad weather. Please await at anchorage. Over.

—Port control, I understood, but there are 35 students practicing on board, permission to enter the harbour for replenishment is urgently requested, over.

—Yu Ying, this is port control. I see, but I cannot give you a fixed answer at present, please wait for further notice and keep watch on channel 13, over.

—Port control, roger, I will wait for further information on channel 13, over.

—Yu Ying, this is port control on channel 13, over.

—Port control, this is Yu Ying answering, come in please, over.

—Yu Ying, you may go to berth number 2 at 2200 hours today for replenishment, please contact with plot station to confirm the details about berthing, over.

—Port control, your message received, I will go alongside at 2200 today for replenishment, I will call pilot station to confirm the details, thank you for your help, over.

—Yu Ying, that is right, nothing more, out.

Example 2

—Pilot station, this is motor vessel Yu Ying on channel 13, do you read me? Over.

—Who is calling me? This is pilot station answering, go ahead please, over.

—Pilot station. This is Yu Ying calling you. Good evening, sir. I have been informed that my ship will go alongside berth number 2 at 2200 hours, please advise at what time will the pilot come on board? Over.

—Yu Ying, this is pilot station, berth number 2 is not clear now, your previous schedule was canceled, and the new berthing time has not been fixed. Please call me again 0400 hours tomorrow on this channel, over.

—Pilot station, OK, I will call you again 0400 hours tomorrow on this channel, out.

—Pilot station, pilot station, Yu Ying calling you on channel 13, over.

—Yu Ying, this is pilot station, new berthing schedule has been fixed, berthing time 0700 hours, pilot will board your ship at 0630, please stand by pilot ladder on your port side, over.

—Pilot station, roger, new berthing time is 0700 hours, pilot will come on board my ship at 0630, is that correct? over.

—Yu Ying. That is correct. Please give me your LOA and max. draft, over.

—Pilot station, my LOA 131 meters, max, draft is 6. 5 meters. I say again: LOA 131 meters, max. draft 6. 5 meters, over.

—Yu Ying, OK, see you then, out.

Example 3

—Sino agent, Sino agent, this is motor vessel Yu Zhi calling on channel 72. Over.

—Motor vessel Yu Zhi, this is Sino agent answering, come in please, over.

—Sino agent, I have arrived at quarantine anchorage and dropped anchor at 1020 local time. How about my berthing schedule? Over.

—Yu Zhi, the quarantine officers are on their way to your ship, please call me again on this channel after quarantine inspection, over.

—Sino agent, roger, I will call you again after quarantine inspection, out.

—Sino agent, this is Yu Zhi on channel 72, over.

—Yu Zhi, this is Sino agent, have you passed the quarantine inspection? Over.

—Sino agent, yes, the inspection is over, I have got the free pratique at 1105, over.

—Yu Zhi, that is fine, you will go alongside Jetty number 2 at 1630, do you read me? Over.

—Sino agent, your message received, my ETB is 0630 today, is that correct? Over.

—Yu Zhi, negative, your ETB is 1630 hours, repeat: 1630. Please stand by engines 2 hours before entering, over.

—Sino agent, roger, my ETB is 1630, and stand by engines 2 hours before entering, over.

5. Communication for preventing collision

5.1 Useful expressions

(1) Unknown vessel.

(2) The vessel ahead of me/astern of me (following me).

(3) The vessel is ××× miles on my port (starboard) bow/quarter/beam.

(4) The vessel on opposite/same course.

(5) The vessel head-on and ××× miles ahead of me.

(6) The vessel crossing ahead ××× of my port (starboard) bow.

(7) Unknown vessel bearing ××× degrees distance ×× miles from me (light house).

(8) The vessel in lat.××× N(S), long.××× E(W), course ××× degrees, speed ×× knots.

(9) The white passenger ship/black container ship/bulk carrier/oil tanker/LPG (LNG) ship/war ship/dredger.

(10) North/South/West/East bound vessel.

(11) Incoming (Inward)/Outgoing (Outward) vessel.

(12) The vessel intending to overtake/cross/turn.

(13) What is your intention?

(14) I intend (want) to…

(15) I intend to alter course, new course ××× degrees.

(16) Alter course to port (star board)/reduce speed/keep course and speed/stop engine.

(17) Advise you make (steer) course ××× degrees.

(18) Please keep well clear of me/give me a wide berth.

(19) Keep out of the way of me/give way to me.

(20) Do not pass on my/I will pass on your port (starboard) side.

(21) Shall we pass port (starboard) side to port (starboard) side?

(22) Do not pass ahead/astern of me.

(23) I will overtake on your port (starboard) side.

(24) You should navigate with caution.

(25) I am manoeuvring with difficulty, keep clear of me.

5.2 Examples

Example 1

—Inward vessel Jin Jiang, this is outward vessel Yu Qing on channel 06, over.

—Yu Qing, this is Jin Jiang, this is Jin Jiang, come in please, over.

—Jin Jiang, what is your intention? Now you are crossing ahead of me, it is dangerous, please alter your course to starboard, over.

—Yu Qing, I want to proceed to the quarantine anchorage, I will follow your advice to alter my course to starboard, over.

—Jin Jiang, thank you very much. Shall we pass port side to port side? Over.

—Yu Qing, OK, pass port side to port side. out.

Example 2

—Container ship Han Tao He, container ship Han Tao He, this is Panama vessel Trans Bridge, Trans Bridge, over.

—Panama vessel Trans Bridge. This is Han Tao He, go ahead please, over.

—Han Tao He, please tell me your present course and destination, over.

—Trans Bridge, my present course is 080 degrees and I am proceeding to Yokohama Japan, what can I do for you? over.

—Han Tao He, my course is 350 degrees, you are crossing ahead of my port bow, please keep out of way of me, over.

—Trans Bridge, I intend pass ahead of your port bow, no problem with you, over.

—Han Tao He, do not pass ahead of my port bow, pass astern of me, please, over.

—Trans Bridge, OK, I will alter course to starboard and pass your stern. Please keep your present course and speed, over.

—Han Tao He, thank you for your cooperation. I will keep my present course and speed, out.

Example 3

—Securite navigation, securite navigation, this is Fu Zhou on channel 16, my present position at time 1130: latitude 38 degrees 40 minutes north, longitude 121 degrees 22 minutes east, course 270 degrees, speed 7 knots, bound for Qinhuangdao, visibility less than 1.5 cables, vessels navigate with caution, out.

—The vessel in position: lat. 38 degrees 40 minutes north, long. 121 degrees 22 minutes east and course 270 degrees, this is east bound vessel Da Qing, this is Da Qing, please repeat your ship's name, over.

—Da Qing, Da Qing, this is west bound vessel Fu Zhou: Foxtrot Uniform, Zulu Hotel Oscar Uniform. What is your present position, course and speed? Over.

—Fu Zhou, my present position: 3.2 miles south of Light House, course 090 degrees, speed 6 knots, over.

—Da Qing, I have located you on my radar, you are 2 miles ahead of me. What is your Intention? Over.

—Fu Zhou, this is Da Qing, I am going to alter my course to starboard, advise you alter course to starboard too, over.

—Da Qing, roger, but I can not alter course to starboard because there is a shoal on my starboard bow. I have to keep my present course, over.

—Fu Zhou, I understood. Please keep your present course, please call me on this channel if necessary, over.

—Da Qing, thank you for your cooperation. I will keep watch on this channel, over.

—Fu Zhou, nothing more, out.

Example 4

—LPG vessel Anabella, LPG vessel Anabella, this is oil tanker Esabella, this is oil tanker Esabella, you are dragging and drifting to me, I say again: you are dragging and drifting to me, it is dangerous, please pay attention. Over.

—Esabella, Esabella, this is Anabella, your message received, I have got my engine ready, and commenced heaving up anchor, the vessel is under command, over.

—Anabella, that is fine. Do you need any help? Over.

—Esabella, help is not required, thank you, over.

—Anabella, OK, nothing more, out.

Example 5

—East bound vessel on my port bow, east bound vessel on my port bow, this is west bound vessel Seaway, this is west bound vessel Seaway calling you, over.

—Seaway, Seaway, this is east bound vessel Sheng Li on your port bow answering, go a-head please, over.

—Sheng Li, this is Seaway, I intend to alter my course to port after period 10 minutes, new course 193 degrees, please navigate with caution, over.

—Seaway, roger, you will make a new course 195 degrees after period 10 minutes. I will keep sharp lookout and maintain my present course, over.

—Sheng Li, thank you for your cooperation, out.

Example 6

—The ferry ship crossing traffic lane, the ferry ship crossing traffic lane, this is north bound vessel Hua Shan, this is north bound vessel Hua Shan, do you read me? Over.

—Hua Shan, Hua Shan, this is Ferry number 2, this is Ferry number 2, what can I do for you? Over.

—Ferry number 2, this is Hua Shan, my steering gear was out of order. I wish to proceed to separation zone and anchor for repairing, I am manoeuvring with difficulty. Please clear of me, over.

—Hua Shan, your message received, I will keep clear of your ship, please report your situation to the VTS center on channel 16, over.

—Ferry number 2, thank you for your advice. I will report my situation to VTS center immediately. Out.

6. Communication in VTS areas

6.1   Useful expressions

（1）Way point/Reporting point/CIP（calling in point）.

（2）I am at（I am passing）way point...

(3) I am approaching CIP..., course ×××...speed ××× knots.

(4) Please report at next reporting point (or reporting line).

(5) Say again your position for identification.

(6) You are entering area...

(7) You are in the fairway.

(8) You are approaching starboard/port limit of fairway.

(9) You must keep to the starboard side of fairway.

(10) You are not keeping to your correct traffic lane.

(11) You are not complying with traffic regulations.

(12) You are proceeding at a dangerous speed.

(13) May I enter traffic lane (route)?

(14) Advise you make course ××× degrees.

(15) Advise speed ××× knots.

(16) I have located you on my radar.

(17) You will meet crossing traffic at way point...

(18) There are many fishing vessels at CIP.

(19) There is a vessel ahead obstructing your movements.

(20) There is a vessel anchored ahead of you in position...

(21) There is a vessel ahead of you passing your starboard (port) side on opposite course.

(22) Vessel following will overtake you on port (starboard) side.

(23) You must avoid (keep clear of) this area.

(24) There is a vessel with a difficult tow on passage from... to...

(25) There is a vessel turning at...

(26) Vessel... is leaving...

(27) Vessel... has entered the fairway at... hours.

(28) Transit canal will begin at... hours.

(29) Your station in convoy will be number...

(30) I am underway/I am ready to get underway.

(31) I will proceed by west (east) channel.

(32) Wait for vessel... to clear, before entering fairway/getting underway/leaving berth.

(33) What is the anchor position for me?

(34) You have anchored in wrong position.

6.2 Examples

Example 1

—Hong Kong Mardep, Hong Kong Mardep, this is Sea World: Novenine Hotel Echo Whiskey on channel 16, over.

—Sea World, Novenine Hotel Echo Whiskey, this is Hong Kong Mardep, channel 14 please, over.

—Hong Kong Mardep, roger, channel 14, over.

—Hong Kong Mardep, this is Sea World, I am approaching CIP Po-Toi from sea, my ETA at Po-Toi is 1630 local time. May I enter the east Lamma channel? Over.

—Sea world, this is Hong Kong Mardep, your nationality, GRT and NRT please, over.

—Hong Kong Mardep, my nationality is Panama, GRT 9390, NRT 7384, over.

—Sea World, roger, please advise your port of departure and destination, any dangerous cargo on board? Over.

—Hong Kong Mardep, I sailed from Busan, Korea, I bound for Shen Zhen, no dangerous cargo on bard. Over.

—Sea World, understood, you may enter Lamma channel, next reporting position is Buoy Lamma number 1, what is your ETA at Green Island pilot station? Over.

—Hong Kong Mardep, my ETA at Green Island pilot station is about 1805 local time, I will report at Buoy Lamna number 1, over.

—Hong Kong Mardep, this is Sea World, I am passing Buoy Lamma number 1 1715 local time, over.

—Sea World, OK, there is a VLCC turning ahead of you, she is obstructing your movement, you should reduce your speed and wait for VLCC to clear the fairway, advise speed 6 knots, over.

—Hong Kong Mardep, I understood. I will reduce my speed to 6 knots immediately and wait for VLCC to clear fairway, over.

—Sea World, you may pick up pilot at Green Island. Pilot wants to rig pilot ladder on your starboard side. Your next reporting point is Mawan, over.

—Hong Kong Mardep, I will get pilot ladder ready on my starboard side, please repeat the next reporting position, over.

—Sea World, next reporting point is Mawan: Mike Alfa Whiskey Alfa November, over.

—Hong Kong Mardep, I see, I will report at Mawan, thank you, over.

—Sea World, this is Hong Kong Mardep, you are not complying with the traffic regulations, you are approaching to port limit of fairway, there is a vessel on opposite course ahead of you, you should keep to starboard side of fairway, over

—Hong Kong Mardep, this is Sea World, wilco, I have located the vessel ahead of me on my radar. I will alter my course to starboard, over.

—Sea World, there is a crossing traffic at CIP Mawan, please navigate with caution, over.

—Hong Kong Mardep, information received, thank you, over.

—Sea World, nothing more, out.

Example 2

Issuing navigational warning

—Attention all vessels, attention all vessels, this is Hong Kong Mardep on VHF channel

12, this is Hong Kong Mardep on VHF channel 12, navigational warning.

One: Waglan Light House was extinguished.

Two: A pipe laying operation is commenced in Mawan area.

Three: There is a vessel with a difficult tow on passage from Lamma anchorage to refinery quay, vessels should proceed with great caution, out.

Example 3

Issuing weather report

—Attention all vessels, attention all vessels, this is Hong Kong Mardep on VHF channel 14, this is Hong Kong Mardep on VHF channel 14, weather report for Hong Kong area: Time 1200 GMT wind north-west, force 4, sea moderate, weather fog, visibility is reduced by fog and expected to decrease to 350 meters, pressure 1,000 HPa falling, navigate with caution, out.

Example 4

Issuing typhoon warning

—Attention all vessels, attention all vessels, this is traffic information service, this is traffic information service, tropical storm warning: the latest storm center is reported at 0600 GMT in position 20 degrees 18 minutes north, 115 degrees 05 minutes east, the atmospheric pressure is 987 HPa. And the center is moving in direction 300 degrees at 11 knots with maximum winds force 10. Out.

—Traffic information service, this is motor vessel Sea World, request: position and moving direction of tropical storm center, over.

—Motor vessel Sea World, this is traffic information service, request received: tropical storm center is reported in position 20 degrees 18 minutes north, 115 degrees 05 minutes east, moving in direction 300 degrees at 11 knots, over.

—Traffic information service, this is Sea World, information received, out.

7. Communication for agent service

7.1 Useful expressions

(1) PENAVICO ××/Sino agent ××/×× shipping agency.

(2) Ship owner's agent/charterer's agent.

(3) I want to make a telephone call to my agent.

(4) The telephone number of my agent is...

(5) The line is connected, please go ahead.

(6) Hold on for minutes.

(7) Your station (turn) is number...

(8) What is your QRC (accounting code)?

(9) My QRC is CN 01.

(10) Is it a collect-call?

（11）Please advise your ROB（Remaining on Board）.

（12）My ROB is FO（fuel oil）… tons, DO（diesel oil）… tons, FW（fresh water）… tons.

（13）Please arrange bunkering FO/DO… tons.

（14）Please arrange supplying provisions/fresh water.

（15）Please recommend a ship chandler to come on board my ship.

（16）My deratting（deratting exemption）certificate has expired, please arrange renewing it.

（17）Fumigation will be carried out on my ship, please arrange crew's lodging ashore.

（18）Is it for owner's account or charterer's account?

（19）… crew members will sign off（sign on）from my vessel, arrange their repatriation please.

（20）Will you hand me the repatriates' passports or seaman's books for immigration formalities and visas?

（21）Please go through all the necessary formalities connected with our arrival/departure as soon as possible.

（22）I will do my best to arrange it.

（23）I am afraid I cannot meet your request,

7.2　Examples

Example 1

Communication with agent through port radio

—Port radio, port radio, this is motor vessel Yu Qing, over.

—Motor vessel Yu Qing. This is port radio, channel 25 please, over.

—Port radio, channel 25, over.

—Yu Qing, this is port radio, what can I do for you? Over.

—Port radio, I want to make a telephone call to my agent, over.

—Yu Qing, is it a collect-call? Over.

—Port radio, that is right, it is a collect-call, over.

—Yu Qing, what is the agency's name and telephone number? Over.

—Port radio, my agent is Hai Da shipping agency, telephone number 262239, over.

—Yu Qing, please spell your ship's name and advise your QRC, over.

—Port radio, my QRC is Charlie-November-Zero-One, ship's name is Yankee-Uniform-Quebee-India-November-Golf, over.

—Yu Qing, roger, hold on for minutes, your station is number 2, over.

—Port radio, thank you, I will hold on for minutes, over.

—Yu Qing, the line is connected, go ahead please, over.

—Hai Da shipping, Hai Da shipping, this is motor vessel Yu Qing speaking, over.

—Yu Qing, this is Hai Da shipping, come in please, over.

—Good morning, Mr. agent, I have arrived at anchorage of this port at 0645 hours today, it is ready in all respects for discharging cargo, what is my berthing schedule? Over.

—Yu Qing, you are welcome to this port, quarantine inspection will be carried out at 0900 today. I will board your ship together with cargo surveyor to go through formalities of arrival and cargo survey as soon as you get free pratique, please open hatch covers. You will go alongside at 1340 local time. Please contact with pilot station to confirm pilot's boarding time, over.

—Roger, quarantine inspection will be carried out at 0900, ETB is 1340 today, is that all correct? Over.

—Yu Qing, that is correct, over.

—Ok, thank you for your information, nothing more, out.

—Port radio, this is Yu Qing, over.

—Yu Qing, this is port radio, come in please, over.

—Port radio, that is all for my telephone call, thank you, out.

Example 2

Agent's arrangements for bunkering

—Sino-agent Shanghai, Sino-agent Shanghai, this is Mei Jiang, Bravo Alfa Charlie Delta, over.

—Mei Jiang, this is Sino-agent Shanghai, come in please, over.

—Sino-agent Shanghai, I need some fuel oil and diesel oil, please arrange bunkering as soon as possible, over.

—Mei Jiang, please advise the quantity and quality, over.

—Sino-agent Shanghai, I need 250 tons of fuel oil with viscosity 2,000 seconds, light diesel oil 70 tons 40 seconds, I repeat: fuel oil 250 tons viscosity 2,000 seconds, light diesel oil 70 tons 40 seconds, over.

—Mei Jiang, understood, fuel oil 250 tons viscosity 2,000 seconds, light diesel oil 70 tons 40 seconds, I will contact with bunker supply company immediately, over.

—Sino-agent, thank you, I will wait for your information, over.

—Mei Jiang, this is your agent, I want to talk to chief engineer, over.

—Sino-agent, this is chief engineer speaking, go ahead please, over.

—Chief engineer, I inform you that the oil barge will core alongside your ship at 0900 tomorrow, please get every thing ready for bunkering, over.

—Sino-agent, roger, oil barge will go alongside my ship at 0900 tomorrow. I will have every thing ready, thank you for your good work, out.

Example 3

Agent's arrangements for crew members repatriation

—Sea land shipping, sea land shipping, this is motor vessel Yu Long, over.

—Motor vessel Yu Long, this is your agent sea land shipping answering, what can I do for you? Over.

—Good afternoon, Mr. Agent, this is Captain speaking. Two crew members will sign off, they will leave ship for Shanghai China by air on Friday this week, please arrange their repatriation, over.

—Mr. Captain, I understood. I will do my best to do that. Please hand me their passports or seaman's books for immigration formalities and emergency visas, over.

—Mr. Agent, OK, I will do that. At the same time, two crew members will signed on and join the ship, please pay attention to meet them, over.

—Mr. Captain, I see. I will meet them at the airport, then they will be taken to your ship in my car, over.

—Thank you, Mr. Agent, see you then, out.

8. Distress, urgency and SAR operation communication

8.1   Useful expressions

(1) I am in distress and require immediate assistance.

(2) I am in danger, please come to assist me.

(3) My generator is out of order (break down), I am drifting.

(4) I have a damaged steering gear.

(5) I need help, I am aground/drifting.

(6) I am on fire in the hold/cargo tanks/engine room/accommodation/living space.

(7) Man overboard, please take action to pick him up.

(8) I have lost a man overboard, help with search and rescue.

(9) I have collided with unknown vessel/unknown object/navigation buoy/underwater object/surface craft.

(10) What damage have you received?

(11) I have received damage to stem/stern frame/boiler room/engine room/hatchways/bottom-plate.

(12) The extent of the damage is still unknown.

(13) I have received serious/minor damage.

(14) I have sprung a leak.

(15) My hold is flooded/leaking.

(16) I have a dangerous list.

(17) What assistance is required?

(18) I require (need) fire-fighting assistance/a tug/a lifeboat/a helicopter/medical assistance.

(19) Please make fullest use of your... equipment to save your ship.

(20) I am coming to your assistance.

(21) Can you get the fire under control without assistance?

(22) I am sending a boat/a helicopter to you (to search and rescue).

(23) I expect to reach you at... hours.

(24) Take command of search and rescue.

（25）Assistance is no longer required, you may proceed.

8.2　Examples

Example 1

（1）Distress and SAR operation communication

①Initial call

—Mayday, Mayday, Mayday, this is motor vessel Tuan Jie, Tuan Jie, Tuan Jie Mayday, Tuan Jie, Bravo-Alfa-Foxtrot-Zulu.

　Position: Latitude 32 degrees 50 minutes north, longitude 132 degrees 43 minutes east. I am on fire in engine room and living space. I require immediate assistance.

②Acknowledgement

—Mayday, motor vessel Tuan Jie, Tuan Jie, Tuan Jie, Bravo-Alfa-Foxtrot-Zulu, this is port Kobe, port Kobe, port Kobe, Mayday received, I have sent a helicopter and fire-fighting vessel to your assistance. Do your best to get the fire under control, over.

③Mayday relay

—Mayday relay, Mayday relay, Mayday relay. All vessels, this is port Kobe, port Kobe, port Kobe, Mayday, Tuan Jie, Bravo-Alfa-Foxtrot-Zulu, following received from Tuan Jie. Position: Latitude 32 degrees 50 minutes north, longitude 132 degrees 45 minutes east. I am on fire in engine room and living space, I require immediate assistance. Over.

④Inquiring about distress information from relay station

—Port Kobe, port Kobe, this is Chinese vessel Dong Feng, this is Chinese vessel Dong Feng. I can give the quickest assistance, say again what is the position of vessel in distress?

—Chinese vessel Dong Feng, this is Port Kobe answering, position: Latitude 32 degrees 50 minutes north, longitude 13 degrees 55 minutes east, correction: Latitude 32 degrees 50 minutes north, longitude 132 degrees 45 minutes east, over.

—Port Kobe, this is Dong Feng, message understood, position: Latitude 32 degrees 50 minutes north, longitude 132 degrees 45 minutes east. What can I do for Tuan Jie? Over.

—Dong Feng, this is port Kobe, take command of on-scene search and rescue, over.

—Port Kobe, this is Dong Feng, I will take command of search and rescue, out.

⑤Information issued from SAR Center

—Attention all vessels, attention all vessels. this is port Kobe, Chinese vessel Dong Feng is in command of SAR, all the vessels are advised to keep clear of sea area in distress, search and rescue is in operation, over.

⑥On-scene communication

—Mayday, motor vessel Tuan Jie, Bravo Alfa Foxtrot Zulu, this is Dong Feng, Dong Feng, I am coming to your assistance, my present position: Latitude 32 degrees 54 minutes north, longitude 132 degrees 48 minutes east, course 210 degrees, speed 12 knots. I expect to reach you at time 1300 local time. Over.

—Mayday. Dong Feng, this is Tuan Jie, information received, you are coming to me, your present position: Latitude 32 degrees 54 minutes north, longitude 132 degrees 48 minutes east, course 210 degrees, speed 12 knots, ETA 1300 local, out.

—Dong Feng, Dong Feng, this is helicopter on channel 16, over.

—Helicopter, this is motor vessel Dong Feng, I am in charge of co-ordinating search. Information: I have picked up 5 survivors on board. Request: Proceeding to me for casualties. Over.

—Dong Feng, this is helicopter, I am proceeding to you, question: What is visibility, wind direction and force in your position? Over.

—Helicopter, this is motor vessel Dong Feng, answer: Visibility 3 miles, wind direction north west, force 5, over.

—Dong Feng, this is helicopter, message received, request: Identify yourself by directing signal light at me, over.

—Helicopter, this is Dong Feng, request received, I am ready and making identification signal, over.

—Dong Feng, this is helicopter, you are identified, request: Permission to land on your deck, over.

—Helicopter, this is Dong Feng, request received, do not land on deck, operation should be carried out using hoist, over.

—Dong Feng, this is helicopter, roger, I am commencing operation using hoist now, over.

—Port Kobe, this is Dong Feng, SAR operation finished, helicopter flew away with survivors, assistance no longer required. I am proceeding, out.

—Dong Feng, this is port Kobe, message received, out.

Example 2

Urgency call: steering gear damaged

—Pan-Pan, Pan-Pan, Pan-Pan, this is Victory, Victory, Victory, Pan-Pan, Victory, Whiskey-Alfa-Uniform-Sierra. Position: Bearing 030 degrees, distance 0.5 mile from way point number 2 in east fairway. I have a damaged steering gear. I am not under command. over.

—Pan-Pan, Victory, Whiskey-Alfa-Uniform-Sierra, this is Traffic Service, question: What assistance do you require? Over.

—Traffic service, this is Victory, answer: I intend to anchor for repairing immediately, over.

—Victory, this is Traffic service, instruction: Do not anchor at where you are, reason: Other traffic in fairway will be obstructed, over.

—Traffic service, instruction received, request: I need a tug for manoeuvring, over.

—Victory, this is Traffic service, request received, I will send a tug to assist you, over.

—Traffic service, information received, question: Where may I anchor for repairing, over.

—Victory, this is Traffic service, answer: You may anchor at traffic separation zone, over.

—Traffic service, roger, I will proceed to traffic separation zone with the help of tug, over.

第八课　甚高频无线电话明语通信示例综合

1. 初始呼叫、建立通信联系用语

1.1　常用通信短语

（1）Calling/Answering 呼叫/回答

（2）Who is calling? 谁在呼叫?

（3）Which ship is calling me? 哪条船在呼叫我?

（4）Come in/Go ahead/Send your message please.有话请讲。

（5）Wilco/Roger/Over/Out.收悉照办/知道了/我讲完了,请你讲/完毕。

（6）Do you read me? 你听到我没有?

（7）How do you read me? 你听我信号怎么样?

（8）I read you bad/poor/fair/good/excellent.
　　我听你信号不好/不太好/还好/良好/非常好。

（9）Nothing more. 没事了。

（10）I cannot read you,我听不清你的信号。

（11）Change to channel/switch to channel... 转到……频道

（12）Agree channel... 同意使用……频道。

（13）I will switch to channel... 我将转到……频道。

（14）Do not use this channel, shift another channel. 不要用这个频道,请转另一频道。

（15）Keep watch（listening）on channel.../Stand by channel... 在……频道守听。

（16）Hold on/Read back please. 不要放下话筒/请重复。

（17）Say again/repeat it. 请再讲一遍。

（18）I cannot follow you. 我没有听清你的话。

（19）Speak slowly please. 请讲慢一点。

（20）I understood/That is correct. 我明白了/完全正确。

（21）Please spell your ship's name and call sign. 请拼读你的船名和呼号。

（22）Motor vessel（MV）/motor tanker（MT）/steam ship（SS）
　　内燃机船/内燃机油船/蒸汽机船

（23）Is that correct? 我说的对吗?

（24）Negative/Positive. 不对、不是、不同意/对的、正确、同意。

（25）Mistake/Correction. 错误/更正。

（26）Please confirm/Advise. 请证实/通知。

（27）There is a message for you. 有你的消息。

1.2　通信示例

例1　船舶与港口话台间通信

—Yantai radio, Yantai radio, this is motor vessel Yu Ying calling, how do you read me? Over.

—Motor vessel Yu Ying, this is Yantai radio, I read you good, please change to channel 12. Over.

—Yantai radio, this is motor vessel Yu Ying, I agree, change to channel 12, over.

—Yantai radio, this is motor vessel Yu Ying calling, over.

—Motor vessel Yu Ying, this is Yantai radio, go ahead please, over.

译文

—烟台话台,烟台话台,"育英"轮呼叫,你听我信号怎么样,请回答。

—"育英"轮,我是烟台话台,我听你信号不错,请转12频道讲话。

—烟台话台,"育英"轮明白,12频道讲话。请回答。

—烟台话台,"育英"轮呼叫,请回答。

—"育英"轮,我是烟台话台,请讲。

例2　船舶与引航站之间通信

—Singapore pilot station, Singapore pilot station, this is motor vessel Sincere Gemini calling, over.

—Sincere Gemini, Sincere Gemini, this is Singapore pilot station, please change to channel 08, over.

—Singapore pilot station, this is motor vessel Sincere Gemini, channel 08, over.

—Singapore pilot station, this is motor vessel Sincere Gemini calling, over.

—Sincere Gemini, this is Singapore pilot station, please go ahead, over.

译文

—新加坡引航站,新加坡引航站,我是"信友双辉"轮,请回答。

—"信友双辉"轮,我是新加坡引航站,请转到08频道通话,请回答。

—新加坡引航站,我是"信友双辉"轮,08频道通话,请回答。

—新加坡引航站,"信友双辉"轮呼叫,请回答。

—"信友双辉"轮,我是新加坡引航站,请讲。

2. 招请引航员通信

2.1　常用通信短语

（1）I require a pilot. 我需要引航员。

（2）Please send a pilot to meet me. 请给我船派一名引航员。

（3）Please arrange a pilot to board my ship. 请安排一名引航员上我船。

（4）No pilot is available at present, please wait. 现在派不出引航员,请等候。

（5）When (At what time) will the pilot be available? 何时可以派出引航员?

（6）Pilot can be available at short notice. 接到申请即可派出引航员。

（7）Where shall we wait for pilot? 在哪等待引航员？

（8）Where and when the pilot come on board? 何时何地引航员登我船？

（9）Where can I take（pick up，meat）pilot? 在哪接引航员？

（10）Please advise pilot boarding time and position. 请告知引航员登船时间和地点。

（11）Please meet（pick up，take）pilot at... hours and position...
请在……时间……地点接引航员。

（12）You can meet（pick up，take）pilot at...hours and position...
你可以在……时间……地点接引航员。

（13）Pilot is coming to you. 引航员正前往你处。

（14）Pilot is on his way to you. 引航员正在前往你船的路上。

（15）Pilot boat is approaching your vessel. 引航船正在接近你船。

（16）Pilot will board your ship at... hours（in twenty minutes），please get pilot ladder
ready. 引航员将在……时间（20 分钟内）登船，请准备好引航梯。

（17）Owing to（Due to）strong wind and rough sea outside, pilot cannot board your ship.
外面风浪大，引航员无法登你船。

（18）Sea is too rough, pilot can not proceed to you. 外面风浪大，引航员无法登你船。

（19）Stop where you are and wait for pilot. 原地停车并等候引航员。

（20）What's your ETA at pilot station? 预计何时到达引航站？

（21）On which side do you want pilot ladder? 引航梯悬挂在哪一舷？

（22）On which side is pilot ladder to be rigged? 引航梯悬挂在哪一舷？

（23）On which side shall I get pilot ladder ready? 引航梯悬挂在哪一舷？

（24）Please rig pilot ladder on your lee（starboard/port）side.
将引航梯悬挂在下风（右舷/左舷）舷。

（25）1 want pilot ladder on lee（starboard/port ）side，2 meters above water.
将引航梯悬挂在下风舷（右舷/左舷），距水面 2 米。

（26）Put on lights at pilot ladder position. 把引航梯照亮。

（27）Have a heaving line ready at pilot ladder position. 在引航梯部位备好撇缆。

（28）Make a lee for pilot boat. 给引航艇做个下风舷。

（29）Keep pilot boat on you lee（starboard/port）side.
将引航艇保持在你的下风舷（右舷/左舷）。

2.2 通信示例

例 1

—Xiamen pilot station, Xiamen pilot station, this is Zheng He calling, over.

—Zheng He, Zheng He, this is Xiamen pilot station, please change to channel 12, over.

—Xiamen pilot station, this is Zheng He calling, over.

—Zheng He, this is Xiamen pilot station, come in please, over.

—I am coming to entrance light house and expect to arrive there in thirty minutes. Please
send a pilot to meet me. Over.

—Pilot will meet you there on your arrival. Over.

—Roger，anything else？Over.

—Nothing more，good-bye，out.

—Good-bye，out.

译文

—厦门引航站，厦门引航站，"郑和"轮呼叫，听到请回答。

—"郑和"轮，这里是厦门引航站，请转 12 频道。请回答。

—厦门引航站，厦门引航站，"郑和"轮呼叫，听到请回答。

—"郑和"轮，这里是厦门引航站，请讲。

—我正前往进口灯塔处，预计 30 分钟后到达那里，请派一名引航员。请回答。

—你到达时引航员将会登你船，请回答。

—知道了，还有什么事吗？请回答。

—无事，再会。

—再会。

例 2

—Canal pilot station, canal pilot station, this is Chinese vessel Jiang Guan calling, over.

—Jiang Guan, this is Canal pilot station, please change to channel 68, over.

—Change to channel 68, over.

—Canal pilot station, this is Chinese vessel Jiang Guang calling, over.

—Go ahead please, over.

—My ETA at pilot station is 1700 local time. I require a pilot, please advise pilot boarding time. Over.

—You can pick up pilot at 1900 local time, near Light buoy number 2, drop anchor and wait for pilot, over.

—Near Light buoy number 2, I will drop anchor and wait for pilot, on which side do you want pilot ladder？Over.

—Please stand by your pilot ladder on lee side and put on light at pilot ladder position, over.

—I understood, I will have pilot ladder ready on my lee side and put on light at pilot ladder position. Over.

—Thank you, nothing more, out.

—Nothing more, out.

译文

—运河引航站，运河引航站，中国船"江关"轮呼叫，请回答。

—"江关"轮，这里是运河引航站，请转 68 频道，请回答。

—转 68 频道，请回答。

—运河引航站，中国船"江关"轮呼叫，请回答。

—请讲。

—"江关"轮预计在地方时 1700 抵达引航站，我需要引航员，请通知引航员登船时间。

请回答。

—1900 时引航员将登你船,在 2 号灯浮附近抛锚等待引航员,请回答。

—在 2 号灯浮附近抛锚等待引航员,引航梯挂在哪一舷?请回答。

—请将引航梯放在下风舷处,并在那点亮照明灯,请回答。

—明白,引航梯放在下风舷处,并在那点亮照明灯。请回答。

—谢谢你,无事,再会。

—无事,再会。

3. 通报船舶资料

3.1　常用通信表达

（1）Ship's particulars. 船舶资料。

（2）Advise（Give）the following ship's particulars：ship's name/call sign/Gross Register Tonnage（GRT）/Net Register Tonnage （NRT）/Length Overall （LOA）/Breadth. 请告知下列船舶资料:船名/呼号/总吨/净吨/船舶总长/船宽。

（3）What is your port of registry/port of destination/port of departure/next port of call/last port of call. 你船登记港/目的港/起航港/下一停靠港/上一停靠港。

（4）What is your nationality （ship's flag）? 你船国籍(船旗)是什么?

（5）What is your ship's draft fore and aft/maximum draft in fresh water/air draft/drafts in ballast? 你船前后吃水/淡水中的最大吃水/水面以上高度/压载吃水是多少?

（6）What is your dead weight （DW）/displacement? 你船载重量/排水量是多少?

（7）What is your maximum height from bottom? 你船自船底的最大高度是多少?

（8）I am on even keel. 我船平吃水。

（9）What is your ship's owner/operator? 你船船东/经营者是谁?

（10）Advise the type of your ship/cargo quantity. 告知你船类型和货物数量。

（11）What is your cargo capacity （grain and bale）?
　　　你船舱容(散粮和包装)货物是多少?

（12）Please confirm the lifting capacity of your cargo gear/derrick/crane.
　　　请告知你船装卸设备/吊杆/克令吊起重能力是多少。

（13）What is the SWL （safety working load） of your cargo gear?
　　　你船起货设备的安全工作负荷是多少?

（14）The SWL（safety working load） of crane is... tons.
　　　克令吊的安全工作负荷是……吨。

（15）The lifting capacity of heavy derrick/crane is... tons.
　　　重吊杆/克令吊的起货能力是……吨。

3.2　通信示例

例 1

—Port control, port control, this is Golden Bear, Golden Bear calling, over.

—Golden Bear, Golden Bear, this s port control, please change to channel 14, over.

—Channel 14, over.

—Port control, port control, this is Golden Bear, Golden Bear calling, over.

—Go ahead and spell your call sign, over.

—My call sign is HTTY, Hotel-Tango-Tango-Yankee, over.

—Roger, your ETB will be tomorrow morning, please tell me your maximum draft, over.

—Thank you. My maximum draft is 9. 0 meters even keel, over.

—Golden Bear, this is port control, what is the type of your cargo gear? over.

—There are 4 cranes on deck, over.

—Please advise the safety working load of the crane, over.

—Three cranes' safety working load is 5 tons, one crane's safety working load is 15 tons, over.

—Which one's safety working load is 15 tons? Over.

—Number 2 crane's safety working load is 15 tons, over.

—Thank you for your co-operation, please call me tomorrow morning to confirm the berthing time, over.

—Understood, I will call you again tomorrow morning, out.

—Good-bye, out.

译文

—港调,港调,我是"金熊"轮,"金熊"轮呼叫,请回答。

—"金熊"轮,"金熊"轮,这里是港调,请转 14 频道,请回答。

—14 频道,请回答。

—港调,港调,"金熊"轮呼叫,请回答。

—请讲,拼出你船的呼号,请回答。

—我船呼号是 HTTY,Hotel-Tango-Tango-Yankee,请回答。

—明白,你将明天早晨靠泊,请告知你船最大吃水,请回答。

—谢谢,我船最大平吃水 9 米,请回答。

—"金熊"轮,这里是港调,你船装卸设备是什么类型? 请回答。

—4 个克令吊,请回答。

—请告知克令吊的安全工作负荷,请回答。

—有 3 个克令吊的安全工作负荷是 5 吨,另一个克令吊的安全工作负荷是 15 吨,请回答。

—哪一个克令吊的安全工作负荷是 15 吨? 请回答。

—2 号克令吊的安全工作负荷是 15 吨,请回答。

—谢谢你的合作,明天早上再叫我,以便确认靠泊时间,再会。

—明白,我明天早上会叫你,再会。

—再会。

例2：

—Yokohama pilot station，Yokohama pilot station，this is motor vessel Prince，Prince calling，over.

—Prince，Prince，this is Yokohama pilot station，please spell your ship's call sign，over.

—My call sign is GHYU，Golf-Hotel-Yankee-Uniform，over.

—Roger，please advise the following ship's particulars：LOA，GRT，NRT，drafts fore and aft，over.

—My ship's particulars：LOA is 167.8 meters，GRT is 9,834，NRT 6,590，drafts fore is 6.7 meters and aft is 7.8 meters，over.

—Thank you，what is your port of registry，last port of call? over.

—My port of registry is Singapore，my last port of call is Kobe，over.

—Your message received，nothing more，out.

—out.

译文：

—横滨引航站,横滨引航站,我是"王子"轮,"王子"轮呼叫,请回答。

—"王子""王子",这里是横滨引航站,请拼读你船呼号,请回答。

—我船呼号是 GHYU，Golf-Hotel-Yankee-Uniform,请回答。

—收到,请告知下列船舶资料:总长、总吨、净吨、前后吃水,请回答。

—我船船舶资料是:总长167.8米,总吨9 834,净吨6 590,前吃水6.7米,后吃水7.8米,请回答。

—谢谢,你船的船籍港和上一停靠港是哪里? 请回答。

—船籍港是新加坡,上一停靠港是神户,请回答。

—信息收到,无事,完毕。

—完毕。

4. 询问船舶动态

4.1　常用通信表达

（1）port control/port operation 港口调度

（2）Any berthing information/schedule/instruction for me?
　　有我船的靠泊消息/计划/指示吗?

（3）Port is congested，there is no vacant berth now. 港口拥挤,没有空泊位给你。

（4）No berth for you these two days. 这两天没有你的泊位。

（5）Your berth will be clear this afternoon. 你的泊位下午清爽。

（6）The previous berthing time/schedule/instruction was canceled.
　　先前的靠泊时间/计划/指示取消。

（7）Permission to go alongside the wharf is urgently requested. 迫切请求靠泊。

（8）When shall we go alongside the wharf/what is the berthing schedule?

我们什么时候靠码头/靠泊计划是什么?

（9）You will go to berth at...hours. 你将在……时间靠码头。

（10）What is the berth number? 几号泊位?

（11）Which berth are we going to take? 我们计划靠哪个泊位?

（12）You will moor buoys number 1 and number 2. 你将系泊在 1、2 号浮筒上。

（13）Wait for further notice please. 等待进一步通知。

（14）Stand by engine... hours before berthing. 靠泊前……小时备妥主机。

（15）Please give me notice... hours before to stand by main engine.
　　　提前……小时通知我备车。

4.2　通信示例

例 1

—Pilot station, pilot station, this is Japanese vessel Tokyo Maru calling, over.

—Who is calling me? this is pilot station answering, go ahead please, over.

—Pilot station, this is Japanese vessel Tokyo Maru calling you. Good morning, sir, I have been informed that my ship will go alongside berth number 4 at 1900 hours, please advise when will the pilot come on board? Over.

—Tokyo Maru, this is pilot station, berth number 4 is not clear, your previous schedule was canceled, and new berthing schedule time have not been fixed. Please call me again 0600 hours tomorrow on this channel, over.

—Pilot station, OK, I will call you again 0600 hours tomorrow on this channel, out.

—Pilot station, pilot station, this is Japanese vessel Tokyo Maru calling, over.

—Tokyo Maru, this is pilot station, new berthing schedule have been fixed, berthing time is 0800 hours, pilot will board your ship at 0730 hours, please stand by pilot ladder on your port side, over.

—Pilot station. Roger, berthing time is 0800 hours, pilot will board your ship at 0730 hours, please stand by pilot ladder on your port side, over.

—Please give me your LOA and maximum draft, over.

—My LOA 178. 9 meters and maximum draft 11. 3 meters, over.

—See you after a while, out.

—Out.

译文

—引航站,引航站,日本船"东京丸"轮呼叫,请回答。

—哪条船呼叫引航站? 请讲。

—引航站,日本船"东京丸"轮呼叫,早上好,先生,我得到通知今天 19 点靠 4 号码头,请告知引航员何时登我船,请回答。

—"东京丸"轮,引航站,4 号泊位没有空出来,原定靠泊计划取消,新的靠泊时间未定,请明天早上 6 点在本频道呼叫我,请回答。

—好的,引航站,我明天早上 6 点在本频道呼叫你,完毕。

—引航站,引航站,日本船"东京丸"轮 呼叫,请回答。

—"东京丸"轮,这里是引航站,新的靠泊时间已定,早晨 0800 时靠码头,引航员 0730 时登你船,左舷备好引航梯,请回答。

—明白,引航站,早晨 0800 时靠码头,引航员 0730 时登你船,左舷请备好引航梯,请回答。

—请告知你船的总长和最大吃水,请回答。

—我船的总长是 178.9 米,最大吃水 11.3 米,请回答。

—一会儿见,完毕。

—完毕。

例 2

—Sino-agent, Sino-agent, this is motor vessel Yu Feng, Yu Feng calling, over.

—Motor vessel Yu Feng, Yu Feng, this is Sino-agent, come in please, over.

—Sino-agent, I have arrived at quarantine anchorage and drop anchor at 1300 local time, anchor position is bearing 080 degrees, distance 3 miles from light house, how about my berthing schedule? Over.

—Yu Feng, the quarantine office are on their way to your ship, please call me again on this channel after quarantine inspection, over.

—Sino-agent, roger, I will call you again on this channel after quarantine inspection, out.

—Sino-agent, Sino-agent, this is motor vessel Yu Feng Yu Feng calling, over.

—Yu Feng, this is Sino-agent, have you passed quarantine inspection? Over.

—Sino-agent, yes, the inspection is finished, I have got the free pratique at 1100, over.

—You will go alongside Jetty number 3 at 1400, do you read me? Over.

—Sino-agent, your message received, my ETB is 1300 today, is that correct? Over.

—Negative, your ETB is 1400 today, please stand by main engine 1 hours before entering, over.

—Sino-agent, roger, my ETB is 1400 today, stand by main engine 1 hour before entering, out.

—Out.

译文

—外运代理,外运代理,我是"育峰","育峰"轮呼叫,请回答。

—"育峰"轮,"育峰"轮,外运代理听到,请讲。

—"育峰"轮到达检疫锚地并于 1300 时抛锚,锚位是相对灯塔方位 080°,距离 3 海里。靠泊计划怎么样? 请回答。

—检疫官员正前往你船,检疫结束后在本频道呼叫我,请回答。

—外运代理,"育峰"轮明白,检疫结束后在本频道呼叫你,完毕。

—外运代理,外运代理,"育峰"轮呼叫,请回答。

—"育峰"轮,外运代理听到,检疫通过了吗? 请回答。

—检疫结束,在 1100 时获得检疫证书,请回答。

—在 1400 时常凸 3 号泊位,听清没有? 请回答。

—外运代理,信息收到,1300 时靠码头,对吗? 请回答。

—错,1400 时靠泊,进港前 1 小时备好主机。请回答。

—外运代理,明白,1400 时靠泊,进港前 1 小时备好主机,完毕。

—完毕。

5. 船舶间协调避让行动通信

5.1 常用通信表达

（1）Unknown vessel 不知名船

（2）The vessel ahead of me/astern of me（follow me）. 我前方/后方的船。

（3）The vessel... on my port bow（starboard bow）/quarter/beam.
在我左（右）前方/后方/正横相距……的船。

（4）The vessel on opposite/same course. 航向相反/相同的船。

（5）The vessel head on and... miles ahead of me. 与我相距……海里的对遇船。

（6）The vessel crossing ahead of my port（starboard）bow. 从我左（右）穿越船头的船。

（7）Unknown vessel bearing... degrees, distance... miles from my ship（light house）.
距我（灯塔）……海里、方位……度的不知名船。

（8）The vessel in latitude... N(S), longitude... E(W), course...degrees, speed... knots.
在纬度……北（南）,经度……东（西）处,航向……度,速度……节的船。

（9）The white passenger ship/black container ship/bulk carrier/oil tanker/LPG ship/LNG
ship/war ship/dredger...
白色客船/黑色集装箱船/散货船/油船/液化石油气船/液化天然气船/军舰/挖泥
船……

（10）North/South/West/East bound ship. 北/南/西/东行船。

（11）Incoming（Inward）/Outgoing（Outward）vessel. 进口船/出口船。

（12）The vessel intending to overtake/cross/turn. 打算追越/交叉/掉头的船。

（13）What is your intention? 你的意图是什么?

（14）I intend（want）to... 我打算……

（15）I intend to alter course, new course... degrees. 我准备转向,新航向……度。

（16）Alter course to port（starboard）/reduce speed/keep course and speed/stop engine.
向左（右）舷转向/减速/保持航向和航速/停车。

（17）Advise you make（steer）course... degrees. 建议你走航向……度。

（18）Please keep well clear of me/give me a wide breadth. 请宽让我。

（19）Keep out of the way of me/give way to me. 给我让路。

（20）Don't pass on my port side/starboard side. I will pass on your port side/starboard
side. 不要过我的左/右舷。我将过你的左/右舷。

（21）Shall we pass port side（starboard side）to port side（starboard side）?
我们左（右）舷对左（右）舷通过好吗?

（22）Don't pass ahead/astern of me. 不要过我船头/船尾。

（23）I will overtake on your port side（starboard side）. 我将从你左（右）舷追越。

（24）You should navigate with caution. 你应小心航行。

（25）I am manoeuvring with difficulty, keep well clear of me. 我操纵困难，请宽让我。

5.2　通信示例

例 1

—Container ship Western Wood, Container ship Western Wood, this is panama vessel Sincere Gemini calling, over.

—Sincere Gemini, Sincere Gemini, this is Western Wood, Western Wood, please change to channel 06, over.

—Channel 06, over.

—Sincere Gemini, Sincere Gemini, this is Western Wood, Western Wood, go ahead please, over.

—Please tell me your present course and speed, over.

—My present speed is 25 knots and course is 180 degrees, over.

—My course is 060 degrees, you are crossing ahead of my port bow, please keep out of way of me, over.

—I intend pass ahead of your port bow, no problem with you, over.

—Don't pass ahead of my port bow, pass astern of me, please, over.

—OK, I will alter course to starboard and pass your stern. Please keep your present course and speed, over.

—Thank you for your co-operation, I will keep my present course and speed, out.

译文

—集装箱船"西部森林"，集装箱船"西部森林"，这是巴拿马籍"信友双辉"轮的呼叫，请回答。

—"信友双辉"轮，"信友双辉"轮，我是"西部森林"，"西部森林"，请转 06 频道，完毕。

—已转 06 频道，请回答。

—"信友双辉"轮，"信友双辉"轮，我是"西部森林"，我是"西部森林"，请讲。

—请告诉我你现在的航向、航速，请回答。

—我现在的航向是 180 度，航速 25 节，请回答。

—我现在航向是 060°，你船将从我左舷穿越船头，请给我让路，请回答。

—我打算过你船头，对你没有危险，请回答。

—不要过我的船头，建议你过我的船尾，请回答。

—好的，我向右转向过你的船尾。请你保向保速，请回答。

—谢谢你的合作。我将保向保速，完毕。

例 2

—The head-on vessel 4 miles ahead of me, the head-on vessel 4 miles ahead of me, this is oil tanker Kobe maru, Kobe maru calling, over.

—Kobe maru, Kobe maru, this is Ping Xing Guan, Ping Xing Guan come in please, over.

—Ping Xing Guan, this is Kobe maru, please change to channel 06, over.

—Kobe maru, channel 06, over.

—Ping Xing Guan, this is Kobe manu, we are meeting nearly on opposite course, shall we alter course to starboard respectively? Over.

—Kobe maru, I have found your both navigation lights ahead of me, agree alter course to starboard respectively and passing on port side, over.

—Ping Xing Guan, thank you, please contact on this channel, out.

译文

—在我前方 4 海里的对遇船,这里是油船"神户丸","神户丸"号呼叫,请回答。

—"神户丸",我是"平型关"轮,请讲。

—"平型关",我是"神户丸"轮,请转 06 频道,请讲。

—"神户丸",已转 06 频道,请讲。

—"平型关",我是"神户丸",我们在接近相反的航向上相遇,我们各自向右转向好吗? 请回答。

—"神户丸",我发现你船的两个航行灯在我正前方,同意向右转向,从面左舷通过。请回答。

—"平型关",谢谢你,在本频道上保持联系,完毕。

6. 船舶在 VTS 水域中的通信

6.1　常用通信表达

（1）Way point/Reporting point/CIP（calling in point）航路点/报告点/呼叫点

（2）I am at（I am passing）way point... 我在(我正通过)……航路点。

（3）I am approaching CIP（calling in point）... course..., speed...

我正接近呼叫点……,航向……,航速……

（4）Please report at next reporting point（or reporting line）.

请在下一报告点（或报告线）报告。

（5）Say again your position for identification. 再说一遍你的位置以便识别。

（6）You are entering area... 你正在进入……区域。

（7）You are in the fairway. 你船在航道中。

（8）You are approaching starboard/port limit of fairway. 你正驶近航道的左/右边缘。

（9）You must keep to the starboard side of fairway. 你必须保持在航道右侧。

（10）You are not keeping to your correct traffic lane. 你没有保持在正确的通航分道内。

（11）You are not complying with traffic regulation. 你船没有遵守通航规则。

（12）You are proceeding at dangerous speed. 你正以危险的速度航行。

（13）May I enter traffic lane（route）? 我可以进入通航分道(航路)吗?

（14）Advise you make course... degrees. 建议你走航向……度。

（15）Advise speed... knots. 建议你航速……节。

（16）I have located you on radar. 我在雷达上发现你船。

（17）You will meet crossing traffic at way point... 你将在……报告点遇到交叉船。

（18）There are many fishing boats at CIP. 在呼叫点有很多渔船。

（19）There is a vessel ahead obstructing your movement. 你船前方有一船妨碍你的行动。

（20）There is a vessel anchored ahead of you in position...

在你船前方……处有一锚泊船。

（21）There is a vessel ahead of you passing your starboard/port side on opposite course.

你前方有一对驶船过你右/左舷。

（22）Vessel following you will overtake you on port side/starboard side.

你后边的船将在你左/右舷追越。

（23）You must avoid（keep clear of）this area. 你必须避开（让开）此区域。

（24）There is a vessel with difficult towing on passage from... to...

从……到……的航线上有从事困难拖带作业的船。

（25）There is a vessel turning at... ……处有一船在掉头。

（26）Vessel... is leaving... berth. ……船正在离开……泊位。

（27）Vessel... has entered the fairway at... hours... ……船于……时间进入航道。

（28）Transit canal will begin at... hours. 在……时间开始进入运河。

（29）Your station in convoy will be number... 你船在编队中的位置是……号。

（30）I am underway/I am ready to get underway. 我船在航/我船准备好起航。

（31）I will proceed by west/east channel. 我准备走西/东航道。

（32）Wait for vessel... to clear... before entering fairway/getting underway/leaving berth.

等……轮让清……后再进入航道/起航/离泊。

（33）What is the anchor position for me? 给我船的锚位在哪里？

（34）You have anchored in wrong position. 你抛错了锚位。

6.2 通信示例

例1

—Wismar Traffic，Wismar Traffic，this is King Point，King Point calling，over.

—King Point，King Point，this is Wismar Traffic，go ahead please，over.

—Wismar Traffic，I am passing reporting line at time 1600 local time. My present course is 095 degrees，speed is 12 knots，May I enter harbour now? Over.

—King Point，this is Wismar Traffic，What is your gross tonnage and net tonnage? Over.

—Wismar Traffic，this is King Point，My gross tonnage is 6,587，net tonnage 2,435，over.

—King Point，What is your maximum draft? Over.

—Wismar Traffic，my maximum draft is 4.5 meters，over.

—King Point，You may enter the harbour，the pilot will board your ship at pilot boarding position，please make a lee for the pilot boat and put pilot ladder on starboard side，1 m above water，over.

—Roger，the pilot will board my ship at pilot boarding position，make a lee for the pilot boat and put pilot ladder on starboard side，1 m above water，over.

—Yes，that is correct，anything else? Over.

—Nothing more，good-bye，out.

译文

—Wismar Traffic, King Point 呼叫,请回答。

—King Point,请讲。

—Wismar Traffic,我在 1600 地方时正通过报告线。我目前航向 095°,航速 12 节,我可以进港吗? 请回答。

—King Point,这里是 Wismar Traffic,你船的总吨和净吨是多少? 请回答。

—Wismar Traffic,这里是 King Point,我船总吨是 6 587,净吨是 2 435。请回答。

—King Point,你船最大吃水是多少? 请回答。

—Wismar Traffic,我船最大吃水是 4.5 米。请回答。

—King Point,你可以进港,引航员在引航登船处登你船,请你给引航艇做一下风舷,引航梯放在右舷距水面 1 米处,请回答。

—收到,引航员在引航登船处登我船,给引航艇做一下风舷,引航梯放在右舷距水面 1 米处,请回答。

—正确,还有什么事吗? 请回答。

—无事,再会。

例 2

—Hong Kong Mardep, Hong Kong Mardep, this is Yu Long, Yu Long calling, over

—Yu Long, this is Hong Kong Mardep, please change to channel 14, over.

—Hong Kong Mardep, roger, channel 14, over.

—Hong Kong Mardep, Hong Kong Mardep, this is Yu Long, Yu Long calling, over.

—Yu Long, this is Hong Kong Mardep, go ahead please, over.

—Hong Kong Mardep, this is Yu Long, I am approaching CIP Po-Toi from sea, my ETA at Po-Toi is 1600 local time, may I enter the east Lamma chanel? Over.

—Yu Long, this is Hong Kong Mardep, your nationality, GRT and NRT please, over.

—Hong Kong Mardep, my nationality is Chinese, GRT 9,865 and NRT 3,657, over.

—Roger, please advise your port of departure and destination, any dangerous cargo on board? Over.

—Hong Kong Mardep, I sailed from Busan Korea, I bound for Shenzhen, no dangerous cargo on board, over.

—Yu Long, you may enter east Lamma channel, next reporting position is Buoy Lamma number 1, what is your ETA at Green Island pilot station? Over.

—Hong Kong Mardep, my ETA at Green Island pilot station is about 1930 local time. I will report at Buoy Lamma number 1, over.

—Hong Kong Mardep, Hong Kong Mardep, this is Yu Long, Yu Long, I am passing Buoy Lamma number 1 at 1825 local time. Over.

—Yu Long, this is Hong Kong Mardep, roger, there is a VLCC turning ahead of you, she is obstructing your movement, you should reduce your speed and for VLCC to clear the fairway, advise speed is 6 knots, over.

—Hong Kong Mardep, I understood, I will reduce my speed to 6 knots immediately and wait for VLCC to clear the fairway, over.

—Yu Long, you may pick up the pilot at Green Island. Pilot wants to rig the pilot ladder on your port side, your next reporting point is Mawan, over.

—Hong Kong Mardep, I will put the pilot ladder on port side, next reporting point is Mawan, over.

—Nothing more, good-bye, out.

译文

—香港海事处,香港海事处,"育龙"轮呼叫,请回答。

—"育龙"轮,我是香港海事处,请转 14 频道,请回答。

—香港海事处,收到,已转 14 频道,请回答。

—香港海事处,香港海事处,"育龙"轮呼叫,请回答。

—"育龙"轮,我是香港海事处,请讲。

—香港海事处,"育龙"轮正由海上驶近呼叫点蒲台岛,预计到达蒲台岛时间是地方时 1600 时,我可以进入薄寮东水道吗? 请回答。

—"育龙"轮,请告知你轮的国籍、总吨、净吨,请回答。

—香港海事处,我轮国籍是中国,总吨是 9 865,净吨是 3 657,请回答。

—"育龙"轮,你的起航港和目的港是哪里? 船上有危险品货物吗? 请回答。

—香港海事处,我从韩国釜山港出发,驶往深圳港,船上没有危险品,请讲。

—收到,你可以进入薄寮东水道,下一报告点是薄寮 1 号浮,请告知你船到达绿岛引航站的时间。请回答。

—香港海事处,我轮预计到达绿岛的时间是地方时 1930,我将在薄寮 1 号浮向你报告,请回答。

—香港海事处,"育龙"轮正通过薄寮 1 号浮,地方时 1825。请回答。

—"育龙"轮,明白,这是香港海事处,你前方有一艘 VLCC 正在掉头,妨碍你船航行,你应减速等待 VLCC 让清航道,建议航速 6 节,请回答。

—香港海事处,"育龙"轮明白,我将立即减速到 6 节,等待 VLCC 让清航道,请回答。

—"育龙"轮,引航员在绿岛登你船。引航员要求在你船左舷安放引航梯。你的下一报告点是马湾,请回答。

—香港海事处,我将在船左舷安放引航梯,下一个报告点是马湾,再会。

—无事,再会。

例 3

Typhoon Information

—SECURITE, SECURITE, SECURITE. All ships, all ships, all ships. This is BH VTS. Warning: The No. 21 typhoon/tropical storm DU JUAN center is reported at GPS position: N22.1°, E129.4°. The maximum wind force/Beaufort is 14, pressure is 955 milliards/hectopascals in center. The typhoon/tropical storm center is moving in direction northwest at 12 knots/km. It is expected to imagine BH port at 0800 LT on September 29th. Advise all ships in area of BH keep on sharp watch and take effective action in advance.

—所有船舶请注意,这里是北海交管,现在发布台风消息:第 21 号台风/热带风暴"杜鹃",中心位置位于北纬 22.1°,东经 129.4°,中心最大风力有 14 级,中心气压 955 百帕,目前台风/热带风暴中心正以每小时 12 千米的速度朝西北方向移动,将于当进时间 9 月 29 日 8 时经过北海港。建议在北海水域所有船舶加强值班,提前做好抗台准备。

—SECURITE, SECURITE, SECURITE. All ships, all ships, all ships. This is BH VTS. Warning:Owing to the No. 21 typhoon, BH port has come into third class against typhoon from 1800 on September 27th. Advice. All ship call back your crewmembers immediately, stop repairing important mechanical apparatus, hydrographic operation get ready for departure. All vessels keep on sharp watch, standby on channel 16/08, take effective action against typhoon in advance, and report to BH VTS immediately when finding abnormal condition.

—所有船舶请注意,这里是北海交管。现在发布防台消息:因受 21 号台风影响,从 9 月 27 日 1800 时开始,北海港进入三级防台,港内所有船舶应立即召回所有船员,停止检修重要机械属具,水工作业船舶做好随时撤离准备;所有船舶应加强值班,保持规定频道守听,做好各项防台准备,发现异常情况立即向交管中心报告。

—SECURITE, SECURITE, SECURITE. All ships, all ships, all ships. This is BH VTS Warning:Owing to the No.21 typhoon, BH port has come into second class against typhoon from at 1600 LT on September 28th. Instruction. All hydrographic operation and tanker transshipment stop working, and proceed to anchorage. Some berthing vessels add more lines and make them tight. Other vessels depart wharf and proceed to anchorages. All vessels keep on sharp watch, standby on channel 16/08, take effective action against typhoon in advance, and report to BH VTS immediately when finding abnormal condition.

—所有船舶请注意,这里是北海交管,现在发布防台消息:因受 21 号台风影响,从 9 月 28 日 1600 时开始,北海港进入二级防台,所有水工作业和水上过驳作业船舶立即停止作业,进入锚地避风。部分靠泊船舶增加缆绳,并使缆绳紧固。其他船舶应离开码头到锚地避风。所有船舶应加强值班,保持规定频道守听,做好各项防台准备,发现异常情况立即向交管中心报告。

—SECURITE, SECURITE, SECURITE. All ships, all ships, all ships. This is BH VTS. Warning:Owing to the X typhoon, BH port has come into first class against typhoon from at 0000 LT on September 29th. Instruction. All vessels keep on navigational watch and captain come on bridge and manage, report to BH VTS immediately when finding abnormal condition.

—所有船舶请注意,这里是北海交管,现在发布防台消息:因受 21 号台风影响,从 9 月 29 日 0000 时开始,北海港进入一级防台,所有船舶应进入航行值班状态,船长上驾驶台指挥,发现异常情况立即向交管中心报告。

—SECURITE. All ships. This is BH VTS. Warning canceled:the No.21 typhoon reduced to tropical storm on at 0850 LT on September 29th and depart BEIHAI far away gradually.

From 1700 LT, typhoon warning cancels. All vessels can heave up anchor timely or depart wharf at the demand of BH VTS. Do not cross or overtake the fairway, navigate with caution, report to BH VTS immediately if found some navigational aids abnormal.

—所有船舶请注意,这里是北海交管,现在发布防台警报解除消息:21 号台风 9 月 29 日 0850 时已减弱为热带风暴,并逐渐远离北海港,从 1700 时起北海港解除防台警报,所有船舶应听从指挥,有秩序地起锚撤离避风锚地,或离码头开航,不得抢越航道,谨慎驾驶,发现航标异常等情况,立即向交管中心报告。

例 4

Information Broadcast 信息发布

—Information：VHF CH08 has been interfered by unidentified station, BH VTS working channel change to CH27 temporarily.

—VHF CH08 受到干扰,北海 VTS 工作频道临时改到 CH27。

—SECURITE, SECURITE, SECURITE. All ships, all ships, all ships. This is BH VTS. Gale Warning：The wind force beaufort is 7 in Beihai port area today, gust force beaufort is 8, wind direction is northeast, will increase to northeast wind, force beaufort 8, gust force beaufort 9. All vessels keep on sharp watch, standby on channel 08, check your anchor position timely in case of anchor dragging. Report to BH VTS immediately when finding abnormal condition.

—所有船舶请注意,这里是北海交管,现在发布大风信息:北海港区今天风力 7 级,阵风 8 级,风向东北,夜里(明天)起增强至东北风 8 级,阵风 9 级。所有抛锚船舶应加强值班,保持规定频道守听,定期检查核对锚位,防止船舶走锚。发现异常情况立即向交管中心报告。

—SECURITE, SECURITE, SECURITE. All ships, all ships, all ships. This is BH VTS. Visibility Warning：Visibility is reduced by fog/rain in main channel. Visibility is expected to decrease to 1,000 m. Advise you navigate with caution and take ample time action for avoiding collision, contact in time when you enter this channel.

—所有船舶请注意,这里是北海交管,现在发布能见度信息:因受雾(雨)的影响,主航道能见度下降至 1 000 米,严重影响船舶航行安全,请航经以上水域船舶注意瞭望,加强联系,谨慎驾驶,及早避让。

—SECURITE, SECURITE, SECURITE. All ships, all ships, all ships. This is BH VTS. Visibility Information：Visibility is reduced by fog/rain in the vicinity of buoy No.11. Advise you navigate with caution, take ample time action for avoiding collision, contact in time when you enter this area.

—所有船舶请注意,这里北海交管,现在发布能见度信息:因受雾(雨)的影响,11 号灯浮附近水域能见度下降,严重影响船舶航行安全,请航经以上水域船舶注意瞭望,加强联系,谨慎驾驶,及早避让。

例 5

Tide Information Broadcast 大潮汛信息发布

—SECURITE, SECURITE, SECURITE. All ships, all ships, all ships. This is BH VTS.

Spring tide warning: The falling tide is about 5 knots in port, anchor dragging easily. Advise all anchoring vessels keep on sharp watch, standby on channel 16/08, check your anchor position timely, report to BH VTS immediately when finding your anchor or others dragging. Advise all vessels proceed inbound/outbound to the anchorage when the tide is against you. Avoiding turning around in anchorage. Do not cross the anchorage.

——所有船舶请注意,这里是北海交管,现在发布大潮汛信息:北海港正值天文大潮汛期间,港内落流最大可达 5 节,容易引起船舶走锚。所有锚泊船应加强值班,保持规定频道守听,定期检查核对锚位,发现本船或他船走锚及其他险情立即向交管中心报告;避免在锚地内调头;禁止过路船穿越锚地航行。

例 6

Navigation Security Information 航行安全信息

——SECURITE, SECURITE, SECURITE. All ships, all ships, all ships. This is BH VTS. Navigational warning: More small ships proceed in main channel, navigate with caution, maintain safe speed, and keep safe when entering this area.

——所有船舶请注意,这里是北海交管,现在发布航行安全信息:现在主航道(港区)航行的小船很多,请在主航道(港区)航行的船舶加强值班,保持安全航速,谨慎驾驶,保障安全。

——SECURITE, SECURITE, SECURITE. All ships, all ships, all ships. This is BH VTS. Navigational warning: Salvage operation in position N24°34′, E118°12′. Wide berth requested, pass it slowly. (At the demand of patrol boat on scene, pass it slowly.)

——所有船舶请注意,这里是北海交管,现在发布航行安全信息:在 N24°34′, E118°12′位置正在打捞沉船,航经该水域船舶应保持安全距离航行,慢速通过。(航经该水域船舶应听从现场巡逻艇的指挥,慢速通过。)

——SECURITE, SECURITE, SECURITE. All ships, all ships, all ships. This is BH VTS. Navigational warning: MV SUN RISE has main engine problem in position N24°34′, E118°12′, and adrift to JIUJIEJIAO now, please navigates with great caution, keep on sharp watch, and take ample action to avoid collision when entering this area.

——所有船舶请注意,这里是北海交管,现在发布航行安全信息:在 N24°34′, E118°12′位置有一货船"日升"轮主机发生故障,该船正朝九节礁方向漂移,请航经以上水域船舶注意瞭望,谨慎驾驶,及早避让。

——SECURITE, SECURITE, SECURITE. All ships, all ships, all ships. This is BH VTS. Navigational warning: MV SUN RISE has constrained by her draft in position N24°34′, E118°12′, and proceed to JIUJIEJIAO now. Please navigate with great caution and take ample action to avoid collision in time when entering this area.

——所有船舶请注意,这里是北海交管,现在发布航行安全信息:在位置 N24°34′, E118°12′有一大型机动船"日升",该轮限于吃水,操纵不便,正朝九节礁方向行驶,请航经以上水域船舶谨慎驾驶,注意避让。

——SECURITE, SECURITE, SECURITE. All ships, all ships, all ships. This is BH VTS. Navigational warning: Power-off vessel SUN RISE in position N24°34′, E118°12′, and move to JIUJIEJIAO by tug boat now. Please keep sharp watch, navigate with caution, and take ample action to avoid collision.

—所有船舶请注意,这里是北海交管,现在发布航行安全信息:在位置 N24°34′, E118°12′, 有一货船"日升",失去动力,现由拖船拖带,正朝九节礁方向移动,请航经以上水域船舶注意瞭望,谨慎驾驶,及早避让。

—SECURITE, SECURITE, SECURITE. All ships, all ships, all ships. This is BH VTS. Navigational warning: Overwater and submarine operation in position N24°34′, E118°12′. Please maintain at least safety distance, and pass it slowly. (And guided by pastrol ship.)

—所有船舶请注意,这里是北海交管,现在发布航行安全信息:在 N24°34′, E118°12′ 位置正在进行水上(水下)施工作业,航经该水域船舶应保持安全距离航行,慢速通过。(航经该水域船舶应听从现场巡逻艇的指挥。)

—SECURITE, SECURITE, SECURITE. All ships, all ships, all ships. This is BH VTS. Navigational warning: military exercise in achorage No.4, please maintain at least safety distance, and pass it slowly. (And guided by patrol ship.)

—所有船舶请注意,这里是北海交管,现在发布航行安全信息:在 4 号锚地正在进行军事演习,航经该水域船舶应保持安全距离航行,慢速通过。(航经该水域船舶应听从现场巡逻艇的指挥。)

例 7

交通管制信息 (Traffic Control Information)

—PAN-PAN, PAN-PAN, PAN-PAN. All ships, all ships, all ships. This is BH VTS. Warning: Traffic prohibited in Qingyu channel owing to the poor visibility by the fog from now. All ships are prohibited to enter inbound or outbound this channel.

—所有船舶请注意,这里是北海交管,现在发布雾航管制信息:因受雾的影响,青屿水道能见度下降,现对青屿航道实施雾航管制,禁止所有船舶进出青屿航道。

—PAN-PAN, PAN-PAN, PAN-PAN. All ships, all ships, all ships. This is BH VTS. Warning: Traffic prohibited in Beihai port area owing to the poor visibility by the fog from now. All ships must select someplace for anchoring, heaving up anchor and berthing/departing are prohibited. All ships must keep sharp watch and demand by BH VTS.

—所有船舶请注意,这里是北海交管,现在发布雾航管制信息:因受雾的影响,北海港区能见度下降,现对北海港区实施雾航管制,所有航行船舶必须择地抛锚,禁止船舶起锚,禁止船舶进行靠离泊作业,所有船舶应加强值班,并听从交管中心的指挥。

—PAN-PAN, PAN-PAN, PAN-PAN. All ships, all ships, all ships. This is BH VTS. Warning: Traffic prohibited temporarily in JIUJIEJIAO owing to the collision accident, now are organizing for salvage. Please deviate this area.

—所有船舶请注意,这里是北海交管,现在发布临时交通管制信息:在九节礁发生船舶碰撞事故(沉船事故),现正在组织救助,以上水域实施临时交通管制,禁止船舶通行,请航经船舶绕道航行。

—PAN-PAN, PAN-PAN, PAN-PAN. All ships, all ships, all ships. This is BH VTS. Warning: Traffic prohibited temporarily in Western Fairway area owing to the overwater and submarine operation from 1500 to 1600 LT.

—所有船舶请注意,这里是北海交管,现在发布临时交通管制信息:从 1500 时至 1600 时在西航道水域进行水上(水下)施工作业,在上述时间内对以上水域实施临时交通管制,禁止船舶通行。

—SECURITE, SECURITE, SECURITE. All ships, all ships, all ships. This is BH VTS. Traffic clearance in Qingyu channel owing to the visibility increasing to 1,500 m. Please proceed inbound and outbound timely at the demand of BH VTS.

—所有船舶请注意,这里是北海交管,现在发布雾航管制解除信息:青屿水道能见度上升至 1 500 米,请船舶听从指挥,有秩序地进出航道。

—SECURITE, SECURITE, SECURITE. All ships, all ships, all ships. This is BH VTS. Traffic clearance in Western Fairway area owing to the overwater/submarine operation finished. Please proceed inbound and outbound this area timely at the demand of BH VTS.

—所有船舶请注意,这里是北海交管,现在发布临时交通管制解除信息:水上(水下)施工作业结束,对西航道水域实施的临时交通管制现在解除,各船舶应听从指挥,有秩序地进出该水域。

7.　代理业务通信

7.1　常用通信表达

(1) ... shipping agency……船务代理公司

(2) Ship owner's agent/charterer's agent 船东代理/租家代理

(3) I want to make a telephone call to my agent. 我想与我的代理通话。

(4) The telephone number of my agent is... 我的代理的电话是……

(5) The line is connected, please go ahead. 线路接通,请讲话。

(6) Hold on for minutes. 请稍等,别放下电话。

(7) Your station(turn) is number... 你排在……位。

(8) What is your QRC(accounting code)? 你船通信费结算单位是哪里?

(9) Is it a collect call? 是对方付费电话吗?

(10) Please advise your ROB (remaining on board). 请告知你船存油、水数量。

(11) My ROB is FO (fuel oil)/DO(diesel oil)/FW(fresh water)... tons.
　　 我船存燃油/柴油/淡水……吨。

(12) Please arrange bunkering FO/DO/... tons. 请安排加燃油/柴油……吨。

(13) Please arrange supplying provisions/FW. 请安排供应伙食/淡水。

(14) Please recommend a ship chandler to come on board my ship.
　　 请推荐一位船舶供应商来我船。

(15) My deratting certificate (deratting exemption) has expired, please arrange renewing it. 我船除鼠证书(免予除鼠证书)到期,请安排换新。

(16) Fumigation will be carried out on my ship, please arrange crew's lodging ashore.

我船将进行熏舱,请安排船员在岸上的食宿。

(17) Is it for owner's account or for charterer's account? 是船东还是租家付费?

(18) ... crew members will sign off (sign on) from my vessel, arrange their repatriation, please.我船将有……船员离任(到任),请安排他们的遣返事宜。

(19) Will you hand me the repatriates' passports or seaman's books for immigration formalities and visas.

请将遣返者的护照或海员证交给我,以便办理移民局手续和签证。

(20) Please go through all the necessary formalities connected with our arrival/departure as soon as possible. 请尽快办理所有与我船到/离港有关的手续。

(21) I will do my best to arrange it. 我将尽力安排。

(22) I am afraid I can not meet your request. 我恐怕难以满足你的要求。

7.2 通信示例

例 1

—Sino-agent Dalian, Sino-agent Dalian, this is Merry Trans, Merry Trans calling, over.

—Merry Trans, this is Sino-agent Dalian, come in please, over.

—Sino-agent Dalian, I need some fuel oil and diesel oil, please arrange bunkering as soon as possible, over.

—Merry Trans, this is Sing-agent Dalian, I will contact with bunker supply company immediately, over.

—Sino-agent Dalian, thank you, I will wait for your information, over.

—Merry Trans, this is Sino-agent Dalian, I want to talk to chief engineer, over.

—Sino-agent Dalian, this is Chief Engineer speaking, go ahead please. Over.

—Chief Engineer, I inform you that the oil barge will come alongside your ship at 0900 tomorrow, please get every thing ready for bunkering, over.

—Sino-agent Dalian, roger, oil barge will come alongside my ship at 0900 tomorrow, I will have everything ready, thank you for you good work, out.

译文

—大连外运代理,我是"美全"轮,请回答。

—"美全"轮,大连外运代理听到,请讲。

—大连外运代理,我需要燃油和柴油,请尽快安排加油,请回答。

—"美全"轮,我是大连外运代理,我将立即与燃料供应公司联系,请讲。

—大连外运代理,谢谢,我等候你的消息,请讲。

—"美全"轮,我是大连外运代理,我想与轮机长通话,请回答。

—大连外运代理,我是轮机长,请讲。

—轮机长,我通知你加油船将在明天0900时靠你船,请做好各项加油准备,请讲。

—大连外运代理,我明白,加油船将在明天0900时靠我船,我将做好各项加油准备,谢谢你出色的工作,完毕。

例 2

—Strait shipping agency, strait shipping agency, this is Blue Sky, Blue Sky calling, over.

—Blue Sky, this is strait shipping agency, please change to channel 10, over.

—Strait shipping agency, channel 10, over.

—Strait shipping agency, this is Blue Sky, Blue Sky calling, over.

—Blue Sky, come in please, over.

—Strait shipping agency, my deratting certificate has expired, please arrange renewal of it, over.

—Blue Sky, wilco, I will arrange it immediately, over.

—Strait shipping agency, fumigation will be carried out at quarantine anchorage tomorrow morning, please arrange crew's lodging ashore, over.

—Blue Sky, roger, please advise it is for owner's account or charterer's account, over.

—Strait shipping agency, according to the charter party, it is for charterer's account, by the way, I need some fresh provision and bounded store, please arrange a ship chandler for me, over.

—Blue Sky. I will recommend a reliable ship chandler for you as soon as possible, over.

—Strait shipping agency, thank you, nothing more, out.

译文：

—海峡船务代理,"蓝天"轮呼叫,请回答。

—"蓝天"轮,我是海峡船务代理,请转 10 频道,请讲

—海峡船务代理,10 频道,请讲

—海峡船务代理,"蓝天"轮呼叫,请回答。

—"蓝天"轮,请讲。

—海峡船务代理,我船除鼠证书已到期,请安排换新,请讲。

—"蓝天"轮,收悉照办,我会马上安排,请讲。

—海峡船务代理,我轮明天将在检疫锚地进行货物熏蒸,请代为安排船员在岸上的食宿,请讲。

—"蓝天"轮,我明白,请告知是船东付费还是租家付费,请讲。

—海峡船务代理,根据租约规定是租家付费。另外,我需要一些新鲜食品和免税烟酒,请安排一位供应商来船,请讲。

—"蓝天"轮,我将尽快为你推荐一个可靠的船舶供应商,请讲。

—海峡船务代理,谢谢,无事,再会。

例 3

—Mediterranean shipping agency, Mediterranean shipping agency, this is Ever Green, Ever Green calling, over.

—Ever Green, this is Mediterranean shipping agency, please change to channel 14, over.

—Channel 14, over.

—Mediterranean shipping agency, this is Ever Green calling, over.

—Ever Green, go ahead, please. Over.

—Mediterranean shipping agency, this is Captain speaking, three crew member will sign off, they will leave ship for Tokyo by air on Sunday morning, please arrange their repatriation, over.

—Mr. Captain, I understood, I will do my best to do that, please hand me their passports or seaman's books for immigration formalities and emergency visas, over.

—Mr. Agent, OK, I will do that, at the same time, three crew members will sign on and join the ship, please pay attention to meet them, over.

—Mr. Captain, I see, I will meet them at airport, then I will take them to your ship in my car, over.

—Thank you, Mr. Agent, see you then, out.

译文

—地中海船务代理公司,"永青"轮呼叫,请回答。

—"永青"轮,这里是地中海船务代理公司,请转14频道,请讲。

—已转14频道,请讲。

—地中海船务代理公司,"永青"轮呼叫,请回答。

—"永青"轮,请讲。

—地中海船务代理公司,我是船长,3名船员合同期满,他们将在星期天早上乘飞机回东京,请安排他们遣返事宜,请讲。

—船长先生,我明白,我尽力办此事。请将他们的护照或海员证交给我去办理移民局手续和紧急签证,请回答。

—代理先生,我会照办的。还有3名船员来任职,请你留意接他们,请讲。

—船长先生,我明白,我会到机场接他们,并会用我的车送他们上船,请讲。

—多谢您,代理先生,一会儿见,完毕。

8. 遇险、紧急和搜救通信

8.1　常用通信短语

(1) I am in distress and require immediate assistance. 我船遇险需要立即援助。

(2) I am in danger, please come to assist me. 我船危险,请来援助我。

(3) My generator is out of order (break down), I am drifting.
我船发电机故障,我正在漂流。

(4) I have a damaged steering gear. 我船操舵装置损坏。

(5) I need help, I am aground/drifting. 我需要援助,我船搁浅/漂流。

(6) I am on fire in the hold/cargo tanks/engine room/accommodation/living space.
我船货舱/液货舱/机舱/住舱/生活区失火。

(7) Man overboard, please take action to pick him up/keep look sharp out.
有人落水,请设法救起/保持认真瞭望。

(8) I have lost a man overboard, help with search and rescue.
我船有人落水,请帮助搜救。

(9) I have collided with unknown vessel/unknown object/navigation buoy/underwater object/surface craft.我船与不知名船/不明物体/助航浮筒/水下物体/水面船只碰撞。

（10）What damage have you received? 你船受损情况如何？

（11）I have received damaged to stem/stern post/boiler room/engine room/hatchways/bottom plate.我船首柱/尾柱/锅炉舱/机舱/舱口/船底板受损。

（12）The extent of the damage is still unknown. 损坏程度尚不详。

（13）I have received serious/minor damage. 我船严重/轻微受损。

（14）I have sprung a leak. 我船已漏水。

（15）My hold is flooded/leaking. 我船的货舱被水淹/正在漏水。

（16）I have a dangerous list. 我船严重倾斜。

（17）What assistance is required? 需要什么援助？

（18）I require fire-fighting assistance/a tug/a lifeboat/a helicopter/medical assistance.
我需要消防援助/一条拖船/一只救生艇/一架直升机/医疗援助。

（19）Please make fullest use of your... equipment to save your ship.
请充分利用你船的……设备来挽救你船。

（20）I am coming to your assistance. 我船正前往救助你。

（21）I am sending a lifeboat/a helicopter to you（to search and rescue）.
我正派一只救生艇/一架直升机去你处（搜救）。

（22）Can you get the fire under control with out assistance?
在无外援情况下你能控制火势吗？

（23）I expect to reach you at... hours. 我预计……时抵达你处。

（24）Take command of search and rescue. 请指挥搜救。

（25）Assistance is no longer required, you may proceed. 不再需要援助，你可继续航行。

8.2　通信示例

遇险搜救通信：

—Mayday, Mayday, Mayday, this is White Star, White Star, White Star, Mayday, White Star. My call sign：Charlie-Oscar-Hotel-Delta. Position：Latitude 30 degrees 45 minutes north, longitude 122 degrees 55 minutes east. Due to strong wind, I have a dangerous list and I will capsize at once. I abandoned my ship and boarded on lifeboat. I require immediate assistance, over.

—White Star, White Star, White Star, this is Coastguard, Coastguard, Mayday received, I sent a helicopter to your assistance, over.

—Mayday relay, Mayday relay, Mayday relay, this is Coastguard, Coastguard, following received from White Star. Position：latitude 30 degrees 45 minutes north, longitude 122 degrees 55 minutes east. Due to strong wind, I have a dangerous list and I will capsize at once, I abandoned my ship and boarded on lifeboat. I require immediate assistance, over.

—Coastguard, Coastguard, this is motor vessel Yu Long, Yu Long, I can give the fastest assistance, repeat the position of the vessel in distress, over.

—Motor vessel Yu Long, Yu Long, this is Coastguard, Position：Latitude 30 degrees 45 minutes north, longitude 122 degrees 55 minutes east, over.

—Coastguard, roger, what should I do? Over.

—Yu Long, you take command of on-scene search and rescue, over.

—Coastguard, roger, I will take command of on-scene search and rescue, out.

—Attention all vessels, Attention all vessels, this is Coastguard, motor vessel Yu Long, Yu Long is in command of search and rescue, all search and rescue units can communicate with Yu Long on VHF channel 06, over.

—Mayday, White Star, this is Yu Long, I am coming to your assistance, my present position: latitude 31 degrees 30 minutes north, longitude 122 degrees 50 minutes east, course 260 degrees, speed 14 knots, ETA at your position is 1500 local time, over.

—Yu Long, Yu Long, this is helicopter, over.

—Helicopter, this is Yu Long, I am in charge of co-ordinating search and rescue, information: I have pick up 10 survivors on board, request: proceeding to me for casualties, over.

—Yu Long, this is helicopter, I am proceeding to you, question: what is the visibility, wind direction and force in your position? Over.

—Helicopter, this is Yu Long, visibility 4 miles, wind direction north east and force 8, over.

—Yu Long, this is helicopter, message received, request: put on deck light for identification, over.

—Helicopter, this is Yu Long, request received, I put on deck light for identification, over.

—Yu Long, this is helicopter, can I land on your deck? Over.

—Helicopter, this is Yu Long, you cannot land on deck, operation should be carried out by using hoist, over.

—Yu Long, this is helicopter, I am commencing operation using hoist, over.

—Coastguard, this is Yu Long, search and rescue operation finished, helicopter flew away with survivors, assistance no longer required, I am proceeding, out.

—Yu Long, this is Coastguard, message received, out.

译文

—Mayday, Mayday, Mayday, 我是"白星"轮。呼号：COHD，位置：北纬 30 度 45 分，东经 122 度 55 分，由于大风，我轮严重倾斜即将倾覆，我已弃船并登上救生艇，我需要立即援助，请讲。

—"白星"轮，海岸警卫队收到你的遇险呼叫，我已派一架直升机前往你处救援，请讲。

—遇险转发，这里是海岸警卫队，收到来自"白星"轮的如下遇险信文。位置：北纬 30 度 45 分，东经 122 度 55 分，由于大风，我轮严重倾斜即将倾覆，我已弃船并登上救生艇，我需要立即援助，请讲。

—海岸警卫队，我是机动船"育龙"，我可以迅速提供援助，请重复一下船位，请讲。

—"育龙"轮，遇险船的位置是：北纬 30 度 45 分，东经 122 度 55 分。

—海岸警卫队，"育龙"轮明白，我应该做些什么？请讲。

—"育龙"轮，你负责现场搜救，请讲。

—海岸警卫队，"育龙"轮明白，我负责现场搜救，完毕。

—各船注意,机动船"育龙"轮负责搜救,各搜救单元可以在 VHF 06 频道与"育龙"轮通信,请讲。

—"白星"轮,我是"育龙"轮,我正前往你处救助,我现在位置是:北纬 31 度 30 分,东经 122 度 50 分,航向 260 度,航速 14 节,预计到达你处 1500 时,请讲。

—"育龙"轮,直升机呼叫,请回答。

—直升机,我是"育龙"轮,我负责现场搜救,信息:我救起 10 名幸存者,要求:速来我处接伤员,请回话。

—"育龙"轮,我是直升机,正飞往你处,问题:请报告你处能见度、风向和风速。

—直升机,我是"育龙"轮,能见度 4 海里、风向东北和风速是 8 级,请讲。

—"育龙"轮,我是直升机,信文收到,要求:请开甲板灯以便识别你船,请讲。

—直升机,我是"育龙"轮,要求收到,我已开甲板灯,请讲。

—"育龙"轮,我是直升机,我能在你甲板降落吗?请讲。

—直升机,我是"育龙"轮,不能在甲板降落,请使用升降器接伤员,请讲。

—"育龙"轮,我是直升机,我开始操作升降器,请讲。

—海岸警卫队,我是"育龙"轮,救助作业完毕,直升机已带幸存者飞离,不再需要援助,我已恢复航行,完毕。

—"育龙"轮,我是海岸警卫队,信文收到,完毕。

9. 应急搜救基础句式

9.1   通用（General）

（1）What is your vessel's name/call sign/MMSI number?

你船的船名、呼号及海上移动业务识别码是什么?

（2）When and where did the accident happen? 何时何地发生事故?

（3）I am/MV SUN RISE is on fire/aground/flooding/sinking/disabled/dragging/under attack by pirates.

我(船)/"日升"轮失火/搁浅/进水/正在下沉/失控/走锚/遭到海盗袭击。

（4）I have/MV SUN RISE has dangerous list to port/starboard. Lost person in position N24°20′, E118°10′.

我(船)/"日升"轮左/右倾危险。在 N24°20′, E118°10′位置人员落水。

（5）Who is your owner/operator/local agent in this port?

你的船东/经营人/当地代理是谁?

（6）What's the number of persons on board? 在船人数多少?

How many persons on board your vessel? 你(船)在船人数多少?

（7）What kind of assistance is required? 需要什么样的救助?

（8）How many tugs do you require? 你需要几艘拖船?

（9）Do you require medical assistance? 你船需要医疗援助吗?

（10）I/MV SUN RISE requires fire fighting assistance/breathing apparatus/fire pumps/medical assistance.

我（船）/"日升"轮需要消防援助/氧气面罩/消防泵/医疗援助。

（11）I/MV SUN RISE requires escort/tug assistance/navigational assistance.

我（船）/"日升"轮需要护航/拖船协助/导助航服务。

（12）Are there any passenger? Number of passengers：five.

船上有旅客吗？船上有 5 名旅客。

（13）No passenger on board. 船上没有旅客。

（14）Report injured persons. No persons injured. Number of injured persons/casualties：two. 报告人员伤亡情况。没有人员伤亡。有 2 人受伤/死亡。

（15）Can you pick up survivors? 你能救起幸存者吗？

（16）Report injured persons. 报告受伤人员

（17）I have 12 survivors on board. Request tug boat/patrol boat/helicopter for casualties.

我船上有 12 名幸存者，要求拖船/巡逻艇/直升机运送伤员。

（18）Tug boat/Patrol boat/Helicopter is now proceeding to you. Be ready.

拖船/巡逻艇/直升机正向你靠近，准备接应。

（19）How many tons of cargo on board? 船上载有几吨货？

Are there any dangerous cargoes? 有否危险货物？

What's the IMO-Class? 它们属于哪类危险品？

What's the UN-number? 它们的联合国编号是多少？

（20）Vessel in position N24° 20′, E118° 10′ on fire/had explosion/aground/flooded/listing/in danger of capsizing/sinking/disabled and adrift/abandoned.

位于 N24°20′, E118°10′（位置）的船舶发生火灾/发生爆炸/搁浅/进水/正在横倾/有倾覆的危险/正在下沉/失控并在漂移/弃船。

（21）Attention：MV SUN RISE is not under command. Keep clear of her. Navigate with caution. 注意："日升"轮失控，（附近船舶）远离，谨慎航行。

9.2　溢油（Spilling）

（1）Can you identify the polluter? 你能识别污染船吗？

（2）MT OCEAN TANKER spilling oil/chemicals in position N24°34′, E118°12′. Wide berth requested. 油轮 OCEAN TANKER 在 N24°34′, E118°12′处溢出油/化学品。请宽让。

（3）Located oil spill in position N24°34′, E118°12′ extending length of 100 meters to bearing 080 degrees. 在 N24°34′, E118°12′处发现有长度 150 米的油污正朝 080 方位延伸。

（4）Located oil spill in your wake/in the wake of MV SUN RISE.

发现你船航迹上有油污/"日升"轮的航迹上有油污。

（5）How many tons/kilograms/liters of crude oil/fuel oil/diesel oil/gasoline overboard?

多少吨/千克/公升原油/燃油/柴油/汽油入海？

（6）Is the oil pollution prevention plan available? 防止油污计划可用吗？

9.3　漏气（Leaking gas）

（1）LNG-tanker（name）OCEAN TANKER is leaking gas in position N24°34′, E118°12′.

Do not pass to leeward.

液化天然气船 OCEAN TANKER 在 N24°34′，E118°12′处泄漏气体。请勿在下风通过。

9.4　清除油污（Oil clearance）

（1）Oil clearance operations near MT OCEAN TANKER in position N24°34′，E118°12′. Wide berth requested.

油轮 OCEAN TANKER 附近的清除油污作业在 N24°34′，E118°12′处进行。请宽让。

（2）I require/MV SUN RISE requires oil clearance assistance/floating booms/oil dispersant. 我船/"日升"轮需要清除油污援助/围油栏/消油剂。

（3）Stay in vicinity of pollution and co-operate with oil clearance team. 停留在污染区附近，并与油污清除队合作。

9.5　弃船（Abandon vessel）

（1）Will you abandon vessel？你是否将弃船？

（2）Close all of oil valves and report. 关闭所有的油路阀门并报告。

（3）How many lifeboats/life rafts（with how many persons）will you launch？
你将放下多少救生艇/筏（能载多少人员）？

（4）If the situation gets worse, all persons should stand by evacuation station.
如果情况变坏的话应尽快做好撤离准备。

（5）Advice you. Please
- check the situation of your vessel frequently.
- all lifeboat should be standing by.
- everybody should be on life jacket.
- all persons should stand by evacuation station.

建议你船
- 密切关注船舶状况。
- 所有救生艇均应做好释放前的准备工作。
- 所有人员均应穿好救生衣。
- 所有人员应做好随时撤离的准备。

（6）Instruction：All sea chests and valves of oil pipes should be closed before evacuation if possible. 指示：如果可能的话，在人员撤离前应将所有海底阀和油路阀门关闭。

9.6　着火（On fire）

（1）Where is the fire？船上什么地方着火？
Fire is in superstructure/accommodation/forecastle/poop/bosun store/paint store.
上层建筑/生活区/首楼甲板/船尾甲板/水手长（工作）间/油漆间着火。

（2）What is on fire？什么东西着火？
Fuel/Cargo/Car(s)/Truck(s)/Containers（with dangerous cargoes）on fire.
燃油/货物/汽车/卡车/装有危险货物的集装箱着火。

（3）What's condition of your vessel？船舶状况怎样？

（4）Is the fire under control？火势能否得到控制？

（5）What's the acting you are taking? 你船正在采取什么措施？

I am taking all necessary actions to control the development of the fire.

我船正在采取一切必要措施来控制火势的发展。

（6）Advice you. Please
- close all openings and ventilator(s) in fire area.
- remove all flammable cargoes in vicinity to separate from the fire area.
- turn bow/stern/port side/starboard side to windward.

建议你船
- 关闭火区内的所有开口和通风装置。
- 移开附近的易燃物品，隔离火区。
- 将船首/船尾/左舷/右舷摆在下风。

9.7 进水（Flooding）

（1）Check flooding. 察看进水情况。

（2）What part of your vessel is flooding? 船上什么部位进水？

Engine-room/Hold No. 3/Fore peak tank/Bottom is flooding.

机舱/第三货舱/首尖舱/船底进水。

（3）What's the size of flooding point? 进水点的尺寸？

The size of flooding point is 3 meters by 1 meter. 进水点的尺寸是3米乘1米。

About 3 square meters. 约3平方米。

（4）What's the shape of flooding point? 进水点的形状？

The sharp of flooding point is triangle/circle/semicircle/oval.

进水点的形状是三角形的/圆形的/半圆形的/椭圆形的。

（5）I require pumps/divers/collision mats/timber wedges/leaking stopper/tug assistance to beach/some barge to transfer cargo/escort/assistance to stop flooding from outside.

我船需要水泵/潜水员/堵漏毯/木楔/堵漏器材/拖船协助冲滩/驳船来转运货物/护航/一些援助以便从舷外实施堵漏。

（6）Is danger imminent? 情况危急吗？

Yes, danger of
- heavy listing to port/starboard.
- decreasing stability.
- damage by sea.
- breaking apart.
- environmental pollution.

是的，船舶有
- 严重左/右倾的危险。
- 稳性减少的危险。
- 浪损的危险。
- 解体的危险。
- 环境污染的危险。

（7）Can you beach? 你船能冲滩吗？

（8）Advice：You should take all necessary actions to make fast the vessel after beaching.

建议：冲滩（成功）后，你应该采取所有必要的措施来固定船体。

9.8　碰撞（Collision）

（1）What part of your vessel collided? 你船遭到碰撞的部位在哪里？

　　The hull/the bow/the bridge of my vessel collided. 我船船体/船首/驾驶台被撞。

（2）What is the damage? 损失情况如何？

　　I am not under command. 我船失控。

　　I am flooding. 我船正在进水。

（3）What's the condition of the another vessel involved collision?

　　She is damaged severely too/sinking/damaged slightly/no damaged.

　　另一碰撞船的状况如何？

　　她同样受损严重/正在下沉/受损轻微/没有受损。

（4）Have you called her to rescue you?

　　Yes, I have called her. She is rescuing me. She is anchoring nearby. She has escaped
　　to outside/northward/westward.

　　No, I have not called her.

　　你有没有呼叫她来救你？

　　是的,我已呼叫她来。她正在实施救援。她在(我船)附近锚泊。她已向外/向北/
　　向西方向逃逸。

　　不,我没有叫她。

9.9　搁浅（Grounding ）

（1）What part of your vessel is aground? 你船哪部分搁浅？

（2）Aground forward/Amidships/Aft/Full length. 船首/船中/船尾/全船搁浅。

　　I cannot establish which part is aground. 我不能确定哪部分搁浅。

（3）What is your draft forward/aft before aground? 搁浅前你船的首尾吃水？

　　My draft forward/aft is 5 meters before aground. 搁浅前我船的首尾吃水是 5 米。

　　What is your present maximum draft? My present maximum draft is 12 meters.

　　你现在的最大吃水是多少？ 目前我船的最大吃水是 12 米。

（4）Check flooding. 查看进水情况。

　　Flooding in starboard side. 在右舷部位进水。

（5）Is danger imminent? 情况危急吗？

（6）What is nature of sea bottom? 底质怎样？

　　Sea bottom rocky. 底质为岩石底。

　　Sea bottom soft. 底质为软底。

（7）When do you expect to refloat? 你船准备何时起浮？

（8）Request a (diving) survey is necessary before sailing due to aground.

　　由于搁浅你船开航前申请(船底)检验是必要的。

（9）Can you beach? I can/will beach in position bearing 225 degrees distance 1.5 nautical
　　miles. I cannot beach.

　　你船能冲滩吗？我船可以/将在据此处方位 225°,距离 1.5 海里位置冲滩。我船不能冲滩。

9.10 下沉 (Sinking)

(1) What's condition of you/your vessel? 你船的状况如何？

I am sinking after collision/grounding/flooding/explosion.

我船因碰撞、搁浅、进水、爆炸等船体正在下沉。

(2) I am/Salvage boat is proceeding to your assistance. 我船/救助船正前来援助你。

(3) Advice：Check the situation of your vessel frequently. 建议：密切关注船舶状况。

All life boat should be standing by! 所有救生艇均应做好释放前的准备工作。

Everybody should be on life jacket! 所有人员均应穿好救生衣。

All persons should stand by evacuation station. 所有人员应做好随时撤离的准备。

9.11 失控、漂流、机械故障 (Disabled, adrift, technical failure)

(1) What's condition of you/your vessel? 你船的状况如何？

I am/MV SUN RISE is not under command/adrift/drifting at 6 knots to bearing 080 degrees (cardinal points)/drifting into danger.

我船/"日升"轮失控/随波漂流/正向 080°方位漂移, 速度 6 节/正在漂向危险中。

9.12 人员落水 (Person overboard)

(1) I have lost person overboard in position N24°20′, E118°10′.

我船有人落水, 位置在 N24°20′, E118°10′。

Where did the person overboard from? 人员从何处落水？

The person overboard from the poop deck/the main deck。

人员从尾甲板/主甲板落水。

(2) Sea Patrol 08179/rescue boat is proceeding to you for assistance—ETA at 0800 UTC/within 1 hours.

"海巡 08179" 轮/搜救船正前来你处救助。预计在格林尼治时间 0800 时/在 1 小时内抵达你处。

(3) I am searching in vicinity of position N24°20′, E118°10′.

我船正在 N24°34′, E118°10′ 位置处附近进行搜寻。

Aircraft ETA at 1000 UTC/within 1 hour to assist in search.

飞机将在格林尼治时间 1000 时/在 1 小时内抵达以协助搜寻。

(4) I located/picked up person(s) in position N24°20′, E118°10′.

我船在 N24°20′, E118°10′ 位置处找到/救捞起落水人员。

Person picked up is crewmember/passenger of MV SUN RISE.

被救起的人员是"日升"轮的船员/旅客。

(5) What is condition of person(s)? 落水人员的情况怎样？

Condition of person(s) bad/good. 落水人员的情况不好/良好。

9.13 医疗援助 (Medical assistance)

(1) Report injured persons. 报告受伤人员。

Two patients have fracture. 两人骨折。

（2）What is your position? 你船位置在哪里？

（3）Report name and age of patients. 报告受伤人员的姓名和年龄。

（4）Report patient's respiration, pulse rate, temperature and blood pressure.
病人的呼吸情况、脉搏、体温和血压。

Wang：the rate of breathing per minute is 25, the pulse rate per minute is 80, the temperature is 38 ℃, and the blood pressure is 140/90.

Li：The rate of breathing per minute is 20, the pulse rate per minute is 80, the temperature is 38℃, and the blood pressure is 130/70.

王：每分钟的呼吸频率是每分钟 25 次，脉搏是每分钟 80 次，体温是 38 ℃，血压是 140/90。

李：每分钟的呼吸频率是每分钟 20 次，脉搏是每分钟 80 次，体温是 38 ℃，血压是 130/70。

（5）What is the location of fracture? 骨折位置是哪里？

Wang has fracture on his left lower arm. Li has fracture on his right leg.
王是左前臂骨折。李是右腿骨折。

（6）Is bleeding present? 有发生出血吗？

Bleeding is absent. 没有出血。

（7）Report patients' previous health. 报告受伤人员既往病史。

They have no serious previous illness. 没有严重的过往疾病史。

（8）Are there any medically trained persons on board?
船上有任何经过医疗训练的人员吗？

Yes, Captain and Chief Officer are medically trained.
是的，船长和大副有接受过医疗训练。

（9）What treatment has been carried out? 已经进行了哪些治疗？

Well padded splints are applied. 已经对骨折部位用夹板固定。

（10）You should keep patients cool, refer back to VTS in 1 hour or before if patients worsen. The patients will be arranged for hospital admission on your arrival. Over.
你应该保持病人镇静，1 小时后给我回信，如果病情恶化提前报告，船到港后我将安排病人入院。

9.14 执行、协调搜救行动（Performing/Co-ordinating SAR-operations）

（1）Vessels are advised to proceed to position N24°20′, E118°10′ to start rescue.
通知各船舶前往 N24°20′, E118°10′开始救助。

（2）Can you proceed to distress position? 你能驶往遇险地点吗？

Sighted vessel in position N24°34′, E118°12′. Lifeboats/Liferafts/persons in water in position N24°34′, E118°12′.

发现目标船/救生艇/筏/落水人员位置在 N24°34′, E118°12′。

（3）Can you pick up survivors? 你能捞起幸存者吗？

（4）MV SUN RISE, you are advised to proceed to position N24°34′, E118°12′ to pick up survivors. "日升"轮，通知你前往 N24°34′, E118°12′处去救幸存者。

（5）Picked up 3 survivors/1 lifeboat（liferaft）（with 3 persons/3 casualties）/3 persons/3 casualties in lifejackets in position N24°34′, E118°12′.

在 N24°34′, E118°12′ 位置处捞起 3 名幸存者/1 个救生艇（筏），上有 3 人/3 伤亡者/3 名穿着救生衣的人员/伤亡者。

（6）What's the condition of survivors? 幸存者状况如何？

（7）Try to obtain information from survivors. 设法从幸存者中获得信息。

（8）There are still 12 lifeboats/liferafts with survivors.

这里还有载有 12 名幸存者的救生艇/筏。

（9）All persons/8 persons rescued. 所有人员/8 人被救起。

9.15 演习（Exercises）

（1）S：BH VTS, this is oil tanker Sea Star. I'm asking for permission to carry out lifesaving drill and firefighting drill from 1400−1500 local time. Repeat：I'll carry out exercises on board from 1400 to 1500 local time, and I'm asking for permission to lowered down the lifeboat into water and manoeuvre the boat not more than 100 meters from my vessel. Over.

S：北海交管，我是油轮"海星"号。我申请当地时间 1400−1500 时开始进行救生及消防演习。重复：我轮将在 1400−1500 时举行演习，我申请将救生艇放到水面并在海上进行操纵练习，操艇范围不超过我轮 100 米的范围内。

V：Sea Star, this is BH VTS. You have permission to carry out drill. And advice you lowered down the lifeboat up 1 meter of water, but don't manoeuvre the boat at anchorage No.4. Heavy traffic in No.4 anchorage and the tide is strong. I don't think it is safe enough for you to do that, over.

V："海星"号，我是北海交管。你可以进行演习，建议你将救生艇放到水面即可，不要在四号锚地操纵救生艇，因为 4 号锚地交通比较拥挤且潮流较大，我认为在四号锚地操艇练习是不安全的。

（2）Gunnery/Rocket firing/Missile/Torpedo/Underwater ordnance exercises are in abounded circle of position N24°42.33′, E118°43.75′, direction 51 degree to 117 degree and radius 12 kilometers from 0800 hours to 2100 hours local time on 10th November 2015. Wide berth requested（if requested）.

枪炮/火箭/导弹/鱼雷/水下演习将于 2015 年 11 月 10 日 0800 时至 2100 时在以 N24°42.33′, E118°43.75′为圆心，方位角 51 度~117 度，12 千米为半径的范围内进行，请宽让（如果需要）。

9.16   巡逻艇(Patrol boat)

(1) Patrol boat is in attendance (on scene). 现场有巡逻艇。

(2) Patrol boat/tug boat is proceeding to you now. 巡逻艇/拖轮正朝你开来。

(3) Patrol boat/tug boat will arrive you within 30 min. 巡逻艇/拖船 30 分钟内抵达。

10. 日常工作通信范例

下文例句中包含 10 段日常工作通信对话,对话中的"V"代表的是北海 VTS 中心,"S"代表船方,包括 1~9 段对话中的"日升"轮,以及第 10 段对话中的油船"海星"轮。

10.1   一般动态报告(General report)

S:BH VTS, this is MV SUN RISE calling. Over.

S:北海交管,"日升"轮呼叫。完毕。

V:MV SUN RISE, this is BH VTS.Change to CH 08. Over.

V:"日升"轮,我是北海交管。请转 08 频道。完毕。

S:BH VTS, this is MV SUN RISE. Changing to CH 08. Over.

S:北海交管,我是"日升"轮。已转到 08 频道。完毕。

V:MV SUN RISE, this is BH VTS. What is your intention? Over.

V:"日升"轮,我是北海交管。报告你船意图。

S:BH VTS, MV SUN RISE is passing JIUJIEJIAO lighthouse. Over.

S:北海交管,"日升"轮通过九节礁。完毕。

V:MV SUN RISE, this is BH VTS. What is your pilot boarding time? Over.

V:"日升"轮,我是北海交管。你船引航时间是几点? 完毕。

S:BH VTS, my pilot boarding time is 0300 local time. Over.

S:北海交管,我船引航时间预计 0300。完毕。

V:MV SUN RISE, this is BH VTS. Advise slow down your speed. Over.

V:"日升"轮,我是北海交管。建议你船减车慢速进港。

S:BH VTS, MV SUN RISE copy. Over.

S:北海交管,"日升"轮收到。完毕。

V:MV SUN RISE, this is BH VTS. Please stand by on Channel 08 and 16 all the time. Out.

V:"日升"轮,我是北海交管。请保持 08 和 16 频道守听。通话完毕。

10.2   锚泊申请(Anchoring application)

S:BH VTS, this is MV SUN RISE calling. Could you give me an anchor position? Over.

S:北海交管,"日升"轮呼叫。请为我船安排一个锚位。

V:MV SUN RISE, this is BH VTS. You can select anchor position near reporting line or No.2 anchorage by yourself, over.

V:"日升"轮,这是北海交管。你可以在报告线附近或 2 号锚地自己选择合适的锚位。

S:BH VTS, this is MV SUN RISE calling. I arrive BH PORT for the first time, could you please give me a pointed anchor position? Over.

S：北海交管，"日升"轮呼叫，我是首次抵港，请为我船指定一个锚位。

V：SUN RISE, this is BH VTS. You can proceed to anchorage No.2, northeast of No.11 buoy, distance about 1.5 nautical miles. Over.

V："日升"轮，这是北海交管。你可以在 2 号锚地抛锚，锚位选择在 11 号浮筒东北方向距离约 1.5 海里的位置。

S：MV SUN RISE, this is BH VTS. What is your LOA and maximum draught? Over.

S："日升"轮，我是北海交管。报告你船船长和最大吃水。

V：BH VTS, my LOA is 261 m and my maximum draught is 8.2 m. Over.

V：北海交管，我船船长 261 米，最大吃水是 8.2 米。

S：Do you have any dangerous cargo on board? Over.

S：你船有装载危险货物吗？

V：No, I don't have any dangerous cargo on board. Over.

V：我船没有装载任何危险货物。

S：What is your berthing schedule? Over.

S：报告你船靠泊计划。

V：1000 LT in tomorrow morning. Over.

V：明天上午 10 点。

V：MV SUN RISE, this is BH VTS. Advise you proceed to Anchorage No.2 to drop anchor. After dropping anchor, report your anchor position and anchor time to VTS. Over.

V："日升"轮，我是北海交管。建议你船到 2 号锚地抛锚。抛锚后请向交管中心报告你船的抛锚时间和抛锚位置。

S：BH VTS, MV SUN RISE copy. Over.

S：北海交管，"日升"轮收到。

V：MV SUN RISE, this is BH VTS. Navigation with caution. Out.

V："日升"轮，我是北海交管。请谨慎驾驶。通话完毕。

10.3　锚位确认（Anchoring confirmation）

V：MV SUN RISE, BH VTS calling. Report anchor position from JIUJIEJIAO lighthouse bearing and distance. Over.

V："日升"轮，北海交管呼叫。请报告你船抛锚后距九节礁灯塔的方位和距离。

S：BH VTS, my anchor position, bearing two zero five degree, distance two decimal one four nautical miles from JIUJIEJIAO lighthouse. Out.

S：北海交管，我船锚位距九节礁灯塔方位 205 度，距离 2.14 海里。通话完毕。

10.4　抛锚前提醒（Remind before anchoring）

S：BH VTS, MV SUN RISE calling. What are the wind direction and speed and what is the tide stream doing? Over.

S：北海交管，"日升"轮呼叫。请问风向、风速和流向？

V：MV SUN RISE, this is BH VTS. Wind direction is northeast and speed is 15 knots. And the tide is slack/rising/falling, speed is about 2 knots. Over.

V：“日升”轮这里是北海交管。风向东北风风速 15 节。平潮/涨潮/落潮,流速约 2 节。

Heavy traffic in No.4 anchorage and the tide is strong. You should adjust your speed and navigate with great caution. Slack away enough shackles and make certain for bringing up when anchoring. You should keep at least 500 m distance from other vessel. Out.

由于 4 号锚地交通拥挤且流压很大。请谨慎驾驶,调整你船航速。松出足够长的锚链并确认锚已经抓牢。请与他船保持至少 500 米距离。通话完毕。

10.5　走锚确认（Dragging confirmation）

V：MV SUN RISE, BH VTS calling. Located your speed on my radar is over than 1.8 knots, so I am afraid you are dragging. Please check your anchor position immediately. Over.

V：“日升”轮,北海交管呼叫。通过雷达发现你船船速超过 1.8 节,你船可能正在走锚,请立即检查锚位。

S：BH VTS, this is MV SUN RISE. My anchor is dragging now, thank you. Over.

S：北海交管,我是“日升”轮。确定我船走锚,谢谢。

V：MV SUN RISE, this is BH VTS. Standby engine immediately, heave up anchor, shift to other position to drop anchor, pay attention to the strong tidal stream at this anchorage. Over.

V：“日升”轮,我是北海交管。请立即备车起锚,重新抛锚,锚泊时请注意强流。

S：BH VTS, your message understood. I will heave up anchor immediately and drop anchor in right position. Over.

S：北海交管,信息收到。我会马上备车起锚移锚位,谢谢。

10.6　交通组织一（Traffic organization Ⅰ）

V：MV SUN RISE, this is BH VTS. According to BH PORT regulation, you must apply for BH VTS before entering main Channel. Over.

V：“日升”轮,根据北海 VTS 的规定,你在进入主航道前必须经北海 VTS 同意。

S：Roger, BH VTS, I will obey the regulation, thank you. Out.

S：收到,北海交管。我船会遵守规定,谢谢。通话完毕。

10.7　交通组织二（Traffic organization Ⅱ）

V：MV SUN RISE, this is BH VTS. You are too close to the west limit of the traffic lane. You must keep in the starboard side of the channel and proceed in the established direction of traffic flow. Over.

V：“日升”轮,这是北海交管。你船太靠近航道的西边界了,请保持在航道右侧航行,并按照规定的交通流向行驶。

S：Roger, BH VTS, I will obey your rules, thank you. Out.

S：收到,北海交管。我船会遵守规定,谢谢。通话完毕。

10.8　交通组织三（Traffic organization Ⅲ）

V：MV SUN RISE, this is BH VTS. Do not joint the main fairway now/crossing the fairway now. The outbound/inbound vessel MERSKEY LUSSY which is a vessel constrained by her draught/vessel restricted in her ability to manoeuvre/vessel not under command, is severely restricted in her ability to deviate from the course she is unable to keep out of the way of another vessel by the Rules. Inbound Traffic prohibited temporarily in main fairway, Please deviate. Over.

V："日升"轮,现在不要进入主航道/现在不要穿越主航道,主航道现在实行临时交通管制。出港/进港船 MERSKEY LUSSY 是一艘限于吃水船/操纵能力受到限制船/失控船,偏离航向能力无法按避碰规则的要求给他船让路,主航道的进港进行临时交通管制。请绕航。

V：MV SUN RISE, this is BHTS. Outbound towing vessel Russy is a vessel engaged in a towing operation, the towing vessel and her tow severely restricted in their ability to deviate from their course. Please take early and substantial action to keep well clear. Over.

V："日升"轮,这是北海交管。Russy 是一艘出港的从事拖带作业的拖船,该拖船及其被拖船偏离所驶航向的能力严重受到限制。请及早地采取大幅度的行动,宽裕地让清该船。

S：Roger, BH VTS, I will not joint the fairway/not cross the fairway, I will deviate, I can navigate out of the fairway due to the small draught. Over.

S：收到,北海交管。我不会进入航道/穿越航道,我准备绕航,我船吃水小,可以在航道外安全航行。

V：MV SUN RISE, this is BH VTS. Do not overtake other vessel at this channel. Adjust your speed. Avoid to meet other vessel at area of Buoy No.11. Over.

V："日升"轮,这是北海交管。在主航道内不要追越他船,控制好速度,避免在 11 号浮附近与他船会遇。

S：Roger, BH VTS, I will obey the rules, thank you. Out.

S：收到,北海交管。我船会遵守规定,谢谢。通话完毕。

10.9　雾航信息发布(Information broadcast of navigation in fog)

V：Attention. ALL STATION, ALL STATION, ALL STATION this is BH VTS. Visibility is reduced by fog. Visibility is expected to decrease to 500 meters in half an hour. DO NOT enter main channel from now. Advise select safety position to drop anchor. Navigate with great caution. Over.

V：所有船台请注意。这是北海交管。大雾导致能见度降低。预计在一个半小时内能见度将下降至 500 米。所有船舶请不要进入主航道。建议就近择地抛锚,请特别谨慎驾驶。

10.10　作业报告(Operation report)

S：BH VTS. This is oil tanker Sea Star. I am the discharging vessel, the receiving ship Blue Sky has finished mooring. Ship transfer operation will star in 1 hour. Over.

S：北海交管,这是油船"海星"轮。我是母船,接驳船"蓝天"轮已靠妥我船。船对船过驳作业将在 1 小时后开始。

V：Sea Star, this is BH VTS. Information received. Please report the weather and the sea condition of your area. Over.

V："海星"轮，这是北海交管。信息收到。请报告当地的天气和海况。

S：BH VTS, SW wind force 3 and smooth sea. It is suitable for transfer operation. Over.

S：北海交管。西南风 3 级，小浪。适于过驳作业，请讲。

V：MV Sea Star, this is BH VTS. Is the receiving ship Blue Sky well secured to your vessel? Over.

V："海星"轮，这是北海交管。接驳船"蓝天"轮是否已经牢固系于你船？请讲。

S：BH VTS. Yes, she is well secured to my vessel. Over.

S：北海交管。是的，她已经牢固系于我船。请讲。

V：Sea Star, this is BH VTS. Is your pollution and oil emergency muster list and transfer check list available on board? Over.

V："海星"轮，这是北海交管。船上是否备有油污应变部署表和过驳检查清单。请讲。

S：BH VTS. Yes, they are available on board. Over.

S：北海交管。船上已备妥。请讲。

V：Sea Star, this is BH VTS. During your transfer operation, you must keep a good anchor watch to monitor your position and inform traffic. Also you must be sure that weather forecasts are received and favorable. Standing by CH08 and CH16. Over.

V："海星"轮，这是北海交管。在过驳作业过程中你必须加强锚泊值班，监控本船锚位，注意来往船舶动态。你还必须确保天气预报的接收以使其适于作业。守听 08 和 16 频道。请讲。

S：Information received. Over.

S：信息收到。请讲。

S：BH VTS, this is oil tanker Sea Star. Ship to ship transfer operation finished, receiving ship unmooring completed at 0100 hours LT. Over.

S：北海交管，这是"海星"轮。船对船过驳作业已结束，接驳船在当地时间 0100 时离开我船。请讲。

V：Sea Star, this is BH VTS. Information received. Out.

V："海星"轮，这是北海交管。信息收到。完毕。

练习题
Exercises

一、字母与数字拼读、抄收练习

拼读速度为 50 字符/分钟,抄收速度为 45 字符/分钟

（1）练习一

ZYXWV	UTSRQ	PONML	KJIHG	FEDCS
ACEGI	KMOQE	SUWYA	BCFHI	KMRST
WSQEK	GACHI	UYRIM	XVYJC	MFDSA
VHLMP	BDFIK	SUWYZ	JHEAO	TQREM

（2）练习二

01234	56789	35791	24680	19356
27681	39215	48271	56789	14321

（3）练习三

TUFRD	CBIAY	PMLEU	TZDH2	YOJVQ
AW7FD	ZXCFS	468HM	DITSN	KTW57
SENVL	R9Q30	LRXHY	JU61P	EVLGZ
5SFV2	AJHKG	710E8	WYRID	NGF94

（4）练习四

BZLMU	DCRGI	EGYNJ	OPNDZ	DQSTX
VZCHQ	WBKET	FPYVO	JNAUB	HMZXC
JDPHC	WXUBI	2794A	KBZGH	G0236
C3425	RTCHW	ZVLBO	QSKLA	WDOMT

二、甚高频通信实例

首先判断通信类型,然后分组练习

（1）

—OSAKA BAY pilot station. This is Chinese cargo vessel SHANHAIGUAN calling, over.

—SHANHAIGUAN, this is OSAKA BAY pilot station, over.

—OSAKA BAY pilot station, this is SHANHAIGUAN, my ETA pilot station is 1430 hours. I require a pilot, over.

—SHANHAIGUAN, this is OSAKA BAY pilot station. You may enter at 1600 hours and alongside Wharf No.23, pilot boat is coming to you. Please rig pilot ladder on port side.

—OSAKA BAY pilot station. This is SHANHAIGUAN. Yes, I will rig pilot ladder on port side. Over.

—SHANHAIGUAN. This is OSAKA BAY pilot station. Keep watch on channel 20. Out.

—OSAKA BAY pilot station. This is SHANHAIGUAN, keep watch on channel 20. Out.

（2）

—NAGOYA port radio. This is Chinese ship HUANGHAI calling, over.

—HUANGHAI. This is NAGOYA port radio. Change to channel 06, over.

—NAGOYA port radio. This is HUANGHAI. Change to channel 06, over.

—HUANGHAI. This is NAGOYA port radio, over.

—NAGOYA port radio. This is HUANGHAI. My ETD is 1600 hours. At what time will the pilot be available? Over.

—HUANGHAI. This is NAGOYA port radio. Pilot will come to you at 1545 hours. What is your deadweight tons, draught and destination? Over.

—NAGOYA port radio. This is HUANGHAI. My deadweight is 12,000 tons. My draught forward is 8.6 meters. My draught aft is 9.5 meters. My destination is Dalian. Over.

—HUANGHAI. This is NAGOYA port radio. Message is received. Thank you! Out.

—NAGOYA port radio. This is HUANGHAI. Good-by! Out.

（3）

—MARDEP HONG KONG. This is JINGANGLING calling. Over.

—JINGANGLING. This is MARDEP. Change to channel 22. Over.

—MARDEP HONG KONG. This is JINGANGLING calling. Channel 22. Over.

—JINGANGLING. This is MARDEP. What is your ship's name and nationality?

—MARDEP. This is JINGANGLING. JULIET INDIA NOVEMBER GOLF ALFA NOVEMBER GOLF LIMA INDIA NOVEMBER GOLF. Chinese cargo ship. Passing WANGLAN light house. Time 1320. entering East LAMMA Channel now. Over.

—JINGANGLING. This is MARDEP. Your LOA, air draught and max draught. Over.

—MARDEP. This is JINGANGLING. My LOA is 158 m. My air draught is 21 m. My max draught is 10.5 m. Over.

—JINGANGLING. This is MARDEP. Roger. Your ETA quarantine anchorage. Over.

—MARDEP. This is JINGANGLING. ETA quarantine anchorage is 1830 hours. Over.

—Roger. Report when passing LAMMA No.1 buoy. Out.

—Thank you! Out.

（4）

—SINGAPORE port operation. This is Chinese RO/RO ship XIFENGKOU calling. Over.

—XINFENGKOU. This is port operation. Say again your ship's name and call sign. Over.

—Port operation. This is XINFENGKOU X-RAY INDIA FOXTROT ECHO NOVEMBER GOLF KILO OSCAR UNIFORM. My call sign is BRAVO X-RAY FOXTROT GOLF. Over.

—XINFENGKOU. This is port operation. What is your present position, course and speed? over.

—Port operation. This is XINFENGKOU. Present position: passing HORSBURGH light house. Distance 3.8 miles. Course 245 degrees. Speed 15 knots. ETA boarding ground A is 1830 hours. Over.

—XINFENGKOU. This is port operation. Roger, pilot boat will meet you near boarding ground A. You may anchor in eastern working anchorage. Out.

—Port operation. This is XINFENGKOU. Message understood. Thank you! Out.

（5）

—VICTORIA. This is Chinese ship TUMENJIANG calling. Over.

—TUMENJIANG. This is VICTORIA answering. Over.

—VICTORIA. This is TUMENJIANG. Change to channel 12. Over.

—TUMENJIANG. This is VICTORIA. Change to channel 12. Over.

—VICTORIA. This is TUMENJIANG. I wish to overtake from your port side. Advise you alter course to starboard. Over.

—TUMENJIANG. This is VICTORIA. Do not overtake. I can't alter course to starboard. Advise you: stop engine. Over.

—VICTORIA. This is TUMENJIANG. OK. I will stop engine. Out.

—Thank you! Out.

（6）

—Unknown vessel 225 degrees 4.8 miles from LANGANG Island. This is JINJIANG. Come in please. Over.

—JINJIANG. This is DANJIANGKOU. Over.

—DANJIANG KOU. This is JINJIANG. Change to channel 12. Over.

—JINJIANG. This is DANJIANGKOU. Agree channel 12. Over.

—DANJIANG KOU. This is JINJIANG. My position is 105 degrees 5.6 miles from you. What is your course and speed? Over.

—JINJIANG. This is DANJIANGKOU. I have located you on my radar. My course is 129° and speed is 10 knots. What are your intentions? Over.

—DANJIANGKOU. This is JINJIANG. There are fishing gears on my starboard. I will alter course to port. Advise you keep your course and speed. Over.

—JINIANG. This is DANJIANGKOU. Your message understood. I will keep course and speed. Over.

—Thank you! Good-bye! Out.

—Good-bye! Out.

（7）

—TOKYO MARU. This is SHANGHAI port radio. Over.

—SHANGHAI port radio. This is TOKYO MARU replying. Over.

—TOKYO MARU. This is SHANGHAI port radio. Change to channel 20. Over.

—SHANGHAI port radio. This is TOKYO MARU. Change to channel 20. Over.

—TOKYO MARU. This is SHANGHAI port radio. How do you read me? Over.

—SHANGHAI port radio. This is TOKYO MARU. I read you with signal strength 4. Over.

—TOKYO MARU. This is SHANGHAI port radio. There is a vessel not under command at the SOUTH CHANNEL No. H37 light buoy. You must navigate with caution. Keep well clear of her. Over.

—SHANGHAI port radio. This is TOKYO MARU. My present position is near No. H32 light buoy. I will reduce speed and navigate with caution. Thank you! Out.

—Good bye! out.

（8）

—REKJAVIK radio. This is SMITLLOYD calling. Over.

—SMITLLOYD. This is REYKJAVIK radio. Your message please. Over.

—REYKJAVIK radio. This is SMITLLOYD. Is icing expected in the south side of Iceland tomorrow? Over.

—SMITLLOYD. This is REYKJIAVIK radio. Yes, Fast ice is expected in the south side of Iceland tomorrow. Over.

—REYKJAVIK radio. This is SMITLLOYD. At what time can I get icebreaker assistance? Over.

—SMITLLOYD. This is REYKJAVIK radio. Ice-breaker assistance will begin at 1400 hours tomorrow. Your position in the convoy is astern of VISTA. Please keep watch on channel 9. Out.

—REYKJAVIK radio. This is SMITLLOYD. Yes, I will keep watch on channel 9. Thank you! Out.

（9）

—PENAVICO DALIAN. This is Germany cargo vessel BERLIN MAYOR calling. Over.

—MERLIN MAYOR. This is PENAVICO. Spell your ship's name and call sign. Over.

—PENAVICO DALIAN. This is BERLIN MAYOR: BRAVO ECHO ROMEO LIMA INDIA NOVEMBER MIKE ALFA YANKEE OSCAR ROMEO. My call sign is DELTA ALFA ROMEO YANKEE. Over.

—BERLIN MAYOR. This is PENAVICO. What is your anchor position? Over.

—PENAVICO DALIAN. This is BERLIN MAYOR. My anchor position is 298 degrees from DALIAN harbour eastern entrance light beacon, 6.5 miles off. Please deliver 300 tons of fresh water. Over.

—BERLIN MAYOR. This is PENAVICO. Roger. The water boat will meet you at 1500 hours. No berthing instruction for you. Please keep watch on channel 16, out.

—PENAVICO DALIAN. This is BERLIN MAYOR. Yes. Keeping watch on channel 16. O-ver. Thank you out.

（10）

—GREEN ISLAND. This is PENAVICO calling. Over.

—PENAVICO. This is GREEN ISLAND. Over.

—GREEN ISLAND. This is PENAVICO. Please tell me your last cargo. Over.

—PENAVICO. This is GREEN ISLAND. My last cargo was jet petroleum No.4, over.

—GREEN ISLAND. This is PENAVICO. Spell the cargo's name letter by letter. Over.

—PENAVICO. This is GREEN ISLAND. My last cargo was: JULIETT ECHO TANGO PAPA ECHO ROMEO OSCAR LIMA ECHO UNIFORM MIKE No.4. Over.

—GREEN ISLAND. This is PENAVICO. Roger. Are the customs officers on board? Over.

—PENAVICO. This is GREEN ISLAND. They have just come on board. Over.

—GREEN ISLAND. This is PENAVICO. Is the clearance conducting now? Over.

—PENAVICO, this is GREEN ISLAND. Yes, it is just conducting now. Over.

—GREEN ISLAND. This is PENAVICO. Keeping watch on channel 9, out.

—PENAVICO. This is GREEN ISLAND. Keeping watch on channel 09, out.

（11）

—PORT SAID CONTROL. This is ZHICHENG calling. Over.

—ZHICHENG. This is PORT SAID CONTROL. Over.

—PORT SAID CONTROL. This is ZHICHENG. Request: I require a pilot. Over.

—ZHICHENG. This is PORT SAID CONTROL. Request received: you require a pilot.
Instruction: pilot will board your ship soon rig pilot ladder on port side. Out.

—PORT SAID CONTROL. This is ZHICHENG. Instruction received: pilot will board my ship soon. Rig pilot ladder on port side. Thank you out.

（12）

—SONGSHAN. This is PENAVICO calling. Over.

—PENAVICO. This is SONGSHAN. Over.

—SONGSHAN. This is PENAVICO. Question: what is your anchor position? Over.

—PENAVICO. This is SONGSHAN. Answer. Anchor position: bearing 272° distance 4.7 miles from HUANGBAIZUI light house. Over.

—SONGSHAN. This is PENAVICO. Information: you will get alongside berth No.16 at 1100 hours tomorrow morning. Out.

—PENAVICO. This is SONGSHAN. Information received: I will get alongside berth No.16 at 1100 hours tomorrow morning. Out.

（13）

—SEA TRACK. This is BLUE MOUNTAIN calling. Over.

—BLUE MOUTAIN. This is SEA TRACK. Over.

—SEA TRACK. This is BLUE MOUNTAIN. Warning: I am jettisoning dangerous cargo. Over.

—BLUE MOUNTAIN. This is SEA TRACK. Warning received：you are jettisoning danger-
　ous cargo. Over.

—SEA TRACK. This is BLUE MOUNTAIN. Advice：keep well clear of me. Out.

—BLUE MOUNTAIN. This is SEA TRACK. Advice received：I will keep well clear of
　you. Out.

（14）

—SINGAPORE PORT OPERATION. This is DAISY MARU No.1 calling. Over.

—DAISY MARU No.1. This is SINGAPORE PORT OPERATION. Over.

—SINGAPORE PORT OPERATION. This is DAISY MARU No.1.

Question：Do you have any berthing instruction for me？ Over.

—DAISY MARU No.1. This is SINGAPORE PORT OPERATION.

Answer：no berthing instruction for you today. Over.

—SINGGAPORE PORT OPERATION. This is DAISY MARU No.1.

Question：at what time shall I call again？ Over.

—DAISY MARU No.1, this is SINGAPORE PORT OPERATION.

Answer：you should call back at 1000 hours. Out.

—SINGAPORE PORT OPERATION. This is DAISY MARU No.1, thank you, out.

（15）

—GOLD ISLAND. This is STAR LAKE calling. Over.

—STAR LAKE. This is GOLD ISLAND. Over.

—GOLD ISLAND. This is STAR LAKE.

Intention：I will overtake from your port side. Over.

—STAR LAKE. This is GOLD ISLAND. Intention received：you will overtake from my
　port side. Over.

—GOLD ISLAND. This is STAR LAKE. Advice：keep your present course and speed. O-
　ver.

—STAR LAKE. This is GOLD ISLAND. Advice received：I will keep my present course
　and speed. Out.

—GOLD ISLAND. This is STAR LAKE. Thank you！ Out.

（16）

—GAMMON. This is STOWBRIDGE port radio calling. Over.

—STOWBRIDGE port radio. This is GAMMON. Over.

—GAMMON.This is STOWBRIDGE port radio. Information：dredging operations are com-
　pleted in the south fairway. Out

—STOWBRIDGE port radio. This is GAMMON. Information received：dredging operations
　are completed in the south fairway. Thank you！ Out.

（17）

—BREST port. This is SUNRISE calling. Over.

—SUNRISE. This is BREST PORT. Over.

—BREST port. This is SUNRISE. Information: my steering gear is not working. Over.

—SUNRISE. This is BREST port. Information received: steering gear not working.
Question: what is your position? Over.

—BREST port. This is SUNRISE. Answer: position: bearing 350° distance 28 miles from
SILVER ISLAND. Request: I require tugs. Over.

—SUNRISE. This is BREST port. Request received: three tugs coming to your
assistance. Out.

—BREST port. This is SUNRISE. Thank you! Out.

(18)

—RATTLER. This is LANDS END radio calling. Over.

—LANDS END radio. This is RATTLER. Over.

—RATTLER. This is LANDS END radio. Instruction: keep watch on channel 12. Wait for
navigational warning. Out.

—LANDS END radio. This is RATTLER. Instruction received: keep watch on channel 12.
Wait for navigational warning, thank you! Out.

(19)

—MAYDAY, MAYDAY, MAYDAY.

—This is motor vessel PACIFIC OCEAN, PACIFIC OCEAN, PACIFIC OCEAN.

—Call sign JAPZ.

—MAYDAY, PACIFIC, OCEAN.

—I am on fire in No.4 hold and have dangerous goods on fore deck. Position 31 degrees 35
minutes north 124 degrees 24 minutes east. Require immediate assistance. Out.

(20)

—MAYDAY, MAYDAY, MAYDAY.

—This is SEA TRACK, SEA TRACK, GOMZ.

—MAYDAY, SEA TRACK.

—I am aground.

—Position: 293 degrees 4.5 miles from BRAVO beacon. Request tow. Out.

(21)

—PAN-PAN, PAN-PAN, PAN-PAN.

—This is STAR VEGA, STAR VEGA.

—PAN-PAN, STAR VEGA, call sign GEHT.

—Position bearing 124 degrees distance 2.5 miles from SARKAN light house. Lost propeller
and require tow. Over.

(22)

—SECURITE, SECURITE, SECURITE.

—All ships, all ships, all ships.

—This is North channel port control.

—SECURITE.

—North channel port control.

—Navigational warning.

—North channel shore-based radar is not working.

—Out.

（23）

—MAYDAY RELAY, MAYDAY RELAY, MAYDAY RELAY.

—This is SEA STAR, SEA STAR, SEA STAR.

—MAYDAY.

—SUNRISE. GOLF TANGO X-RAY PAPA.

—Following received from SUNRISE：

—Time：1630 GMT.

—MAYDAY.

—SUNRISE, GOLF TANGO X-RAY PAPA.

—Position：latitude 52 degrees 30 minutes north, longitude 139 degrees 20 minutes west.

—Collision with unknown object, firing.

—Request immediate assistance.

—This is SEA STAR.

—Over.

（24）

—All ships in MALACCA straits, all ships in MALACCA straits, all ships in MALACCA straits.

—This is CHINA STAR. NOVEMBER ALFA TANGO FOXTROT.

—CHINA STAR, NATF.

—Weather report.

—Switch to VHF channel 13, over.

—All ships in MALACCA straits, all ships in MALACCA straits.

—This is CHINA STAR on CH13. NATF.

—CHINA STAR, NATF.

—Weather report for MALACCA straits.

—Time：1200 GMT.

—Information

　Wind：south.

　Force：eight.

　Sea：rough.

　Weather：rain showers.

　Visibility：one mile.

　Pressure：998 falling.

—Out.

（25）

—Attention all vessels, attention all vessels, attention all vessels.

—This is NEW HARBOUR radio.

—Navigational information.

—Change to channel 12. Over.

—All vessels, all vessels.

—This is NEW HARBOUR radio on channel 12.

—Navigational information.

—Visibility is reduced by fog. Visibility at No.1 buoy is 1,500 meters and 1,000 meters at entrance buoy. Vessels must navigate with caution.

—Weather report.

—Tropical storm at 1600 GMT was moving in direction 200 degrees at 10 knots with max wind force 12. Storm center pressure is 985 millibars.

—Out.

Appendix

附录

附录 1
标准航海通信用语（摘录）

INTRODUCTION 简介

These SMCP have been compiled：

—to assist in the greater safety of navigation and of the conduct of ship.

—to standardize the language used in communication for navigation at sea，in port-approaches，in waterways，harbors and on board vessels.

《标准航海通信用语》用于：

—提高航海和船舶操纵的安全性；

—使海上航行、进出港操纵、水道航行、港内作业及船上业务的通信语言标准化。

These phrases are not intended to supplant or contradict the International Regulations for Preventing Collisions at Sea，1972 or special local rules or recommendations made by IMO concerning ships' routeing. Neither are they intended to supersede the International Code of Signals nor to supplant normal radiotelephone practice as set out in the ITU Regulations.

这些语句不用作代替《1972 年国际海上避碰规则》、特殊规则以及国际海事组织对于船舶日常作业做出的建议，也不与这些规则相矛盾；这些语句不用作取代《国际信号规则》，也不用作代替《国际电信联盟规则》的正常无线电话通信规则。

These SMCP meet the requirements of the STCW Convention，1978，as revised，and of the SOLAS Convention，1974，as revised，regarding verbal communication；moreover，the phrases cover the communication relevant safety aspects laid down in these Conventions. Knowledge，understanding and the competence to use the SMCP are required by the STCW Convention，1978，as revised，for officers in charge of a navigational watch on vessels of 500 gross tonnage or more. Use of the communication phrases should be made as often as possible in preference to other wording of similar meaning，and they should be part of instruction in maritime education and training.

《标准航海通信用语》符合经修正的《1978 年海员培训、发证和值班标准国际公约》、经修正的《1974 年国际海上人命安全公约》有关口语通信的要求；而且，这些用语也包括了上述两个公约中有关安全事宜的通信。经修正的《1974 年国际海上人命安全公约》对于 500 总吨及以上船舶的值班驾驶员使用《标准航海通信用语》的知识水平、理解能力和应用能力做出要求。在通信中，《标准航海通信用语》的使用应优先于其他具有类似意义的措辞，而且这应成为航海教育与培训内容的一部分。

In this way they are intended to become an acceptable safety language，using the English language，for the verbal interchange of intelligence between individuals of all maritime nations on the many and varied occasions when precise meanings and translations are in doubt, increasingly evident under modern conditions at sea. For that purpose the SMCP build on basic knowledge of the English language, and they have been drafted in a simplified version of maritime English intentionally reducing grammatical, lexical and idiomatic varieties to a tolerable minimum and standardized structures for the sake of the function of the SMCP, i.e. diminishing misunderstanding in safety related verbal communication.

在现代航海生产中,当表达和翻译有异议时,《标准航海通信用语》逐渐成为航运国家所有人员之间口语通信中可接受的有关安全的英语语言。为此,《标准航海通信用语》基于英语的基本知识,其起草中,将语法、词汇和惯用法缩减到了可接受的最低水平,形成了标准结构,也就是,减少了在有关安全的口语通信中有歧义的部分。

The typographical conventions used throughout most of this communication phrases are as follows:

这些用语中使用的常用编排符号如下:

( )   brackets 括号

indicate that the part of the message enclosed within the brackets may be added where it is relevant, or they enclose a brief explanation of the preceding phrase;

括号中的内容是可添加的内容,或是前述内容的简单解释;

/   oblique stroke 后斜线

indicates that the items on either side of the stroke are alternatives;

斜线表示其左右的内容可供选择;

…   dots 三点线

indicate that the relevant information is to be filled in where the dots occur.

省略符表示在其出现处应添加有关内容。

***italic letters* 斜体**

indicate the kind of information requested.

斜体表示所需的信息种类。

PART I—GENERAL 总则

1. Procedure 程序

When it is necessary to indicate that the SMCP are to be used, the following message may be sent:

在使用《标准航海通信用语》时应用下述句子说明:

"Please use Standard Marine Communication Phrases"

"I will use Standard Marine Communication Phrases"

2. Spelling 拼读

When in external communication spelling is necessary, only the following spelling table should be used:

在与船外进行拼读通信时,应按下表的规定进行拼读:

Letter	Code	Letter	Code
A	Alfa	N	November
B	Bravo	O	Oscar
C	Charlie	P	Papa
D	Delta	Q	Quebec
E	Echo	R	Romeo
F	Foxtrot	S	Sierra
G	Golf	T	Tango
H	Hotel	U	Uniform
I	India	V	Victor
J	Juliet	W	Whisky
K	Kilo	X	X-ray
L	Lima	Y	Yankee
M	Mike	Z	Zulu

Figure	Code word
0	Nadazero
1	Unaone
2	Bissotwo
3	Terrathree
4	Kartefour
5	Pantafive
6	Soxisix
7	Setteseven
8	Oktoeight
9	Novenine
Fullstop	Stop
Decimal point	Decimal

3. Message Markers 信文标识

In ship-to-shore and shore-to-ship communication or radio communication in general, the following eight Message Markers may be used (also see " Application of Message Markers" given in section 6 " Vessel Traffic Service Standard Phrases" of PART Ⅲ):

在"船—岸"和"岸—船"通信中及一般的无线电通信中,可使用下述 8 个信文标识。(另见第三部分 第 6 节 船舶交通管理标准用语)

（ⅰ）Instruction 指示

（ⅱ）Advice 建议

（ⅲ）Warning 警告

（ⅳ）Information 信息

（ⅴ）Question 问题

（ⅵ）Answer 回答

（ⅶ）Request 请求

（ⅷ）Intention 意图

4. Responses 回应

4.1 When the answer to a question is in the affirmative, say：

" Yes, ..." followed by the appropriate phrase in full.

若作肯定回答,请用"Yes",后接全句。

4.2 When the answer to a question is in the negative, say：

" No, ..." followed by the appropriate phrase in full.

若作否定回答,请用"No",后接全句。

4.3 When the information requested is not immediately available, say：

" Stand by" followed by the time interval within which the information will be available.

若对方要求的信息不能立即得到,请用"Stand by",后接取得信息所需的时间。

4.4 When the information requested cannot be obtained, say:

"No information."

若对方要求的信息无法得到,请用"No information"。

4.5 When an INSTRUCTION (e.g. by a VTS-Station, naval vessel or other fully authorized personnel) or an ADVICE is given, respond if in the affirmative:

"I will/can … "followed by the instruction or advice in full; and, if in the negative, respond:

"I will not/cannot … "followed by the instruction or advice in full.

对于一项指示(如由交管站、海军船舶或其他经授权人员给出)或建议,若作肯定回答,请用"I will/can …",后接指示或建议的全句;若作否定回答,请用"I will not/cannot …",后接指示或建议的全句。

Example:"Advice. Do not overtake vessel ahead of you."

Respond:"I will not overtake vessel ahead of me."

The responses to orders of special importance, however, are given in wording in the phrases concerned.

对于具有特殊重要意义的命令的回应,在有关句中说明。

5. **Distress, urgency and safety signals 遇险、紧急和安全信号**

5.1 MAYDAY is to be used to announce a distress message 用作标明遇险电话通信

5.2 PAN-PAN is to be used to announce an urgency message 用作标明紧急电话通信

5.3 SECURITE is to be used to announce a safety message 用作标明安全电话通信

6. **Standard organizational phrases 标准语句**

6.1 "How do you read?"

6.1.1 "I read you…"

bad/one with signal strength one	(i.e. barely perceptible)
poor/two with signal strength two	(i.e. weak)
fair/three with signal strength three	(i.e. fairly good)
good/four with signal strength four	(i.e. good)
excellent/five with signal strength five	(i.e. very good)

6.2 When it is advisable to remain on a VHF channel/frequency say:

若建议在 VHF 某一频道或频率上守听,说:

"Stand by on VHF channel …/frequency … "

6.2.1 When it is accepted to remain on the VHF channel/frequency indicated, say:

若同意在某一指定的 VHF 频道或频率上守听,说:

"Standing by on VHF channel …/frequency …"

6.3 When it is advisable to change to another VHF channel/frequency, say:

若建议改用 VHF 的另一频道或频率,说:

"Advise (you) change to VHF channel …/frequency …".

"Advise (you) try VHF channel …/frequency."

6.3.1 When the changing of a VHF channel/frequency is accepted，say：

若同意改用 VHF 的另一频道或频率,说：

"Changing to VHF channel …/frequency …"

7. Corrections 修正

When a mistake is made in a message，say：

"Mistake …"followed by the word：

"Correction … " plus the corrected part of the message.

若通信语句发生错误,说："Mistake …",后接"Correction … ",再加改正的语句部分。

Example："My present speed 14 knots—mistake. Correction, my present speed 12, one-two, knots."

8. Readiness 备妥

"I am/I am not ready to receive your message".

9. Repetition 重复

9.1 If any part of the message are considered sufficiently important to need safeguarding，say：

"Repeat … " followed by the corresponding part of the message.

若语句的某部分特别重要而需要重复,说："Repeat… ",后接相应语句部分。

Example："My draft 12.6 repeat one-two decimal 6 meters."

"Do not overtake—repeat—do not overtake."

9.2 When a message is not properly heard，say：

"Say again（please）."

若某语句未听清楚,说："Say again（please）."

10. Numbers 数字

Numbers are to be spoken in separate digits：

数字应分读：

"One-five-zero" for 150.

"Two decimal five" for 2.5.

Note：Attention！When rudder angles e.g. in wheel orders are given，say：

"Fifteen" for 15 or，"Twenty" for 20，etc.

注意,舵令并不分读。

11. Positions 位置

11.1 When latitude and longitude are used，these shall be expressed in degrees and minutes（and decimals of a minute if necessary），north or south of the Equator and east or west of Greenwich.

使用经纬度时,应用度和分（若必要用分的 10 分位）,后接南、北或东、西。

Example："WARNING. Dangerous wreck in position 15 degrees 34 minutes north 61 degrees 29 minutes west."

11.2 When the position is related to a mark，the mark shall be a well-defined charted object. The bearing shall be in the 360 degrees notation from true north and shall be that of the position FROM the mark.

若位置参照物标给出,则该物标必须在海图上有明确标志。方位应自真北起算以360度给出,自物标量起。

Example:"Your position bearing 137 degrees from Barr Head lighthouse distance 2.4 nautical miles."

12. Bearings 方位

The bearing of the mark or vessel concerned, is the bearing in the 360 degree notation from north (true north unless otherwise stated), except in the case of relative bearings. Bearings may be either FROM the mark or FROM the vessel.

物标或船舶的方位,应自真北(另有说明除外)起算以360度给出,但相对方位除外。方位可自物标亦可自船舶量起。

Examples:"Pilot boat bearing 215 degrees from you."

Note:Vessels reporting their position should always quote their bearing FROM the mark.

注意:船舶报告自己的船位时,方位应自物标量起。

12.1 Relative bearings 相对方位

Relative bearings can be expressed in degrees relative to the vessel's head or bow. More frequently this is in relation to the port or starboard bow.

相对方位可用相对于船首的角度数表示,常用首或右首表示。

Example:"Buoy 030 degrees on your port bow."

(Relative D/F bearings are more commonly expressed in the 360 degree notation. 测向仪的相对方位常用360度表示)

13. Courses 航向

Always to be expressed in 360 degree notation from north (true north unless otherwise stated). Whether this is to TO or FROM a mark can be stated.

自真北以360度给出(另有说明除外),但可说明量向物标还是自物标量起。

14. Distances 距离

Preferably to be expressed in nautical miles or cables (tenths of a mile) otherwise in kilometers or meters, the unit always to be stated.

最好以海里或链(海里的小数)给出,也可用千米或米给出,但使用单位必须明确说明。

15. Speed 速度

To be expressed in knots:

应以节为单位给出:

15.1 Without further notation meaning speed through the water;

未加说明时系指对水速度;

15.2 "Ground speed" meaning speed over the ground.

"ground speed" 系指对地速度。

16. Time 时间

Times should be expressed in the 24 hour notation indicating whether UTC, zone time or local time is being used.

时间应以 24 小时给出,并表明所作用的是协调世界时、区时还是地方时。

17. Geographical names 地名

Place names used should be those on the Chart or Sailing Directions in use. If these not be understood, latitude and longitude should be given.

地名应为海图或航路指南中所使用的名称,若不明确,应给出经纬度。

18. Ambiguous words 意义不明确的单词

Some words in English have meanings depending on the context in which they appear. Misunderstandings frequently occur, especially in VTS communication, and have produced accidents. Such words are:

英语中有些单词的意义与上下文有关。在分道通航制通信中常发生误解,并曾产生事故。例如:

18.1 The Conditionals "May", "Might", "Should" and "Could".

    May

    Do not say: "May I enter fairway?"

    Say: "QUESTION. Is it permitted to enter fairway?"

    Do not say:"You may enter fairway."

    Say: "ANSWER. It is permitted to enter fairway."

    Might

    Do not say: "I might enter fairway."

    Say: "INTENTION. I will enter fairway."

    Should

    Do not say: "You should anchor in anchorage B3."

    Say: "ADVICE. Anchor in anchorage B3."

    Could

    Do not say: "You could be running into danger."

    Say: "WARNING. You are running into danger."

18.2 The word "Can"

    The word "Can" either describes the possibility or the capability of doing something. In the SMCP the situations where phrases using the word "Can" appear make it clear whether a possibility is referred to. In an ambiguous context, however, say, for example:

英文中,Can 用以表示做某事的能力或用以表示做某事的可能性。在《标准航海通信用语》中,有 Can 的语句出现时,应确切表明是否表示可能性。例如,当不明确时应说:

    "QUESTION. Is it permitted to use shallow draft fairway at this time?", do not say: "Can I use shallow draft fairway at this time?", if you ask for a permission.

    (The same applies to the word "May")

    Note: In cases not covered by PART Ⅰ "General", the regular communication procedures prescribed by the ITU—Radio Regulations will prevail.

    注意,在总论中未说明的情况下,通信中应优先采用国际电信同盟制定的《无线电规则》的规定。

PART Ⅱ—GLOSSARY 术语

Abandon vessel: To evacuate a vessel from crew and passengers following a distress

弃船：遇险时将船员或旅客撤离船舶

Adrift: Floating, not controlled, without a clearly determinable direction

漂航：失控下的无目的漂流

Assembly station: Place on deck, in mess rooms, etc., assigned to crew and passengers where they have to meet according to the muster list when the corresponding alarm is released or announcement made

集合地点：船员和旅客在听到警报或通知时按应急表前往集合的甲板或餐厅等处所

Backing (of wind): When a wind blows round anticlockwise (opposite of veering)

风向逆转：风向逆时针改变，与 veering 相反

Beach (to): To run a vessel upon a beach to prevent its sinking in deep water

抢滩：船舶冲向海滩，以免沉没在深水区

Berth: A sea room to be kept for safety around a vessel, rock, platform, etc., or the place assigned to a vessel when anchored or lying alongside a pier, etc.

泊位：船舶、礁石、平台等周围所保留的安全区，或为船舶指定的锚泊区或靠泊区等

Blast: A sound signal made with the whistle of the vessel

声号：船笛发出的声响

Blind sectors: Areas which cannot be scanned by the radar of the vessel because they are shielded by parts of its superstructure, masts, etc.

盲区：由于上层建筑、桅杆等的遮挡，船舶雷达不能扫描到的区域

Boarding arrangements: All gear, such as pilot ladder, accommodation ladder, hoist, etc., necessary for a safe transfer of the pilot

登船设备：引航员上下船所需的引航员梯、吊绳等索具

Boarding speed: The speed of a vessel adjusted to that of a pilot boat at which the pilot can safely embark

登船速度：使引航员能安全上船的与引航员艇相应的速度

Briefing: A concise explanatory information to crew and passengers

简述：对船员和旅客做出的简要说明

Capsizing: Turning of a vessel upside down while on water

倾覆：船舶在水中翻倒

Cardinal buoy: A sea-mark, i.e. a buoy, indicating the north, east, south or west from a fixed point, e.g. a wreck

方位标：标明固定点如沉船的东、南、西、北方向的海上浮标

Casualty: Case of death or serious injury to a person in an accident or shipping disaster, also said of a distressed vessel

遇难：人员在事故或海难中死亡或受伤的案件，亦指遇难船舶

Close coupled towing: A method of towing vessels through polar ice by means of ice-breaking tugs with a special stern notch suited to receive and hold the bow of the vessel to be towed

　　紧连拖带：在极地冰区中,破冰船利用其尾部的特殊凹槽与被拖船船首相连的拖带方法

　　Compatibility(of goods)：States whether different goods can be stowed together in one hold

　　相容性：货物可否同舱装载的特性

　　Convoy：A group of vessels which sail together, e.g. through a canal or ice

　　编队：同时通过运河或冰区的船舶

　　Crude oil washing(COW)：A system of cleaning the tanks by washing them with the cargo of crude oil while it is being discharged

　　原油洗舱：卸原油时利用所卸油进行洗舱的系统

　　CPA：Closest point of approach

　　最小会距：最小会遇距离

　　Co-ordinator surface search(CSS)：A vessel, other than a rescue unit, designated to co-ordinate surface search and rescue operation within a specified area

　　协调船：在某一区域中,指定为水面搜救作业进行协调而不实际进行救助的船舶

　　Damage control team：A group of crew members trained for fighting flooding in the vessel

　　堵漏队：经训练在船上进行堵漏的一组船员

　　Datum：The most probable position of a search target at a given time

　　基点：在给定时间,搜寻目标最可能存在的位置

　　Derelict：Goods or any other commodity, specifically a vessel abandoned at sea

　　遗骸：在海上遗弃的货物或船舶

　　Destination：Port which a vessel is bound for

　　目的港：船舶驶往的港口

　　Disabled：A vessel damaged or impaired in such a manner as to be incapable of proceeding its voyage

　　失控船：受到损坏导致不能航行的船舶

　　Disembark (to)：To go from board a vessel

　　离船：(人员)离开所在船

　　Distress alert：A radio signal from a distressed vessel automatically directed to a RCC giving position, identification, course and speed of the vessel as well as the nature of distress

　　遇险报警：遇险船自动将船位、标识、航向、速度及遇险性质传送到搜救协调中心的无线电信号

　　Dredging (of anchor)：Moving of an anchor over the sea bottom to control the movement of the vessel

　　拖锚：锚在水下拖动以控制船舶移动

　　Drifting：Floating, caused by winds and current with a determinable direction

　　漂航：因风流作用而向某一方向漂移

　　Drop back (to)：To increase the distance to the vessel ahead by reducing one's own speed

　　减速：本船减速以增加与前方船的距离

　　Embark (to)：To go aboard a vessel

登船:登上船舶

Escape route:A clearly marked way in the vessel which has to be followed in case of an emergency

撤离路线:在船上做出醒目标志的路线,以便紧急时撤离用

Escort:Attending a vessel, to be available in case of need, e.g. ice-breaker, tug, etc.

护航:在必要时对船舶的保护,如利用破冰船、拖船等

ETA:Estimated time of arrival

预抵时间:预计到达时间

ETD:Estimated time of departure

预离时间:预计离开时间

Fairway:Navigable part of a waterway

航道:可航水道

Fairway speed:Mandatory speed in a fairway

航道速度:可航水道规定的行驶速度

Fire party:A group of crew members trained for fire fighting on board

消防队:经训练以扑救船火的一组船员

Fire patrol:A round through the vessel carried out by a crew member of the watch at certain intervals so that an outbreak of fire may be promptly detected; mandatory in vessels carrying more than 36 passengers

防火巡逻:在船上由当值船员以一定时间间隔进行的巡逻,以此可及时发现火灾,载客超过 36 人的船对此有强制要求

Flooding:Major flow of seawater into the vessel

漏损:海水大量进入船舶

Foam monitor:A powerful foam fire extinguisher standing by aboard tankers loading or discharging oil

泡沫灭火器:装卸货油时油船上备用的大型泡沫灭火器

Foul (of anchor):The anchor has its own cable twisted around it or has fouled an obstruction

缠链:锚链绞缠在锚上或其他障碍物上

Foul (of propeller):A line, wire, net, etc., is wound round the propeller

缠桨:绳、线、网等绞缠在螺旋桨上

Full speed:Highest possible speed of a vessel

全速:船舶的最大速度

General emergency alarm:A sound signal of seven short blasts and one long blast given with the vessel's sound system

紧急警报:船舶警报系统发出的 7 短声 1 长声的警报

GMDSS:Global maritime distress and safety system

全球海上遇险与安全系统

GPS:Global (satellite) positioning system

全球定位系统

Hampered vessel: A vessel restricted by its ability to manoeuvre by the nature of its work or its deep draft

操纵受限船：因作业或吃水而操纵能力受到限制的船

Hatch-rails: Ropes supported by stanchions around an open hatch to prevent persons from falling into a hold

舱口拦绳：在开敞的舱口周围由立柱支撑的围绳，以防人员跌落舱下

Hoist: A cable used by helicopters for lifting or lowering persons in a pick-up operation

吊索：直升机吊提作业中用作吊提人员的绳具

IMO-Class: Group of dangerous or hazardous goods, harmful substances or marine pollutants in sea transport as classified in the International Dangerous Goods Code

国际海事组织类别：《国际海运危险货物规则》中规定的危险品、有害物质或海洋污染物

Initial course: Course directed by the OSC or CSS to be steered at the beginning of a search

初搜航向：由现场指挥员或协调员规定的搜索开始的航向

Inoperative: Not functioning

失效：丧失作用

Jettison (to) (of cargo): Throwing overboard of goods in order to lighten the vessel or improve its stability in case of an emergency

弃货：在紧急时为减小船舶重量或增加船舶稳性而将货物抛至舷外

Launch (to): To lower, e.g. lifeboats to the water

落放：将救生艇等落向水面

Leaking: Escape of liquids such as water, oil, etc., out of pipes, boilers, tanks, etc., or a minor inflow of seawater into the vessel due to a damage to the hull

渗漏：管线、锅炉、舱柜等中的水或油的泄漏，或因船壳破损使海水渗入船内

Leeway: Lateral movement of the vessel to leeward of its course

背风移动：船舶向背风向侧移

Let go (to): To set free, let loose, or cast off (of anchors, lines, etc.)

抛放：抛、解、松、放（锚、缆等）

Lifeboat station: The place assigned to crew and passengers where they have to meet before they will be ordered to enter the lifeboats

救生艇站：船员和旅客登艇前的集合地点

List: Inclination of the vessel to port side or starboard side

横倾：船舶向左或向右横倾

Make water (to): Seawater flows into the vessel due to the damage of the hull, or hatches were washed off or not properly closed

进水：因船体损坏、舱盖被冲掉或未盖，海水流入船内

Manoeuvring speed: A vessel's reduced rate of speed in restricted waters such as fairways, Harbors, etc.

操纵速度：船舶在航道或港内减速后的速度

Mass disease: An illness preferably of an infectious nature seizing more than two persons on board at the same time

群疫:船上两名以上人员同时患有的具有传染性的疾病

Moor（to）:To secure a vessel in a particular place by means of chains or ropes made fast to the shore, to anchors, or to anchored mooring buoys, or to ride with both anchors down

系泊:将链或绳系在岸上、锚上、锚泊的浮筒上,或双锚溜锚,以将船固定在某一地点

Muster（to）:To assemble crew, passengers or both in a special place for purposes of checking

集合:将船员和/或旅客集合在某一地点以核查人数

Not under command(NUC): A vessel which through exceptional circumstances is unable to manoeuvre as required by the COLREGs

失控船:船舶因异常情况而不能按避撞规则的要求进行操纵

Obstruction:An object such as a wreck, net, etc., which blocks a fairway, route, etc.

碍航物:阻碍航道的沉船、网具等障碍物

Off air:When the transmissions of a radio station or a Decca chain, etc., have broken down, switched off or suspended

停止发射:无线电台、台卡链站等损坏、关闭或中断发射

Off station（of buoys）:Not at the position charted

漂移:不在海图标称的位置上

Oil clearance:An operation to remove oil from the water surface

油污清除:清除海上污油的作业

Operational:Ready for immediate use

可操作:可即时使用

Ordnance exercise:Naval firing practice

军事演习:海军发射演习

On-scene commander(OSC): The commander of a rescue unit designated to co-ordinate search and rescue operations within a specified area

现场指挥员:在某一指定区域中指定作为搜救作业指挥的人员

Outbound/Inbound vessel:A vessel leaving/entering port

进/出港船:进入或驶离港口的船舶

Overflow:Accidental escape of oil out of a tank when it gets too full because pumping was not stopped in time

溢油:因未及时停泵致使油品溢出舱柜

Polluter:A vessel emitting harmful substances into the air or spilling oil into the sea

污染船:向空气散发出污染物或向海水中漏油的船舶

Proceed（to）:To sail or head for a certain position or to continue the voyage

驶往:向某一位置驶去或继续航行

PA system（Public address system）:Loudspeakers in the vessel's cabins, mess rooms, etc., and on deck via which important information can be broadcast from a central point, mostly from the navigation bridge

广播系统：舱室中、餐厅中或甲板上的高音喇叭，用作从控制中心或驾驶台播送重要信息

RCC（Rescue co-ordination center）：Land-based authority conducting and coordinating search and rescue operations in a designated area

搜救协调中心：在指定区域中从事搜救作业和搜救协调的岸上机构

Receiving point：A mark or place at which a vessel comes under obligatory entry, transit, or escort procedure

接受点：船舶到达进入、通过或护航点的标志或地点

Reference line：A fictive line displayed on the radar screen separating the fairway for inbound and outbound vessels so that they can safely pass each other

参照线：雷达屏幕上显示的分隔进口船和出口船的线，以使相互间安全通过

Refloat（to）：To pull a vessel off after grounding; to set afloat again

重起浮：使船搁浅后重新浮起

Reporting point：(see Way point)

报告点：(见报告点)

Rendezvous：An appointment between vessels normally made on radio to meet in a certain area or position

约见：利用无线电约定在某一区域或地点相见的约定

Rescue team：A group of crew members standing by in case of an emergency in order to assist other teams in action if necessary

救助队：在紧急中，在必要时向其他队组提供援助的一组船员

Restricted area：A deck, space, area, etc., not permitted to be entered for safety reasons

禁入区：因安全原因不得进入的甲板区域、空间或处所

Retreat signal：Sound, visual or other signal to a team ordering it to return to its base

撤回信号：命令搜寻船组回到基点的声号、视觉信号或其他信号

Rig move：The movement of an oil rig, drilling platform, etc., from one position to another

钻井装置移动：钻井装置、钻井平台等从一个位置到另一位置的移动

Roll call：The act of checking who of the passengers and crew members are present, e.g. at assembly stations, by reading aloud a list of their names

点名：利用按名单大声顺序念出名字的方法以核对船员或旅客人员的做法，如在集合点

Safe speed：That speed of a vessel allowing the maximum possible time for effective action to be taken to avoid a collision and to be stopped within an appropriate distance

安全航速：可使船舶有足够时间采取有效行动以避免碰撞并在相应距离内停下的速度

Safety load：The maximum permissible load of a deck, etc.

安全负荷：甲板等所能承受的最大载荷

Safe working pressure：The maximum permissible pressure in cargo hoses

安全工作压力：货油软管中最大许可压力

SAR：Search and rescue

搜索与救助

Scene：The area where the event, e.g. an accident has happened

现场：事故发生的现场

Search pattern：A pattern according to which vessels and/or aircraft may conduct a coordinated search（the IMOSAR offers seven search patterns）

搜索方式：船舶或飞机进行协调搜索的方式（国际海事组织搜救手册中规定了 7 种搜索方式）

Search speed：The speed of searching vessels directed by the OSC or CSS

搜索速度：搜索船由协调员或现场指挥员指定的速度

Segregation（of goods）：Separation of goods which for different reasons must not be stowed together

隔离：货物因种种原因而不能装载在一起

Shifting cargo：Transverse movement of cargo，especially bulk，caused by rolling or a heavy list

货物移动：散货在舱内因横摇或大角度横倾引起的横向移动

Slings：Ropes，nets，and any other means for handling general cargoes

吊货绳扣：装卸杂货用的绳扣、网兜等

Speed of advance：The speed at which a storm center moves

前进速度：风暴中心的移动速度

Spill（to）：To accidentally escape，e.g. oil，etc.，from a vessel，container，etc.，into the sea

漏油：自船或集装箱中向海泄漏油品等

Spill control gear：Special equipment for fighting accidental oil spills at early stages

漏油控制设备：用作漏油初始阶段进行漏油控制的一种特殊设备

Spreader：The step of a pilot ladder which prevents the ladder from twisting

防扭扛：引航员梯上防止梯子扭动的长步蹬

Stand by（to）：To be in readiness or prepared to execute an order

备妥：处于准备执行命令的状态

Stand clear（to）：To keep a boat away from the vessel

远离：使一船离开另一船

Standing orders：Orders of the Master to the officers of the watch which she/he must comply with

日常命令：船长对高级船员下达的其应执行的命令

Stand on（to）：To maintain course and speed

直航：保持航向和速度

Station：The allotted place or the duties of each person on board

岗位：船上分配给每人的位置或责任

Take off（to）：To start with the helicopter from a vessel's deck

起飞：直升机自船舶甲板向上升起

Target：The echo generated e.g. by a vessel on a radar screen

物标：雷达屏幕上由船舶等所产生的回波

Traffic lane：A one-way route which vessels have to comply with within a traffic separation scheme

通航道：分道通航制中供船舶行驶的单行道

Transshipment（of cargo）：The transfer of goods from one vessel to another outside harbors

过驳：将货物从一船卸至外舷的另一船

Transit：The passage of a vessel through a canal，fairway，etc.

通过：船舶航经运河、航道等

Transit speed：Speed of a vessel required for the passage through a canal，fairway，etc.

通过速度：船舶通过运河、航道等的所需的速度

Underway：A vessel which is not at anchor，or made fast to the shore，or aground

在航：未抛锚、未系岸或未搁浅的船

Unlit：When the light characteristics of a buoy or a lighthouse are inoperative

熄灭：浮标或灯塔的灯质无效

UTC：Universal time co-ordinated（ex GMT）

协调时：协调世界时（由 GMT 计算出）

Variable（of winds）：When the wind is permanently changing the direction from which it blows

风向不定：风吹来的方向不断变化

Veering（of winds）：When a wind blows round clockwise；opposite of backing

风向顺转：风向顺时针转变，与 backing 相反

Vessel traffic service（VTS）：The service，designed to improve safety，efficiency，and easiness of vessel traffic and to protect the environment

交管服务：提高通航安全性、通航率和通航便利性及保障环境安全的服务

VTS area：Area controlled by a VTS Center or VTS Station

交管区：由交管中心或交管站所控制的区域

Way point：A mark or position at which a vessel is required to report to establish its position

报告点：要求船舶确定并报告其位置的标志处或位置点

Windward：The general direction from which the wind blows；opposite of leeward

向风：风吹来的方向，与 leeward 相反

Wreck：A vessel which has been destroyed or sunk or abandoned at sea

沉船：在海上毁损、沉没或被遗弃的船

PART Ⅲ—EXTERNAL COMMUNICATION PHRASES 外部通信用语

（Attention：The use of Standard Phrases in ship's external communication does not in any way exempt from applying the relevant ITU—Radio Regulations and Procedures for Radio Telephony）

（注意：在船舶外部通信中使用《标准航海通信用语》并不免除船舶执行国际电信同盟制定的《无线电规则》和《无线电话通信程序》有关规定的责任）

1 Distress Communication 遇险通信

1.1 Distress messages 遇险语句

1.1.1 Fire，explosion 火灾与爆炸

 .1 Vessel on fire（after explosion）in position...

 .2 I am on fire in position...

 .3 What is on fire？

  .3.1 Engine room on fire.

  .3.2 Hold（s）on fire.

  .3.3 （Deck）cargo on fire.

  .3.4 Superstructure on fire.

  .3.5 Accommodation on fire.

  .3.6 ... on fire.

 .4 Are dangerous goods on fire？

  .4.1 Yes，oil/... on fire.

  .4.2 No，dangerous goods not on fire.

 .5 Is danger of explosion？

  .5.1 Yes，danger of explosion.

  .5.2 No，no danger of explosion.

 .6 What is damage？

  .6.1 No damage.

  .6.2 No power supply.

  .6.3 I am not under command.

  .6.4 I am making water.

  .6.5 I am sinking.

 .7 Is fire under control？

  .7.1 Yes，fire under control.

  .7.2 No，fire not under control（fire spreading）.

 .8 Can you get fire under control？

  .8.1 Yes，I can get fire under control.

  .8.2 No，I cannot get fire under control.

 .9 Is smoke toxic？

  .9.1 Yes，smoke toxic.

.9.2   No, smoke not toxic.

.10   What kind of assistance do you require?

    .10.1   I require foam extinguishers.

    .10.2   I require CO_2 extinguishers.

    .10.3   I require fire pumps.

    .10.4   I require fire fighting assistance.

    .10.5   I require …

    .10.6   I do not require assistance.

.11   Report injured persons.

    .11.1   No person injured.

    .11.2   Number of injured persons/casualties: …

    .11.3   I require medical assistance.

1.1.2   Flooding 进水

.1   I have leak below water line.

.2   I am making water.

.3   Can you stop leak?

    .3.1   Yes, I can stop leak.

    .3.2   No, I cannot stop leak.

.4   Can you control flooding?

    .4.1   Yes, I can control flooding.

    .4.2   No, I cannot control flooding.

.5   What kind of assistance do you require?

    .5.1   I require pumps.

    .5.2   I require divers.

    .5.3   I require …

.6   I will send pumps.

    .6.1   I will send divers.

    .6.2   I will send …

    .6.3   I cannot send …

.7   I have dangerous list.

.8   I am in critical condition.

.9   How many compartments flooded?

    .9.1   … compartments flooded.

.10   Flooding under control.

.11   Can you proceed without assistance?

    .11.1   Yes, I can proceed without assistance.

    .11.2   No, I cannot proceed without assistance.

.12   I require escort.

1.1.3　Collision 碰撞

　　.1　I have collided with MV …

　　　　.1.1　I have collided with unknown vessel/object.

　　　　.1.2　I have collided with …(name) light vessel.

　　　　.1.3　I have collided with seamark …(charted name).

　　　　.1.4　I have collided with iceberg.

　　　　.1.5　I have collided with …

　　.2　What is damage?

　　　　.2.1　I have minor/major damage above/below water line.

　　　　.2.2　Propeller/rudder damaged.

　　　　.2.3　I can only proceed at slow speed.

　　　　.2.4　I am not under command.

　　.3　Can you repair damage?

　　　　.3.1　Yes, I can repair damage.

　　　　.3.2　No, I cannot repair damage.

　　.4　What kind of assistance do you require?

　　　　.4.1　I require escort.

　　　　.4.2　I require tugs.

　　　　.4.3　I require …

1.1.4　Grounding 搁浅

　　.1　Are you aground?

　　　　.1.1　Yes, aground in position …

　　　　.1.2　Yes, aground on rocky bottom.

　　　　.1.3　Yes, aground on soft bottom.

　　.2　I went aground in position … require assistance.

　　.3　I went aground at high water.

　　.4　I went aground at half water.

　　.5　I went aground at low water.

　　.6　What part is aground?

　　　　.6.1　Aground forward.

　　　　.6.2　Aground amidships.

　　　　.6.3　Aground aft.

　　　　.6.4　Aground full length.

　　.7　What kind of assistance do you require?

　　　　.7.1　I require pumps.

　　　　.7.2　I require escort.

　　　　.7.3　I require tugs.

　　　　.7.4　I require …

　　　　.7.5　I do not require assistance.

.8   Uncharted rocks in position …

.9   Risk of grounding at low water.

.10   Can you jettison cargo forward/aft to refloat?

    .10.1   Yes, I can jettison cargo forward/aft.

    .10.2   No, I cannot jettison cargo.

.11   Attention! Do not jettison IMO-class cargo.

.12   When do you expect to refloat?

    .12.1   I expect to refloat at …

    .12.2   I expect to refloat when tide rises.

    .12.3   I expect to refloat when weather improves.

    .12.4   I expect to refloat when draft decreases.

    .12.5   I expect to refloat with tug assistance.

.14   Can you beach?

    .14.1   Yes, I can/will beach in position …

    .14.2   No, I cannot beach.

1.1.5   List, danger of capsizing 横倾与倾覆危险

.1   I have heavy list to port side/starboard side.

.2   I have heavy list due to flooding.

.3   I have heavy list due to shifting cargo.

.4   List increasing.

    .4.1   List decreasing.

.5   I am in danger of capsizing.

.6   Can you transfer cargo/bunkers to stop listing?

    .6.1   Yes, I can transfer cargo/bunkers.

    .6.2   No, I cannot transfer cargo/bunkers.

    .6.3   I have transferred cargo/bunkers to stop listing.

.7   Listing stopped after transferring.

    .7.1   Listing did not stop after transferring.

.8   Can you jettison cargo to stop listing?

    .8.1   Yes, I can jettison cargo.

    .8.2   No, I cannot jettison cargo.

    .8.3   I have jettisoned cargo to stop listing.

.9   Listing stopped after jettisoning.

    .9.1   Listing did not stop after jettisoning.

.10   Can you beach?

    .10.1   Yes, I can/will beach in position …

    .10.2   No, I cannot beach.

1.1.6   Sinking 沉没

.1   I am sinking in position … after collision.

.1.1 I am sinking after grounding.

.1.2 I am sinking after flooding.

.1.3 I am sinking after explosion.

.1.4 I am sinking after …

.2 I require assistance.

.3 I proceed to your assistance.

.4 I expect to reach you within … hours/at … UTC.

1.1.7 Disabled and adrift 失控与漂航

.1 I am not under command in position …

.2 I am adrift near position …

.3 I am drifting at … knots to … degrees.

.4 What kind of assistance do you require?

.4.1 I require tug assistance.

.4.2 I require…

1.1.8 Armed attack/piracy 武装袭击/海盗

.1 I am under attack of pirates.

.1.1 MV … under attack of pirates.

.1.2 I require assistance.

.1.3 MV … requires assistance.

.2 I was under attack of pirates.

.2.1 MV … was under attack of pirates.

.3 What kind of assistance do you require?

.3.1 I require medical assistance.

.3.2 I require navigational assistance.

.3.3 I require tug assistance.

.3.4 I require military assistance.

.3.5 I require escort.

.3.6 I require …

.4 What is damage?

.4.1 I have no damage.

.4.2 I have major/minor damage to navigational instruments.

.4.3 I am not under command.

.5 Can you proceed?

.5.1 Yes, I can/will proceed.

.5.2 No, I cannot/will not proceed.

1.1.9 Undesignated distress 其他险情

.1 I have problems.

.2 What problems have you?

.2.1 I have problems with cargo.

.2.2　I have problems with machinery.

.2.3　I have problems with navigation.

.2.4　I have problems with mass disease.

.2.5　I have problems with …

.3　What kind of assistance do you require?

　.3.1　I require …

1.1.10　Abandoning vessel 弃船

.1　I must abandon vessel after collision in position …

　.1.1　I must abandon vessel after grounding in position …

　.1.2　I must abandon vessel after flooding in position …

　.1.3　I must abandon vessel after explosion in position …

　.1.4　I must abandon vessel after piracy in position …

　.1.5　I must abandon vessel after … in position …

1.2　Search and rescue communication 搜救通信

1.2.1　Distress/urgency messages 遇险与紧急语句

.1　I require assistance.

.2　I proceed to your assistance.

.3　What is your position?

　.3.1　My position …

.4　What is your present course and speed?

　.4.1　My present course … degrees, my speed … knots.

.5　How many persons on board?

　.5.1　Number of persons on board: …

.6　Report injured persons.

　.6.1　No person injured.

　.6.2　Number of injured persons/casualties: …

.7　Will you abandon vessel?

　.7.1　I will not abandon vessel.

　.7.2　I will abandon vessel at …

.8　How many lifeboats/life rafts will you launch?

　.8.1　I will launch … lifeboats/liferafts.

.9　How many persons will stay on board?

　.9.1　No person will stay on board.

　.9.2　… persons will stay on board.

.10　What is weather situation in your position?

　.10.1　Wind … (direction) force Beaufort …

　.10.2　Visibility … meters/nautical miles.

　.10.3　Sea/Swell … meters from … (compass points).

　.10.4　Current … knots to … degrees.

.11 Are there dangers to navigation?

    .11.1 No, no dangers to navigation.

    .11.2 Yes, uncharted rocks.

    .11.3 Yes, drifting ice.

    .11.4 Yes, abnormally low tides.

    .11.5 Yes, drifting mines.

    .11.6 Yes, …

    .11.7 Proceed with caution.

1.2.2 Acknowledgement and/or relay of SAR-messages 收到和/或转继搜救语句

.1 Received MAYDAY from MV … at UTC on channel…/frequency …

.2 Vessel in position … on fire/had explosion.

    .2.1 Vessel in position … flooded.

    .2.2 Vessel in position … has collided (with …).

    .2.3 Vessel in position … listing/in danger of capsizing.

    .2.4 Vessel in position … sinking.

    .2.5 Vessel in position … disabled and adrift.

    .2.6 Vessel in position … abandoned.

.3 Vessel requires assistance.

.4 Received your MAYDAY.

    .4.1 My position …

    .4.2 I proceed/MV … proceeds to your assistance.

.5 When will you/assistance arrive?

    .5.1 I/assistance will arrive within … hours/at … UTC.

1.2.3 Performing/coordinating SAR-operations 搜救与协调作业

.1 This is MV …

    .1.1 I am/will act as Coordinator Surface Search.

    .1.2 I will show following signals/lights.

.2 Can you proceed to distress position?

    .2.1 Yes, I can proceed to distress position.

    .2.2 No, I cannot proceed to distress position.

.3 When will you arrive at distress position?

    .3.1 I will arrive at distress position within … hours/at … UTC.

.4 The position given in MAYDAY not correct.

    .4.1 Correct position …

.5 Vessels are advised to proceed to position … to start rescue.

.6 Carry out search pattern … starting at … UTC.

    .6.1 Carrying out search pattern … starting at … UTC.

.7 Initial course … degrees, search speed … knots.

.8 Carry out radar search.

.8.1　　Carrying out radar search.

.9　　MV … is allocated track number …

.10　　MV/MVs … adjust interval between vessels to …kilometres/nautical miles.

　　　.10.1　　Interval between vessels adjusted to … kilometres/nautical miles.

.11　　Adjust track spacing to …kilometres/nautical miles.

　　　.11.1　　Track spacing adjusted to … kilometres/nautical miles.

.12　　Search speed now … knots.

.13　　Alter course to … degrees（at … UTC）.

　　　.13.1　　Course altered to … degrees（at … UTC）.

.14　　Alter course for next leg of track now/at … UTC.

　　　.14.1　　Course altered for next leg of track.

.15　　We resume search in position …

.16　　Crew has abandoned vessel.

.17　　Keep sharp lookout for lifeboats/liferafts.

1.2.4　　Finishing with SAR-operations 搜救作业的结束

.1　　What is result of search?

　　　.1.1　　Result of search negative.

.2　　Continue search in position …

.3　　Sighted vessel in position …

　　　.3.1　　Sighted derelict in position …

　　　.3.2　　Sighted lifeboats/liferafts in position …

　　　.3.3　　Sighted lifejackets in position …

　　　.3.4　　Sighted oil slick in position …

　　　.3.5　　Sighted … in position.

.4　　Can you pick up survivors?

　　　.4.1　　Yes, I can pick up survivors.

　　　.4.2　　No, I cannot pick up survivors.

.5　　I/MV … will proceed to pick up survivors.

　　　.5.1　　Stand by at lifeboats/liferafts.

.6　　Picked up … survivors in position …

　　　.6.1　　Picked up … lifejackets in position …

　　　.6.2　　Picked up … in position …

.7　　Picked up lifeboat/liferaft with … casualties in position …

.8　　Picked up … casualties in lifejackets in position …

.9　　Survivors in bad/good condition.

.10　　Do you require medical assistance?

　　　.10.1　　Yes, I require medical assistance.

　　　.10.2　　No, I do not require medical assistance.

.11　　Try to obtain information from survivors.

.12 There are still .../no more lifeboats/liferafts with survivors.

.13 Total number of persons on board was ...

.14 Rescued all persons/... persons.

.15 You/MV ... can stop search and proceed.

.16 There is no hope to rescue more persons.

.17 We finish with SAR operations.

1.3 Person overboard 人员落水

.1 I/MV ... lost person overboard in position ...

.2 Assist with search in vicinity of position ...

.3 All ships in vicinity of position ... keep sharp lookout and report to ...

.4 I am/MV ... proceeding for assistance and, arriving at ... UTC.

.5 Search in vicinity of position ...

    .5.1 I am/MV ... searching in vicinity of position ...

.6 Aircraft arriving within ... hours to assist in search.

.7 Can you continue search?

    .7.1 Yes, I can continue the search.

    .7.2 No, I cannot continue search.

.8 Stop search and return to base

    .8.1 Search stopped—returning to base.

.9 Stop search and proceed your voyage.

    .9.1 Search stopped—proceeding my voyage.

.10 What is result of search?

    .10.1 Result of search negative.

.11 I/MV ... located person in position ...

.12 I/MV ... picked up person in position ...

.13 Person picked up is crewmember of MV ...

.14 What is condition of person?

    .14.1 Condition of person bad/good.

    .14.2 Person dead.

1.4 Requesting medical assistance 请求医疗协助

.1 I require medical assistance.

.2 What kind of assistance do you require?

    .2.1 I require boat for hospital transfer.

    .2.2 I require radio medical advice.

    .2.3 I require helicopter with doctor.

    .2.4 I require helicopter to pick up person.

.3 I will arrange for boat.

    .3.1 I will arrange for medical advice on channel .../frequency ...

    .3.2 I will arrange for helicopter.

.4   Boat/Helicopter will arrive within … hours/at … UTC.

.5   Have you doctor on board?

    .5.1   Yes, I have doctor on board.

    .5.2   No, I have no doctor on board.

.6   Can you make rendezvous in position … ?

    .6.1   Yes, I can make rendezvous in position … within … hours/at … UTC.

    .6.2   No, I cannot make rendezvous.

.7   I will send boat/helicopter to pick up doctor.

.8   Transfer person to my vessel by boat/helicopter.

.9   Transfer of person not possible.

2   Urgency communication 紧急通信

2.1   Safety of a vessel, aircraft or other vehicle 船舶、飞机与其他交通工具的安全

2.1.1   Engine and equipment 主机与设备

.1   I am not under command in position …

.2   What problems do you have?

    .2.1   I have problems with main engine.

    .2.2   I have problems with steering gear.

    .2.3   I have problems with propeller.

    .2.4   I have problems with …

.3   I am manoeuvring with difficulty.

.4   Keep clear of me.

.5   Navigate with caution.

.6   Vessel not under command in position …

.7   I require tug assistance.

.8   I try to proceed without assistance.

.9   I require escort.

.10   Keep in contact on VHF channel …

.11   Aircraft made forced landing near position …

.12   Vessels in vicinity of position … keep sharp lookout (for …).

2.1.2   Cargo 货物

.1   I have lost dangerous substance of IMO Class … in position …

    .1.1   MV … lost dangerous substance of IMO Class … in position …

.2   Containers with dangerous substance of IMO Class … adrift near position …

    .2.1   Barrels/drums with dangerous substance of IMO Class … adrift near position…

    .2.2   Bags with dangerous substance of IMO Class … adrift near position …

    .2.3   … with dangerous substance of IMO Class … adrift near position …

.3   I am/MV … spilling dangerous substance of IMO Class … in position …

.4   I am/MV … spilling crude oil in position …

.5   Require oil clearance assistance danger of pollution imminent.

    .5.1   MV … in position … requires oil clearance assistance danger of pollution.

.6   I am/MV … dangerous source of radiation.

2.1.3   Ice damage 冰损

.1   I have/MV … has major damage above/below waterline.

.2   Extent of damage unknown.

.3   What kind of assistance do you require？

    .3.1   I require medical assistance.

    .3.2   I require tug assistance.

    .3.3   I require icebreaker assistance.

    .3.4   I require escort.

.4   I have/MV … has stability problems due to heavy icing.

.5   Can you proceed without assistance？

    .5.1   Yes, I can proceed without assistance.

    .5.2   No, I cannot proceed without assistance.

.6   Stand by on VHF channel …

    .6.1   Standing by on VHF channel …

3   Safety communication 安全通信

3.1   Warnings involving meteorological and hydrological conditions 气象与水文警报

3.1.1   Winds, storms, tropical storms, sea state 风、风暴、热带风暴与海况

.1   What is wind direction and force in your position/in position … ？

    .1.1   Wind direction …（compass points）, force Beaufort … in my position/in position … .

.2   Is wind backing/veering？

    .2.1   Wind backing/veering.

.3   What wind direction and force is expected in my position/in position … ？

    .3.1   Wind in your position/in position …expected from … direction（s）, force Beaufort …

    .3.2   Wind in your position/in position …expected variable.

.4   Is wind expected to increase/decrease？

    .4.1   Wind expected to increase/decrease.

.5   What is latest gale warning？

    .5.1   Latest gale warning is as follows：Gale warning. Winds at … UTC in area …（met.area）from direction …（compass points）and force Beaufort … backing/veering to …（compass points）.

.6   What is latest tropical storm warning？

    .6.1   Latest tropical storm warning is as follows：

    （Standard tropical storm warning）（标准热带风暴警报）

    Tropical storm warning at … UTC. Hurricane…（name）/tropical cyclone/tornado/willywilly/typhoon... with central pressure of ... millibars located in position ... Present movement... (compass points) at ... knots. Winds of ... knots within radius of ... miles of center. Seas over ... meters. Further information on VHF channel .../frequency ...

    .7   What is atmospheric pressure in your position/in position ... ?

        .7.1   Atmospheric pressure ... millibars.

    .8   What is barometric change in your position/in position ... ?

        .8.1   Barometric change ... millibars per hour.

        .8.2   Barometric change... millibars within last ... hours.

        .8.3   Barometer steady.

        .8.4   Barometer dropping (rapidly).

        .8.5   Barometer rising (rapidly).

    .9   What is position, path and speed of advance of tropical storm... (name)?

        .9.1   Position of tropical storm ...(name) ..., path... (compass points), speed of advance ... knots.

    .10   What maximum winds are expected in storm area?

        .10.1   Maximum winds of ... knots expected in storm area.

        .10.2   Maximum winds of ... knots expected within radius of ... kilometers/miles of center.

        .10.3   Maximum winds of ... knots expected in ... safe/dangerous semicircle.

    .11   What is sea state in your position/in position ... ?

        .11.1   Sea/swell in my position/in position ... meters from... (compass points).

    .12   Is sea state expected to change (within next hours)?

        .12.1   No, sea state not expected to change (within next hours).

        .12.2   Yes, sea/swell of ... meters from ... (compass points) expected (within next hours).

        .12.3   Tsunami/abnormal wave expected by ... UTC.

3.1.2 Restricted visibility (due to mist/fog, precipitation)能见度受限(因霾、雾或降水所致)

    .1   What is visibility in your position/in position ... ?

        .1.1   Visibility in my position/in position ... meters/nautical miles

        .1.2   Visibility reduced by mist/fog/snow/dust/rain.

        .1.3   Visibility increasing/decreasing/variable.

    .2   Is visibility expected to change in my position/in position ... (within next hours)?

        .2.1   No, visibility not expected to change in your position/in position... (within next hours).

        .2.2   Yes, visibility expected to increase/decrease to ... meters/nautical miles in your position/in position ... （within next hours）.

.2.3　Yes，visibility expected to be variable between ... meters/nautical miles in your position/in position ... （within next hours）.

3.1.3　Ice 冰情

.1　What is latest ice information？

.1.1　Ice warning. Ice/Iceberg(s) located in position ... /reported in area around ...

.1.2　No ice located in position .../reported in area around ...

.2　What kind of ice was located in position .../reported in area around ... ?

.2.1　I/MV ...located ... in position .../reported ... in area around ...

.3　What ice situation is expected in my position/area around ... ?

.3.1　Ice situation expected/not expected to change in your position/area around ...

.3.2　Ice situation expected to improve/deteriorate in your position/area around ...

.3.3　Ice expected to break up in your position/area around ...

.3.4　Ice expected to open in your position/area around ...

.3.5　Ice expected to drift away in your position/area around ...

.3.6　Ice expected to freeze together in your position/area around ...

.3.7　Thickness of ice expected to increase/decrease in your position/area around ...

.4　Navigation dangerous in area around ... due to floating ice/pack ice/iceberg(s).

.5　Navigation in area around ... without icebreaker assistance only possible for highpowered vessels of strong construction.

.6　Navigation in area around ...only possible with icebreaker assistance.

.7　Area around ... temporarily closed for navigation.

.8　Danger of icing in area around ...

3.1.4　Volcanic activities including earth and seaquakes 火山爆发、地震与海啸

.1　Volcanic activities expected in position .../area around ...

.2　Earthquake/Seaquake expected in position .../area around ...

.3　Tsunami/Abnormal wave expected in position .../area around ...

.4　Move to high seas—keep off coast.

3.1.5　Abnormal tides 异常潮汐

.1　Present tide ... meters above datum in position ...

.2　Tide ... above/below prediction.

.3　Tide rising/falling.

.4　Wait until high/low water.

.5　Abnormally high/low tides expected in position ...at about ... UTC/within ... hours.

.6　Is sufficient depth of water in position ... ?

　　.6.1　Yes, sufficient depth of water in position ...

　　.6.2　No, not sufficient depth of water in position ...

　　.6.3　Depth of water ... meters in position ...

.7　My draft ... meters—can I enter/pass ... (charted name of place) ?

　　.7.1　Yes, you can enter/pass (charted name of place).

　　.7.2　No, you cannot enter/pass (charted name of place) at present—wait until ... UTC.

.8　Charted depth of water increased/decreased by ... meters due to sea state/winds.

3.2　Navigational Warnings 航海警告

3.2.1　Land-marks or Sea-marks 陆标与海标

3.2.1.1　Defects 故障

.1　...(charted name of light/buoy) ... (position) unlit.

.2　...(charted name of light/buoy) ... (position) unreliable.

.3　...(charted name of buoy) ... (position) damaged.

　　.3.1　...(charted name of light) ... (position) destroyed.

.4　...(charted name of buoy) ... (position) off station.

.5　...(charted name of buoy) ... (position) missing.

.6　For major lights only: Fog signal at ... (charted name of light) ... (position) inoperative.

3.2.1.2　Alterations 变更

.1　...(charted name of light/buoy) ... (position) changed to ... (full characteristics).

.2　...(charted name of light/buoy) ... (position) temporarily changed to... (full characteristics).

.3　...(charted name of buoy) ... (position) temporarily removed (when appropriate).

.4　...(charted name of light) ... (position) temporarily discontinued (when appropriate).

3.2.1.3　New and moved 新建和移动

.1　... (charted name of light/buoy) ... (full characteristics) established in position ...

.2　... (charted name of light) ... (full characteristics) re-established in position ...

.3　...(charted name of light/buoy) moved ... (in miles and decimal miles) ... (direction) to position ...

3.2.2　Drifting objects 漂流物

.1　Super buoy adrift in vicinity ... (position) at ... (date time if known).

.2　Hazardous mine adrift in vicinity ... (position) at ... (date time if known).

.3　Unlit derelict vessel adrift in vicinity … （position） at … （date time if known）.

.4　…（number） containers adrift in vicinity …（position） at …（date time if known）.

3.2.3　Electronic navaids 电子助航设施

.1　GPS Satellite …（number） unusable from … （date and time） to …（date and time）. Cancel one hour after time of restoration.

.2　LORAN station …（name number master/slave） off air from …（date and time） to …（date and time）. Cancel one hour after time of restoration.

.3　DECCA …（identify chain and colour） off air from …（date and time） to … （date and time）. Cancel one hour after time of restoration.

.4　RACON … （name of station） in position … off air from …（date and time） to…（date and time）. Cancel one hour after time of restoration.

3.2.4　Sea bottom characteristics, wrecks 海底底质与沉船

（Use REPORTED when position is unconfirmed, and use LOCATED when position has been confirmed by survey or other means.）

（若位置不确,请使用 REPORTED 一词表明;若位置经测量或其他方式证实,用 LOCAT-ED 一词表明。）

.1　Uncharted reef/rock/shoal reported in position …

.1.1　Dangerous wreck/obstruction located in position …

.2　Dangerous wreck in position… marked by … （type）buoy …（distance in kilometres/nautical miles ） …（direction）.

3.2.5　Miscellaneous 其他

3.2.5.1　Cable, pipeline and seismic/hydrographic operations 电缆、管线、地震勘探和水文作业

.1　Cable/Pipeline operations by … （vessel） in vicinity/along line joining … （position） from …（date time） to …（date time）. Wide berth requested （if requested）. Contact via VHF channel …（number） （if requested）.

.2　Seismic survey/hydrographic operations by …（vessel） from …（date time） to…（date time） in …（position）. Wide berth requested （if requested）. Contact via VHF channel … （number） （if requested）.

.3　Survey vessel …（name） towing …（length） seismic cable along line joining/ in area bound by/vicinity …（position） from …（date time） to …（date time）. Wide berth requested. （if requested）. Contact via VHF channel … （number） （if requested）.

.4　Hazardous operations by …（vessel） in area bound by/vicinity … （position） from … （date time） to …（date time）. Wide berth requested （if requested）. Contact via VHF channel …（date time） （if requested）.

.5　Current meters/hydrographic instruments moored in …（position）. Wide berth requested （if requested）.

3.2.5.2 Diving operations, tows 潜水与拖带作业

 .1 Diving operations by vessel … (name) from …(date time) to …(date time) in position … Wide berth requested (if requested).

 .2 Difficult tow from …(port of departure)on … (date) to … (destination) on … (date). Wide berth requested.

 .3 Dredging operations by vessel …(name) from … (date time) to … (date time) in …(position). Wide berth requested (if requested).

3.2.5.3 Tanker transshipment 油船过驳

 .1 Transshipment of …(kind of cargo) in position … Wide berth requested.

 .2 I am/MT … spilling oil/chemicals/… in position … Wide berth requested.

 .3 I am/LNG-tanker … leaking gas in position…—do not pass to windward.

 .4 Oil clearance operations near MT … in position … Wide berth requested.

3.2.5.4 Off-shore installations, rig moves 近岸设施与钻井装置的移动

 .1 Platform …(name/number if available) reported/established in position… at … (date and time).Wide berth requested (if requested).

 .2 Platform …(name/number if available) removed from …(position) on … (date).

 .3 Pipeline/Platform …(name/number if available) in position … spilling oil/ leaking gas. Wide berth requested.

 .4 Derelict platform …(name/number if available) being removed from …(position) at … (date time). Wide berth requested.

3.2.5.5 Defective locks or bridges 船闸与桥梁故障

 .1 Lock …(name) defective.

  .1.1 For entering …(charted name of place) use lock …(name).

 .2 Lock/Bridge … (name) defective.

  .2.1 Avoid this area—no possibility for vessels to turn.

3.2.5.6 Military operations 军事演习

 .1 Gunnery/Rocket firing/Missile/Torpedo/Underwater ordnance exercises in area bounded by …(positions) from … (date and time) to… (date and time). Wide berth requested (if requested).

 .2 Mine clearing operations from …(date time) to …(date time) in area bound by … (positions). Wide berth requested. Contact via VHF channel … (number) (if requested).

3.2.5.7 Fishery 渔业作业

 .1 Small fishing boats in area around …/within … nautical miles of me— navigate with caution.

 .2 Is fishing gear ahead of me?

  .2.1 No, no fishing gear ahead of you.

  .2.2 Yes, fishing gear with buoys/without buoys ahead of you—navigate with caution.

   .2.3   Yes, fishing gear in position .../area around ...—navigate with caution.

.3   Fishing gear fouled my propeller(s).

.4   You have caught my fishing gear.

.5   Advise you to recover your fishing gear.

.6   Fishing in area ... prohibited.

.7   You are approaching prohibited fishing area.

3.3   Environmental protection communication 环境保险通信

.1   Located oil spill in position ... extending ... (length and width in meters) to ... (compass points)... Located oil spill in your wake.

   .2.1   I have accidental spillage of oil/...

.3   Can you stop spillage?

   .3.1   Yes, I can stop spillage.

   .3.2   No, I cannot stop spillage.

.4   What kind of assistance do you require?

   .4.1   I require oil clearance assistance.

   .4.2   I require floating booms/oil dispersants/...

.5   Stay in vicinity of pollution and cooperate with oil clearance team.

.6   ... (number) barrels/drums/containers with IMDG Code marks reported adrift near position.....

.7   Located vessel dumping chemicals/waste/... in position ...

   .7.1   Located vessel incinerating chemicals/waste/... in position ...

.8   Can you identify polluter?

   .8.1   Yes, I can identify polluter—polluter MV ...

   .8.2   No, I cannot identify polluter.

.9   What is course and speed of polluter?

   .9.1   Course of polluter ... degrees, speed ... knots.

   .9.2   Polluter left scene.

4   Pilotage 引航业务

4.1   Pilot request 申请引航员

.1   Must I take pilot?

   .1.1   Yes, you must take pilot—pilotage compulsory.

   .1.2   No, you need not take pilot.

.2   Do you require pilot?

   .2.1   Yes, I require pilot.

   .2.2   No, I do not require pilot—I am holder of Pilotage Exemption Certificate (No. ...).

   .2.2.1   You are exempted from pilotage.

.3   Do you require pilot at ...(name) Pilot Station?

.3.1 Yes, I require pilot at … (name) Pilot Station.

.3.2 No, I do not require pilot at … (name) Pilot Station—I require pilot in position …

.4   What is your ETA at …(name) Pilot Station in local time?

　　.4.1 My ETA at …(name) Pilot Station … hours local time.

.5   What is local time?

　　.5.1 Local time … hours.

.6   What is your present position?

　　.6.1 My position …

.7   What is your distance from …(name) Pilot Station?

　　.7.1 My distance from …(name) Pilot Station … kilometres/nautical miles.

.8   Is pilot boat on station?

　　.8.1 Yes, pilot boat on station.

　　.8.2 No, pilot boat not on station.

　　.8.3 Pilot boat on station at … hours local time.

.9   In what position can I take pilot?

　　.9.1 Take pilot in position … at … hours local time.

　　.9.2 Take pilot near … at … hours local time.

.10   When will pilot embark?

　　.10.1 Pilot will embark at … hours local time.

.11   Pilot coming to you.

.12   Pilot boat approaching your vessel.

.13   Keep pilot boat on port side.

.14   Keep pilot boat on starboard side.

.15   What is your freeboard?

　　.15.1 My freeboard … meters.

.16   Stop in present position and wait for pilot.

.17   Change to VHF channel … for pilot transfer.

.18   Stand by on VHF channel … until pilot transfer completed.

.19   Pilotage at …(name) Pilot Station suspended until … (date and local time).

.20   Pilotage at …(name) Pilot Station resumed.

.21   Pilot cannot embark at … (name) Pilot Station due to …

.22   Do you accept shore-based navigational assistance from pilot?

　　.22.1 Yes, I accept shore-based navigational assistance from pilot.

　　　　.22.1.1 I stay in position … until …

.23   You may navigate by yourself (or wait for pilot at … buoy).

.24   Follow pilot boat inward where pilot will embark.

4.2 **Embarking/Disembarking pilot 引航员上下船**

.1 Stand by pilot ladder.

.2 Rig pilot ladder on port side … meters above water.

.3 Rig pilot ladder on starboard side … meters above water.

.4 Pilot ladder on port side.

.5 Pilot ladder on starboard side.

.6 You must rig another pilot ladder

.7 Pilot ladder unsafe.

.8 What is wrong with pilot ladder?

    .8.1 Pilot ladder has broken steps.

    .8.2 Pilot ladder has loose steps.

    .8.3 Pilot ladder has broken spreaders.

    .8.4 Pilot ladder has spreaders too short.

    .8.5 Pilot ladder too far aft.

    .8.6 Pilot ladder too far forward.

.9 Move pilot ladder … meters aft.

.10 Move pilot ladder … meters forward.

.11 Move pilot ladder clear of discharge.

.12 Rig accommodation ladder in combination with pilot ladder.

.13 Rig pilot ladder alongside hoist.

.14 Put lights on at pilot ladder.

.15 Man ropes required/not required.

.16 Have heaving line ready at pilot ladder.

.17 Correct list of vessel.

.18 Make lee on your port side.

.19 Make lee on your starboard side.

.20 Steer … degrees to make lee.

.21 Keep sea on your port quarter.

.22 Keep sea on your starboard quarter.

.23 Make boarding speed of … knots.

.24 Stop engine until pilot boat is clear.

.25 Put helm hard to port.

.26 Put helm hard to starboard.

.27 Alter course to port—pilot boat cannot clear vessel.

.28 Alter course to starboard—pilot boat cannot clear vessel.

.29 Put ahead engine.

.30 Put astern engine.

.31 Embarkation not possible.

    .31.1 Boarding arrangements do not comply with SOLAS Regulations.

    .31.2 Vessel not suited for pilot ladder.

4.3 **Tug assistance** 拖船协助

.1 How many tugs do you require?

    .1.1 I require … tug(s).

.2 Must I take tug(s)?

    .2.1 Yes, you must take … tug(s).

    .2.2 No, you need not take tug(s).

.3 How many tugs must I take?

    .3.1 You must take … tug(s) according to Port Regulations.

    .3.2 You must take … tug(s) fore and … tug(s) aft.

.4 I will order tug(s).

.5 In what position will tug(s) meet me?

    .5.1 Tug(s) will meet you in position … at … local time.

    .5.2 Wait for tug(s) in position …

.6 Must I take my towing lines?

    .6.1 Yes, you must take your towing lines.

    .6.2 No, you must take towing lines of tug.

.7 Tug services suspended until …(date and local time).

.8 Tug services resumed on …(date) at …local time.

5 **Specials** 特殊作业

5.1 **Helicopter operation** 直升机作业

(H：from helicopter 发自直升机；V：from vessel 发自船舶)

.1 V：I require helicopter.

    .1.1 V：I require helicopter to pick up persons.

    .1.2 V：I require helicopter with doctor.

    .1.3 V：I require helicopter with raft.

    .1.4 V：I require helicopter with …

.2 H：MV …, I will drop …

.3 H：MV …, are you ready for helicopter?

    .3.1 V：Yes, ready for helicopter.

    .3.2 V：No, not ready for helicopter (yet).

    .3.3 V：Ready for helicopter in … minutes.

.4 H：MV …, helicopter is on way to you.

.5 H：MV …, what is your position.

    .5.1 V：My position …

.6 H：MV …, what is your course and speed.

    .6.1 V：My course … degrees, speed … knots.

.7 H：MV …, make identification signals.

.8 V：Making identification signals.

    .8.1 V：Making identification signals by smoke (buoy).

.8.2　V：Making identification signals by search light.

.8.3　V：Making identification signals by flags.

.8.4　V：Making identification signals by signalling lamp.

.9　H：MV …, you are identified.

.10　H：MV …, what is relative wind direction in degrees and knots.

　　.10.1　V：Relative wind direction … degrees and … knots.

.11　H：MV …, keep wind on starboard bow.

　　.11.1　V：Keeping wind on starboard bow.

.12　H：MV …, keep wind on port bow.

　　.12.1　V：Keeping wind on port bow.

.13　H：MV …, keep wind on starboard quarter.

　　.13.1　V：Keeping wind on starboard quarter.

.14　H：MV …, keep wind on port quarter.

　　.14.1　V：Keeping wind on port quarter.

.15　H：MV …, indicate landing area.

　　.15.1　V：Landing area …

.16　H：MV …, indicate pickup area.

　　.16.1　V：Pickup area …

.17　H：MV …, can I land on deck？

　　.17.1　V：Yes, you can land on deck.

　　.17.2　V：No, you cannot land on deck（yet）.

　　　　.17.2.1　V：You can land on deck in … minutes.

.18　H：MV …, I will use hoist.

　　.18.1　H：MV …, I will use rescue sling.

　　.18.2　H：MV …, I will use rescue basket.

　　.18.3　H：MV …, I will use rescue net.

　　.18.4　H：MV …, I will use rescue litter.

　　.18.5　H：MV …, I will use rescue seat.

　　.18.6　H：MV …, I will use double lift.

.19　V：I am ready to receive you.

.20　H：MV …, I am landing.

.21　H：MV …, I am starting operation.

.22　H：MV …, do not fix hoist cable.

.23　H：MV …, operation finished.

.24　H：MV …, I am taking off.

5.2　**Icebreaker operation 破冰船作业**

5.2.1　Icebreaker request 申请破冰船

　　.1　I am fast on ice in position …

　　.2　I require icebreaker assistance to …

.2.1　Icebreaker assistance will arrive at …hours local time/within … hours.

.2.2　Icebreaker assistance not available until …hours local time.

.2.3　Icebreaker assistance available only up to latitude… longitude….

.3　Icebreaker assistance suspended until…(date and local time).

.3.1　Icebreaker assistance suspended after sunset.

.3.2　Icebreaker assistance suspended until favourable weather conditions.

.3.3　Icebreaker assistance resumed at …hours local time.

5.2.2　Icebreaker assistance for convoy 破冰船护航

(Icebreaker commands applying to all the vessels in a convoy have to be immediately obeyed and confirmed consecutively by each vessel in turn. Icebreaker commands applying to a single vessel are confirmed only by that vessel, this applies also for close coupled towing.)

(破冰船发出的适用于所有被护航船舶的命令,各船应立即执行并按顺序确认;破冰船发出的适用于单船的命令,只由该船确认,此项要求亦适用于紧连拖带。)

.1　Icebreaker assistance for convoy will start now/at …hours local time..

.2　Stand by on VHF channel …

.2.1　Standing by on VHF channel …

.3　Keep lookout for sound and visual signals.

.3.1　Keeping lookout for sound and visual signals.

.4　Your place in convoy is number …

.4.1　My place in convoy number …

.5　MV … will follow you.

.5.1　MV … will follow me.

.6　You will follow MV …

.6.1　I will follow MV …

.7　Go ahead and follow me.

.7.1　Going ahead and following you.

.8　Do not follow me.

.8.1　I will not follow you.

.9　Proceed along ice channel.

.9.1　Proceeding along ice channel.

.10　Increase your speed.

.10.1　Increasing my speed.

.11　Reduce your speed.

.11.1　Reducing my speed.

.12　Reverse your engine(s).

.12.1　Reversing my engine(s).

.13　Full ahead.

.13.1　Full ahead.

.14　Stop engine(s).

.14.1　Engine(s) stopped.

.15　Keep distance of ... meters/cables between vessels.

　　.15.1　Keeping distance of ... meters/cables between vessels.

.16　Increase distance between vessels to ... meters/cables.

　　.16.1　Increasing distance between vessels to ... meters/cables.

.17　Reduce distance between vessels to ... meters/cables.

　　.17.1　Reducing distance between vessels to ... meters/cables.

.18　Stand by for receiving towing line.

　　.18.1　Standing by for receiving towing line.

.19　Stand by for let go towing line.

　　.19.1　Standing by for let go towing line.

.20　Switch on bow/stern search light

　　.20.1　Bow/stern search light switched on.

.21　Stay where you are.

　　.21.1　I will stay where I am.

.22　Icebreaker assistance for convoy finished.

　　.22.1　Open water ahead.

　　.22.2　Light ice condition ahead.

　　.22.3　Proceed by yourself (to area ...).

　　　　.22.3.1　Proceeding by myself (to area ...).

　　.23.4　Icebreaker ... will escort you.

5.2.3　Icebreaker assistance in close coupled towing 紧连拖带中破冰船的协助

.1　Stand by for close coupled towing.

　　.1.1　Standing by for close coupled towing.

.2　Veer out your anchors under hawsepipes.

　　.2.1　Anchors veered out under hawsepipes.

.3　Pass heaving lines through hawsepipes.

　　.3.1　Heaving lines passed through hawsepipes.

.4　Receive towing line on deck.

　　.4.1　Towing line received on deck.

.5　Lash together eyes of towing line with manila lashing.

　　.5.1　Eyes of towing line lashed with manila lashing.

.6　Fasten towing line on towing bitts.

　　.6.1　Towing line fastened on towing bitts.

.7　I start to draw your bow into stern notch of icebreaker.

.8　Stand by for cutting manila lashing if required.

　　.8.1　Standing by for cutting manila lashing if required.

.9　Keep yourself in centreplan of icebreaker.

　　.9.1　Keeping myself in centreplan of icebreaker.

6 Vessel Traffic Service Standard Phrases 船舶交通管理标准用语
Application of Message Markers 信息标识的使用

In order to especially facilitate shore-to-ship and ship-to-shore communication or radio communication in general or when one of the Standard Marine Communication Phrases will not fit the meaning desired, one of the following eight Message Markers may be used to increase the probability of the purpose of the message being properly understood.

为了方便进行岸—船、船—岸或一般无线电通信,或当《标准航海通信用语》不能表达所要表达的意义时,应使用下述 8 个信息标识之一,以增加准确理解相互意图的可能性。

It is at the discretion of the shore personnel or the ship's officer whether to use one of the message markers and if so which of them to apply depending on his/her qualified assessment of the situation. If used the message marker is to be spoken preceding the message or the corresponding part of the message. The IMO VTS Guidelines recommend that in any message directed to a vessel it should be clear whether the message contains information, advice, warning, or instruction and IMO Standard Marine Communication Phrases should be used where practicable.

是否使用信息标识完全由岸方人员或船方人员决定,而如果使用,则使用哪一个标识由各自对当时情况的判断决定。若使用信文标识,则信文标识应在句子之前或相应语段之前讲出。国际海事组织的交管指南建议,在对船方发出的语句中,必须明确其中是否包括信息、建议、警告或指示,而且应尽可能使用标准航海通信用语。

Message Markers 信息标识

(ⅰ) INSTRUCTION 指示

This indicates that the following message implies the intention of the sender to influence others by a Regulation.

这表示后文是发出者按规则对其他人员做出影响的意图。

Comment: This means that the sender, e.g. a VTS-Station or a naval vessel, must have the full authority to send such a message. The recipient has to follow this legally binding message unless she/he has contradictory safety reasons which then have to be reported to the sender.

评述:这表示发出者有发出该指示的绝对权威,如交管站、海军船舶。收受者必须执行此项具有法律约束作用的指示,除非具有有关安全的原因而不能执行此项指示,这时应将这种原因报告给指示发出者。

Example:"INSTRUCTION.(You must) alter course."

(ⅱ) ADVICE 建议

This indicates that the following message implies the intention of the sender to influence others by a Recommendation.

这表示后文是发出者按建议对其他人员做出影响的意图。

Comment: The decision whether to follow the ADVICE still stays with the recipient. One does not necessarily have to carry out the ADVICE, but should consider it very carefully.

评述:是否执行后文的建议则由收受者决定。收受者并不必须执行此项建议,但应作仔细考虑。

Example:"ADVICE. (Advise you) stand by on VHF channel six nine."

（iii）WARNING 警告

This indicates that the following message implies the intention of the sender to inform others about danger.

这表示后文是发出者向其他人员报告危险物的意图。

Comment：This means that any recipient of a WARNING should pay immediate attention to the danger mentioned. Consequences of a WARNING will be up to the recipient.

评述:这表示警告的收受者应立即注意所提及的危险物。对警告所采取的措施由收受者决定。

Example："WARNING. Obstruction in fairway."

（iv）INFORMATION 信息

This indicates that the following message is restricted to observed facts, situations, etc.

这表示后文是所观测到的事实或情况等。

Comment：This marker is preferably used for navigational and traffic information, etc. Consequences of an INFORMATION will be up to the recipient.

评述:此标识最好用以表示航海和交通等信息。对警告所采取的措施由收受者决定。

Example："INFORMATION. Tanker stop in area Cod End Bank due to poor visibility."

（v）QUESTION 问题

This indicates that the following message is of interrogative character.

这表示后文是具有疑问性。

Comment：The use of this marker removes any doubt on whether a question is being asked or statement being made, especially when interrogatives such as What, Where, Why, Who, How are additionally used at the beginning of the question. The recipient is expected to return an answer.

评述:此标识用以解除是提出问题还是做出陈述的疑问,特别是句首有疑问代词 What, Where, Why, Who, How 等时。收受者应做出回答。

Example："QUESTION. (What is) your draft?"

（vi）ANSWER 回答

This indicates that the following message is the reply to a previous answer.

这表示后文是所做出的回答。

Comment：Note that an answer should not contain another question.

评述:注意,回答中不应再包含一个问题。

Example："ANSWER. My maximum draft seven meters."

（vii）REQUEST 请求

This indicates that the following message is asking for action from others with respect to the vessel.

这表示后文是请求对方对本船采取一项行动。

Comment：The use of this marker is to signal：I want something to be arranged or provided, e.g. ship's stores requirements, tugs, permission, etc.

评述:使用本标识旨在表明:我要求对某事做出安排或提供某物,如要求提供船舶物料、提供拖船或提供许可。

Note：REQUEST must not be used involving navigation, or to modify COLREGs.

注意,REQUEST 一词不得用于有关航行的业务中,不得用于对避碰规则的更改。

Example：“REQUEST.（Please）supply bunkers.”

（viii）INTENTION 意图

This indicates that the following message informs others about immediate navigational action intended to be taken.

这表示后文是通知对方拟立即采取的航行行动。

Comment：The use of this message marker is logically restricted to messages announcing navigational actions by the vessel sending this message.

评述:本标识的使用限于发出船做出航行行动声明。

Example：“INTENTION. I will reduce speed.”

6.1　Phrases for acquiring and providing data for a traffic image 获取和提供交管信息的用语

6.1.1　Acquiring and providing routine traffic data 获取和提供一般航行资料

（The following phrases should normally be preceded by Message Markers：“QUESTION” “ANSWER”“INFORMATION”.）

（下述语句应加的信文标识为:“QUESTION”“ANSWER”“INFORMATION”。）

   .1　What is your name, call sign/identification?

      .1.1　My name …, call sign/identification …

   .2　What is your flag state?

      .2.1　My flag state …

   .3　What is your position?

      .3.1　My position …

   .4　What is your present course and speed?

      .4.1　My present course … degrees, speed … knots.

   .5　From what direction are you approaching?

      .5.1　I am approaching from …

   .6　What is your destination?

      .6.1　My destination …

   .7　What was your last port of call?

      .7.1　My last port of call …

   .8　What is your ETA in position … ?

      .8.1　My ETA … hours local time.

   .9　What is your ETD from … ?

      .9.1　My ETD from … hours local time.

   .10　What is your draft forward/aft?

      .10.1　My draft forward/aft … meters.

   .11　What is your maximum draft ?

.11.1　My maximum draft … meters.

.12　What is your freeboard？

　　.12.1　My freeboard … meters.

.13　What is your air draft？

　　.13.1　My air draft … meters.

.14　Are you underway？

　　.14.1　Yes, I am underway.

　　.14.2　No, I am not underway.

　　.14.3　I am ready to get underway.

.15　What is your full speed？

　　.15.1　My full speed … knots.

.16　What is your full manoeuvring speed？

　　.16.1　My full manoeuvring speed … knots.

.17　What is your cargo？

　　.17.1　My cargo …

.18　Do you carry any dangerous goods？

　　.18.1　Yes, I carry following dangerous goods：… kilogrammes/tonnes IMO

Class …

　　.18.2　No, I do not carry any dangerous goods.

.19　Do you have any deficiencies/restrictions？

　　.19.1　No, I have no deficiencies/restrictions.

　　.19.2　Yes, I have following deficiencies/restrictions：…

.20　MV … hampered by draft.

.21　Maximum permitted draft … meters.

.22　Do you have any list？

　　.22.1　Yes, I have list to port/starboard of … degrees.

　　.22.2　No, I have no list.

.23　Are you trimmed by the head？

　　.23.1　Yes, I am trimmed by the head by … meters.

　　.23.2　No, I am not trimmed by the head.

.24　Are you trimmed by the stern？

　　.24.1　Yes, I am trimmed by the stern by … meters.

　　.24.2　No, I am not trimmed by the stern.

.25　Are you on even keel？

　　.25.1　Yes, I am on even keel.

　　.25.2　No, I am trimmed by the head.

　　.25.3　No, I am trimmed by the stern.

6.1.2　Acquiring and providing distress traffic data 获取和提供遇险航行资料

（The following phrases should normally be preceded by Messages Markers：“WARNING”

"INFORMATION" "ADVICE" "REQUEST" "INTENTION" "QUESTION" "ANSWER".)

(下述语句应加的信文标识为："WARNING" "INFORMATION" "ADVICE" "REQUEST" "INTENTION" "QUESTION" "ANSWER"。)

Fire, explosion 火灾与爆炸

  .1 Vessel on fire (after explosion) in position …

    .1.1 MV … on fire in engine-room.

    .1.2 MV … on fire in holds.

    .1.3 MV … on fire in superstructure.

    .1.4 MV … on fire in accommodation.

  .2 Are dangerous goods on fire?

    .2.1 Yes, dangerous goods on fire.

    .2.2 No, dangerous goods not on fire.

  .3 Is danger of explosion?

    .3.1 Yes, danger of explosion.

    .3.2 No, no danger of explosion.

  .4 MV … no power supply.

  .5 MV … not under command.

  .6 MV … making water/sinking.

  .7 Is fire under control?

    .7.1 Yes, fire under control.

    .7.2 No, fire not under control (fire spreading).

  .8 What kind of assistance required?

    .8.1 MV … does not require assistance.

    .8.2 MV … requires fire fighting assistance.

    .8.3 MV … requires foam extinguishers.

    .8.4 MV … requires CO_2 extinguishers.

    .8.5 MV … requires fire pumps.

    .8.6 MV … requires …

  .9 Report injured persons.

    .9.1 No person injured.

    .9.2 Number of injured persons/casualties：…

  .10 MV … requires medical assistance.

Flooding 进水

  .11 MV … has leak below water line.

  .12 MV … making water.

  .13 MV … can stop leak.

    .13.1 MV … cannot stop leak.

  .14 MV … can control flooding.

    .14.1 MV … cannot control flooding.

.14.2　MV … requires pumps.

.14.3　MV … requires divers.

.14.4　MV … requires …

.15　I will send pumps/divers.

.15.1　I will send …

.15.2　I cannot send …

.16　MV … has dangerous list.

.17　MV … in critical condition.

.18　Flooding under control.

.19　MV … can proceed without assistance.

.19.1　MV … cannot proceed without assistance.

.20　MV … requires escort.

Collision 碰撞

.21　MV … has collided with MV…

.21.1　MV … has collided with unknown vessel/object.

.21.2　MV … has collided with …(name) light vessel.

.21.3　MV … has collided with seamark …(charted name).

.21.4　MV … has collided with iceberg.

.21.5　MV … has collided with …

.22　MV … has major damage above/below water line.

.23　MV … can repair damage.

.23.1　MV … cannot repair damage.

.24　MV … requires …

.25　MV … under command.

.25.1　MV … not under command.

.26　MV … can only proceed at slow speed.

.27　MV … requires escort.

.28　MV … requires … tugs.

.29　MV … requires …

Grounding 搁浅

.30　MV … aground in position …

.31　MV … aground in position … requires assistance.

.31.1　MV … requires pumps.

.31.2　MV … requires escort.

.31.3　MV … requires tugs.

.31.4　MV … requires …

.32　Uncharted rocks in position …

.33　Risk of grounding at low water.

.34　MV … will jettison cargo to refloat.

.35　MV … will beach in position …

List-danger of capsizing 横倾与倾覆危险

.36　MV … has heavy list to port side/starboard side.

.36.1　List increasing.

.36.2　List decreasing.

.37　MV … in danger of capsizing.

.38　MV … jettisoned cargo to stop listing.

.39　MV … will beach in position …

Sinking 沉没

.40　MV … sinking in position … after collision.

.40.1　MV … sinking after grounding.

.40.2　MV … sinking after flooding.

.40.3　MV … sinking after explosion.

.40.4　MV … sinking after …

.41　MV … requires assistance.

.42　MV … proceeds to your assistance.

.43　MV … expects to reach you within … hours/at … UTC.

Disabled and adrift 失控与漂航

.44　MV … not under command in position …

.44.1　MV … adrift near position …

.44.2　MV … drifting at … knots to … degrees.

.45　MV … requires tug assistance.

Undesignated distress 其他险情

.46　MV … has problems.

.46.1　MV … has problems with cargo.

.46.2　MV … has problems with machinery.

.46.3　MV … has problems with navigation.

.46.4　MV … has problems with mass disease.

.46.5　MV … has problems with …

.47　MV … requires …

Abandoning vessel 弃船

.48　MV … must abandon vessel in position …

.48.1　MV … must abandon vessel after collision in position …

.48.2　MV … must abandon vessel after grounding in position …

.48.3　MV … must abandon vessel after flooding in position …

.48.4　MV … must abandon vessel after explosion in position …

.48.5　MV … must abandon vessel after piracy/armed attack in position …

.48.6　MV … must abandon vessel after … in position …

.49　You must keep radio silence unless you have messages about distress.

6.2 Phrases for providing VTS services 提供船舶交通管理服务的用语

6.2.1 Information Service 信息服务

（These phrases are normally transmitted from the shore.）

（这些语句一般由岸方传送出）

6.2.1.1 Navigational Warnings 航海警告

（The following phrases should normally be preceded by the Message Marker "WARNING".）

（下述语句应加的信文标识"WARNING"。）

    .1 Unknown object(s) in position …

    .2 Ice/Iceberg(s) in position …/area around …

    .3 Unlit derelict vessel adrift in vicinity … at … (date and time).

    .4 Dangerous wreck/obstruction located in position … marked by … (type) buoy.

    .5 Hazardous mine adrift in vicinity … at … (date and time).

    .6 Uncharted reef/rock/shoal reported in position …

    .7 Pipeline leaking gas/oil in position …wide berth requested.

    .8 No sufficient depth of water in position …

    .9 U.N. exclusion zone extending … kilometers/nautical miles from … all vessels keep clear.

    .10 Navigation closed in area …

6.2.1.2 Navigational Information 航海信息

（The following phrases should normally be preceded by the Message Markers "INFORMATION" "WARNING".）

（下述语句应加的信文标识为："INFORMATION" "WARNING"。）

    .1 Oil slick in position …

    .2 Current meters/hydrographic instruments moored in position … wide berth requested.

    .3 Platform …(name/number) reported/established in position …wide berth requested.

    .4 …(charted name of light/buoy) in position … unlit.

    .5 …(charted name of light/buoy) in position … unreliable.

    .6 …(charted name of light/buoy) in position … damaged.

    .7 …(charted name of light/buoy) destroyed.

    .8 …(charted name of light/buoy) in position … off station.

    .9 …(charted name of light/buoy) in position … missing.

    .10 …(charted name of light/buoy) in position … changed to …(full characteristics).

    .11 …(charted name of light/buoy) in position…temporarily changed to…(full characteristics).

    .12 …(charted name of buoy) in position … temporarily removed.

.13 …(charted name of light) in position … temporarily discontinued.

.14 …(charted name of light/buoy) …(full characteristics) established in position …

.15 …(charted name of light/buoy) …(full characteristics) re-established in position ….

.16 …(charted name of light/buoy) moved … kilometers/nautical miles in … degrees to position …

.17 (Note: Only for major fog signal stations.) Fog signal …(charted name of light/buoy) in position … inoperative.

6.2.1.3 Traffic Information 交通信息

(The following phrases should normally be preceded by Message Marker "INFORMATION" "WARNING".)

(下述语句应加的信文标识为："INFORMATION" "WARNING"。)

.1 Gunnery/Rocket firing/Missile/Torpedo/Underwater ordnance exercises in area bounded by …(positions) and … from … (date and time) to … (date and time). Wide berth requested.

.2 Cable/Pipeline operations by… (vessel) in vicinity …/along line joining … (position) from …(date and time) to… (date and time). Wide berth requested. Contact via VTS channel …

.3 Salvage operations in position … from … (date and time) to … (date and time). Wide berth requested. Contact via VTS channel …

.4 Seismic/Hydrographic operations by … (vessel)… from … (date and time) to …(date and time) in position … Wide berth requested. Contact via VHF channel …

.5 Oil clearance operations near MT … in position … Wide berth requested.

.6 Transshipment of …(kind of cargo) in position … Wide berth requested.

.7 Difficult tow from …(part of departure) to …(destination) on …(date). Wide berth requested.

.8 Vessel not under command in position …/area …

.9 Hampered vessel in position … area … (course … degrees, speed … knots).

.10 Vessel in position … on course … and speed … not complying with traffic regulations.

.11 Vessel crossing … traffic lane on course … and speed … in position …

.12 Small fishing boats in area around …navigate with caution.

.13 Submarines operating in sea area around … Surface vessels in attendance.

.14 Tanker stop in area … due to poor visibility.

.15 Tanker stop canceled in area … (no more restrictions).

6.2.1.4 Routeing Information 一般信息

(The following phrases should normally be preceded by Message Marker "INFORMATION".)

（下述语句应加的信文标识为：“INFORMATION”。）

  .1 Route …/Traffic Lane … suspended.

  .2 Route …/Traffic Lane … discontinued.

  .3 Route …/Traffic Lane … diverted.

6.2.1.5 Hydrographic Information 水文信息

（The following phrases should normally be preceded by Message Marker “INFORMA-TION”.）

（下述语句应加的信文标识为：“INFORMATION”。）

  .1 Abnormally high tides expected in position … at about … UTC/within … hours.

  .2 Abnormally low tides expected in position … at about … UTC/within … hours.

  .3 Tide rising. It is … hours before high water.

  .4 Tide rising. It is … hours after low water.

  .5 Tide rising. It is … meters below high water.

  .6 Tide rising. It is … meters above low water.

  .7 Tide falling. It is … hours after high water.

  .8 Tide falling. It is … hour before low water.

  .9 Tide falling. It is … meters below high water.

  .10 Tide falling. It is … meters above low water.

  .11 Tide slack.

  .12 Present height of tide above datum … meters in position …

  .13 Tide … meters above prediction.

  .14 Tide … meters below prediction.

  .15 Tidal stream … knots in position …

  .16 Current … knots in position …

  .17 Tide setting in direction … degrees.

  .18 Sufficient depth of water in position …

  .19 No sufficient depth of water in position …

  .20 Charted depth increased by … meters due to winds/sea state.

  .21 Charted depth decreased by … meters due to winds/sea state.

6.2.1.6 Electronic Navigational Aids Information 电子助航设施信息

（The following phrases should normally be preceded by Message Marker “INFORM-ATION”“WARNING”.）

（下述语句应加的信文标识为：“INFORMATION”“WARNING”。）

  .1 GPS Satellite …（name）unusable from …（date and time）to …（date and time）. Cancel one hour after time of restoration.

  .2 LORAN station …（name number master/slave）off air from …（date and time）to …（date and time）. Cancel one hour after time of restoration.

.3　DECCA …（identify chain and colour）off air from …（date and time）to … （date and time）. Cancel one hour after time of restoration.

.4　RACON … （name of station）in position … off air … from … （date and time）to … （date and time）.

6.2.1.7　Meteorological Warnings 气象警报

（The following phrases should normally be preceded by Message Marker "WARNING".）

（下述语句应加的信文标识为："WARNING"。）

.1　Warning：Tropical storm …（name）center in position …

.2　A gale warning/storm warning was issued at …（UTC）starting at …（UTC）.

6.2.1.8　Meteorological Information 气象信息

（The following phrases should normally be preceded by Message Marker " INFORM-ATION" "WARNING".）

（下述语句应加的信文标识为："INFORMATION" "WARNING"。）

.1　Position of tropical storm … （name）…, path … （compass points）, speed of advance … knots.

.2　Wind direction …（compass points）, force Beaufort … in position …

.3　Wind backing and increasing/decreasing.

.4　Wind veering and increasing/decreasing.

.5　Wind expected to increase in position … to force Beaufort … within next hours.

.6　Wind expected to decrease in position … to force Beaufort … within next hours.

.7　Visibility in position … meters/nautical miles.

.8　Visibility reduced by mist/fog/snow/dust/rain/…

.9　Visibility expected to increase to … meters/nautical miles in position … within next hours.

.10　Visibility expected to decrease to … meters/nautical miles in position … within next hours.

.11　Sea/swell in position … meters from …（compass points）.

.12　Sea/swell expected to increase within next … hours.

.13　Sea/swell expected to decrease within next … hours.

.14　Icing expected/not expected to form in area around …

6.2.1.9　Meteorological Questions and Answers 气象问题与回答

（The following phrases should normally be preceded by Message Markers "QUESTION" "ANSWER".）

（下述语句应加的信文标识为："QUESTION" "ANSWER"。）

.1　What is wind direction and force in your position/in position …?

.1.1　Wind direction …（compass points）, force Beaufort … in my position/ in position …

.2　Is wind backing/veering?

.2.1   Wind backing/veering.

.3   What wind direction and force is expected in my position/in position ...?

.3.1   Wind in your position/in position ... expected from ... direction(s),
force Beaufort ...

.3.2   Wind in your position/in position ... expected variable.

.4   Is wind expected to increase/decrease?

.4.1   Wind expected to increase/decrease.

.5   What is latest gale warning?

.5.1   Latest gale warning is as follows:

Gale warning. Winds at ... UTC in area ...(met.area) from direction ...
(compass points) and force Beaufort ... backing/veering to...(compass
points).

.6   What is latest tropical storm warning?

.6.1   Latest tropical storm warning is as follows:

(Standard tropical storm warning 标准热带风暴警报)

Tropical storm warning at ... UTC. Hurricane ...(name)/tropical cyclone/tor-
nado/willy-willy/typhoon ...(name) with central pressure of ... millibars located in position ... Present movement ...(compass points) at ... knots. Winds
of ... knots within radius of ... kilometers/nautical miles of center. Seas over
... meters.

Further information on VHF channel .../frequency ...

.7   What is atmospheric pressure in your position/in position ... ?

.7.1   Atmospheric pressure ... millibars.

.8   What is barometric change in your position/in position ...?

.8.1   Barometric change ... millibars per hour.

.8.2   Barometric change is ... millibars within last ... hours.

.8.3   Barometer steady.

.8.4   Barometer dropping (rapidly).

.8.5   Barometer rising (rapidly).

.9   What maximum winds are expected in storm area?

.9.1   Maximum winds of ... knots expected in storm area.

.9.2   Maximum winds of .... knots expected within radius of ... kilometers/
nautical miles of center.

.9.3   Maximum winds of ... knots expected in safe/dangerous semicircle.

.10   What is sea state in your position/in position ... ?

.10.1   Height of sea/swell in my position/in position ..... meters from ...
(compass points).

.11   Is sea state expected to change (within next hours)?

.11.1   No, sea state not expected to change (within next hours).

.11.2　Yes, sea/swell of … meters from …（compass points）expected（within next hours）.

.12　Tsunami/Abnormal wave expected by … UTC.

.13　What is visibility in position … ?

.13.1　Visibility in position … kilometers/nautical miles.

6.2.2　Navigational Assistance Service 航海报务

（Shore based pilotage by Navigational Assistance Service：see phrases 6.4.3.1.22 to 6.4.3.1.23.2 of this section.）

（有关岸上航海报务机构的引航服务,参见本节 6.4.3.1.22 至 6.4.3.1.23.2 中的语句。）

6.2.2.1　Request, identification, begin and end 请求、识别、开始与结束

（The following phrases should normally be preceded by Message Markers "ADVICE" "INFORMATION" "QUESTION" "ANSWER" "REQUEST".）

（下述语句应加的信文标识为："ADVICE" "INFORMATION" "QUESTION" "ANSWER" "REQUEST"。）

.1　Is shore based radar assistance available?

.1.1　Yes, shore based radar assistance available.

.1.2　No, shore based radar assistance not available.

.2　Shore based radar assistance available from … UTC to … UTC.

.3　Do you want navigational assistance to reach … ?

.3.1　Yes, I want navigational assistance to reach …

.3.2　No, I do not want navigational assistance.

.4　What is your position?

.4.1　My position … degrees from … distance … kilometers/nautical miles.

.5　How was your position obtained?

.5.1　Position obtained by GPS.

.5.2　Position obtained by DECCA.

.5.3　Position obtained by RADAR.

.5.4　Position obtained by cross-bearing.

.5.5　Position obtained by astronomical observation.

.5.6　Position obtained by …

.6　Repeat your position for identification.

.7　I have located you on my radar screen—your position … degrees from …
（NOTE：This message should only be used when the vessel has been positively identified.）
（注意,仅当船舶已确认被识别才可应用本句。）

.8　I cannot locate you on my radar screen.

.9　What is your present course and speed?

.9.1　My present course … degrees, speed … knots.

.10　What is course to reach you?

.10.1   Course to reach me ... degrees.

.11   Is your radar working?

　　.11.1   Yes, radar working.

　　.11.2   No, radar not working.

.12   What range scale are you using?

　　.12.1   I am using ... miles range scale.

　　.12.2   Advise you change to larger range scale.

　　.12.3   Advise you change to smaller range scale.

.13   You are leaving my radar screen.

.14   Change to radar ...（name）VHF Channel ...

　　.14.1   Changing to radar ...（name）VHF Channel ...

.15   I have lost radar contact.

6.2.2.2   Position 位置

（The following phrases should normally be preceded by Message Markers "WARNING" "ADVICE" "INFORMATION" "QUESTION" "ANSWER".）

（NOTE:When possible, positions should be given with reference to a prominent landmark or buoy.）

（下述语句应加的信文标识为:" WARNING "" ADVICE "" INFORMATION " "QUESTION" "ANSWER"。）

（注意,若可能,位置应参照明显的陆标或浮标给出。）

.1   You are entering ...

.2   Your position ...

.3   Your position ... degrees/... kilometers/nautical miles from ...

.4   You are passing ...

.5   You are in center of fairway.

.6   You are in middle of fairway.

.7   You are on reference line.

.8   You are on reference line of fairway.

.9   You are not on reference line of fairway.

.10   You are on ... side of fairway.

.11   You are approaching starboard limit of fairway.

.12   You are approaching port limit of fairway.

.13   You are approaching reference line of fairway.

.14   Your position buoy number ... distance ... meters/cables to port side of reference line.

.15   Your position buoy number... distance... meters/cables to starboard side of reference line.

.16   Your position distance... meters/cables from intersection of reference line... and reference line ...

.17　Your position distance ... meters/cables from intersection of reference line ... and reference line ... and distance ... meters/cables to port side of reference line ...

.18　Your position distance ... meters/cables from intersection of reference line ... and reference line ... and distance ... meters/cables to starboard side of reference line ...

.19　MV ... has reported at way point ...

.20　You are getting closer to vessel ahead.

.21　Vessel on opposite course passing your port side.

.22　Vessel on opposite course passing your starboard side.

.23　MV ... meters/cables ahead of you on your port bow.

.24　MV ...meters/cables ahead of you on your starboard bow.

.25　MV ... ahead of you on opposite course.

.26　MV ... following you will overtake you on your port side.

.27　MV ... following you will overtake you on your starboard side.

.28　Vessel anchored ahead of you in position ...

.29　Vessel ahead of you obstructing your movements.

.30　You will meet crossing traffic in position ...

.31　Vessel entering fairway at ...

.32　Vessel leaving fairway at ...

.33　Buoy ... distance ... meters/cables ahead.

.34　Vessel ahead/Astern/Port/Starboard of you turning/Anchoring/Increasing speed/Decreasing speed/Overtaking you/Not under command.

6.2.2.3　Course 航向

(The following phrases should normally be preceded by the Message Markers "WARNING""ADVICE""INFORMATION""QUESTION""ANSWER".)

(下述语句应加的信文标识为："WARNING"　"ADVICE"　"INFORMATION"　"QUESTION"　"ANSWER"。)

.1　Your track is parallel with reference line.

.2　Your track is diverging from reference line.

.3　Your track is converging to reference line.

.4　Course to ... degrees.

.5　You are steering dangerous course.

(Note：The user of this phrase should be fully aware of the implications of words such as "track", "heading" and "course made good".)

(注意,本句的使用者应确切了解"track", "heading" 和 "course made good"等术语的含义。)

.6　Vessel ahead of you on same course ... degrees.

.7　Advise you make course of ... degrees.

.8　Advise you keep your present course.

.9   Advise you alter course to ... degrees in position ...

.10   Have you altered course?

.11   Yes, I have altered course—new course ... degrees.

.12   No, I have not altered course—my course ... degrees.

.13   What is your present course?

.14   My present course ... degrees.

.15   You are running into danger. Shallow water ahead of you.

.16   You are running into danger. Submerged wreck ahead of you.

.17   You are running into danger. Risk of collision.

.18   Risk of collision with vessel distance... kilometers/nautical miles, bearing... degrees.

.19   You are running into danger. Fog bank ahead of you.

.20   You are running into danger. Bridge defective.

6.2.3   Traffic Organization Service 交通组织服务

6.2.3.1   Clearance, forward planning 清爽与预期计划

(The following phrases should normally be preceded by Message Markers "WARNING" "INSTRUCTION" "ADVICE" "INFORMATION".)

(下述语句应加的信文标识为: "WARNING" "INSTRUCTION" "ADVICE" "INFORMA-TION"。)

.1   Traffic clearance required before entering ...

.2   Do not enter Traffic Lane.

.3   Do not enter ...

.4   Proceed to emergency anchorage.

.5   Vessels are advised to keep clear of ...

.6   Vessels are advised to avoid ...

.8   You may enter traffic lane/route—traffic clearance granted.

.9   You may enter traffic lane/route in position ... at ... UTC.

.10   Do not pass Reporting Point ... until ... UTC.

.11   Report at next way point/way point .../at ... UTC.

.12   You must arrive at way point ... at ... UTC—your berth is clear.

.13   Do not arrive in position ... before ... UTC.

.14   Do not arrive in position ... after ... UTC.

.15   Tide with you.

.16   Tide against you.

6.2.3.2   Anchoring 锚泊

(The following phrases should normally be preceded by Message Markers "INSTRUCTION" "ADVICE" "INFORMATION" "QUESTION" "ANSWER".)

(下述语句应加的信文标识为: "INSTRUCTION" "ADVICE" "INFORMATION" "QUES-TION" "ANSWER"。)

.1   You must anchor at ... UTC.

.2 You must anchor until pilot arrives.

.3 Do not anchor in position …

.4 Anchoring prohibited.

.5 Do not dredge anchor.

.6 You must heave up anchor.

.7 You must anchor in different position.

.8 You must anchor clear of fairway.

.9 Advise you have your crew on stand by for weighing anchor when pilot embarks.

.10 You have permission to anchor at … UTC.

.11 You have permission to anchor in position …

.12 You have permission to anchor until pilot arrives.

.12.1 You have permission to anchor until tugs arrive.

.13 You have permission to anchor until sufficient water.

.14 MV … at anchor in position …

.15 You are obstructing fairway.

.16 You are obstructing other traffic.

.17 You are at anchor in wrong position.

.18 Are you dragging anchor?

.18.1 Yes, I am dragging anchor.

.18.2 No, I am not dragging anchor.

.19 Are you dredging anchor?

.19.1 Yes, I am dredging anchor.

.19.2 No, I am not dredging anchor.

6.2.3.3 Arrival, berthing and departure 到达、靠泊与离开

(The following phrases should normally be preceded by Message Markers "INSTRUCTION" "ADVICE" "INFORMATION" "QUESTION" "ANSWER".)

(下述语句应加的信文标识为:" INSTRUCTION " " ADVICE " " INFORMATION " "QUESTION" "ANSWER"。)

.1 Your orders are to berth on …

.2 Your orders changed.

.3 Proceed to … for orders.

.4 You may enter at … UTC.

.5 You may proceed at … UTC.

.6 Vessel turning/manoeuvring in position …

.7 MV … will turn in position …

.8 MV … will leave … at … UTC.

.9 MV … leaving …

.10 MV … left …

.11　MV … entered fairway in position …

.12　Your berth is not clear（until … UTC）.

.13　Your berth will be clear at … UTC.

.14　You will berth/dock at … UTC .

.15　Berthing delayed by … hours.

.16　Be ready to get underway.

.17　Get underway.

.18　Are you underway？

　.18.1　Yes, I am underway.

　.18.2　No, I am not underway.

　.18.3　I am ready to get underway.

.19　Move ahead … meters.

.20　Move astern … meters.

.21　Your vessel in position—make fast.

.22　Pilot ordered for departing vessel for … UTC.

6.2.3.4　Enforcement 实施

（The following phrases should normally be preceded by Message Markers "WARNING" "INSTRUCTION" "ADVICE" "INFORMATION".）

（下述语句应加的信文标识为："WARNING" "INSTRUCTION" "ADVICE" "INFORMA-TION"。）

.1　According to my radar, your course does not comply with International Regulations for Preventing Collisions at Sea.

.2　According to my radar, your course does not comply with Rule 10 of International Regulations for Preventing Collisions at Sea.

.3　Your actions will be reported to Authorities.

.4　You are not complying with traffic regulations.

.5　You are not keeping to correct lane.

.6　Vessels are advised to have all navigational instruments in operation before entering this area/area …

.7　Your navigation lights not visible.

.8　Advise you recover your fishing gear—you are fishing in fairway.

.9　Fishing gear ahead of you.

.10　Fishing in area … prohibited.

.11　You are approaching prohibited fishing area.

.12　Fairway speed … knots.

6.2.3.5　Avoiding dangerous situations, providing safe movements 避开危险与安全操纵

（The following phrases should normally be preceded by Message Markers "WARNING" "INSTRUCTION" "ADVICE" "INFORMATION".）

（下述语句的信文标识为："WARNING" "INSTRUCTION" "ADVICE" "INFORMATION"。）

.1 It is dangerous to anchor in your present position.

.2 It is dangerous to remain in your present position.

.3 It is dangerous to alter course to port side.

.4 It is dangerous to alter course to starboard side.

.5 Large vessel leaving fairway—keep clear of fairway approach.

.6 Nets with buoys/without buoys in this area—navigate with caution.

.7 Collision in position ...

.8 Keep clear.

.9 MV ... aground in position ...

.10 MV ... on fire in position.

.11 Stand by for giving assistance.

.12 Vessels must keep clear of this are/area ...

.13 Vessels must avoid this area/area ...

.14 Vessels must navigate with caution.

.15 Advise you keep clear of ... search and rescue in operation.

.16 Your present course too close to outbound vessel.

.17 Your present course too close to inbound vessel.

.18 Your present course too close to vessel that you are overtaking.

.19 Your present course too close to starboard limit of fairway.

.20 Your present course too close to port limit of fairway.

.21 Your course deviating from reference line.

.22 You are running into danger. Shallow water ahead of you.

.23 You are running into danger. Submerged wreck ahead of you.

.24 You are running into danger. Risk of collision.

.25 Risk of collision with vessel distance... kilometers/nautical miles, bearing... degrees.

.26 You are running into danger. Fog bank ahead of you.

.27 You are running into danger. Bridge defective.

.28 You are proceeding at dangerous speed.

.29 You must proceed by ... fairway ... route.

.30 You must keep to ... side of fairway line.

.31 You must keep to ... side of reference line.

.32 You must stay clear of fairway.

.33 Do not overtake.

.34 Do not cross fairway.

.35 You must wait for MV ... to cross ahead of you.

.36 You must wait for MV ... to clear ... before entering fairway.

.37 You must wait for MV ... to clear ... before getting underway.

.38 You must wait for MV ... to clear ... before leaving berth.

.39   Advise you alter course to port side.

.40   Advise you alter course to starboard side.

.41   Advise you stop engines.

.42   Advise you pass north/south/east/west of departing/entering/anchored/disabled vessel.

.43   Advise you pass north/south/east/west of … mark.

.44   MV … wishes to overtake on your port side.

.45   MV … wishes to overtake on your starboard side.

.46   MV … agrees to be overtaken.

.47   MV … does not agree to be overtaken.

.48   MV … approaching obscured area … approaching vessels acknowledge.

6.2.3.6   Canal and lock operations 过运河与船闸

（The following phrases should normally be preceded by Message Markers "INSTRUCTION" "INFORMATION".）

（下述语句应加的信文标识为："INSTRUCTION" "INFORMATION"。）

.1   You must close up on vessel ahead of you.

.2   You must drop back from vessel ahead of you.

.3   You must wait at …

.4   You must moor at …

.5   Convoy … must wait at …

.6   Convoy … must moor at …

.7   You must wait for lock clearance at … until … UTC.

.8   You will join convoy … at … UTC.

.9   Transit will begin at … UTC.

.10   Your place in convoy is number …

.11   Transit speed … knots.

.12   Convoy speed … knots.

.13   Convoys/vessels will pass in area …

.14   You will enter canal/lock at … UTC.

6.3   **Phrases between adjacent VTS 相邻 VTS 的交接用语**

Hand off Procedures（Handing over to another VTS）转交程序（转交给其他交管站）

（The following phrases should normally be preceded by Message Marker " INFORMA-TION".）

（下述语句应加的信文标识为："INFORMATION"。）

.1   … VTS this is … VTS：MV … position … degrees, distance … kilometers/nautical miles from … Working Frequency VHF Channel … Your Target. Please Confirm.

.2   … VTS this is … VTS：MV … position … degrees, distance … kilometers/nautical miles from … I confirm. My target.

.3   … VTS this is … VTS：MV … position … degrees, distance … kilometers/nautical miles from … I am unable to take over this target.

6.4 Phrases for communication with Emergency Services and Allied Services 应急服务与联合服务通信用语

6.4.1 Emergency Services (SAR, fire fighting, pollution fighting) 应急服务(搜救、消防与污染处理)

See phrases in section 6.1.2 "Acquiring and providing distress traffic data"

6.4.2 Tug assistance 拖船服务

(The following phrases should normally be preceded by Message Markers "INSTRUCTION" "ADVICE" "INFORMATION" "QUESTION" "ANSWER".)

(下述语句应加的信文标识为:"INSTRUCTION" "ADVICE" "INFORMATION" "QUES-TION" "ANSWER"。)

 .1 How many tugs do you require?

  .1.1 I require … tug(s).

 .2 You must take … tug(s) according to Port Regulations.

 .3 You must take … tug(s) fore and … tug(s) aft.

 .4 Wait for tug(s) in position …

 .5 Tugs will meet you in position … at … local time.

 .6 Tug services suspended until …(date and local time).

 .7 Tug services resumed on…(date) at … local time.

6.4.3 Pilotage 引航

6.4.3.1 Pilot Request 申请引航员

(The following phrases should normally be preceded by Message Markers "ADVICE" "IN-FORMATION" "REQUEST" "INTENTION" "QUESTION" "ANSWER".)

(下述语句应加的信文标识为:"ADVICE" "INFORMATION" "REQUEST" "INTENTION" "QUESTION" "ANSWER"。)

 .1 You must take pilot—pilotage compulsory.

 .2 Do you require pilot?

  .2.1 Yes, I require pilot.

  .2.2 No, I do not require pilot—I am holder of Pilotage Exemption Certifi-cate (No. …).

 .3 You are exempted from pilotage.

  .3.1 You are allowed to proceed without pilot.

 .4 Do you require pilot at …(name) Pilot Station?

  .4.1 Yes, I require pilot at …(name) Pilot Station.

  .4.2 No, I do not require pilot at …(name) Pilot Station—I require pilot in position …

 .5 What is your ETA at …(name) Pilot Station in local time?

  .5.1 My ETA at…(name) Pilot Station … hours local time.

 .6 What is local time?

.6.1　Local time ... hours.

.7　What is your present position?

.7.1　My position ...

.8　What is your distance from ...(name) Pilot Station?

.8.1　My distance from ...(name) Pilot Station ... kilometers/nautical miles.

.9　Is pilot boat on station?

.9.1　Yes, pilot boat on station.

.9.2　No, pilot boat not on station.

.9.3　Pilot boat on station at ... hours local time.

.10　In what position can I take pilot?

.10.1　Take pilot at ...(Pilot Station) at ... hours local time.

.10.2　Take pilot near ... at ... hours local time.

.11　When will pilot embark?

.11.1　Pilot will embark at ... hours local time.

.12　Pilot coming to you.

.13　Pilot boat approaching your vessel.

.14　Keep pilot boat on port side.

.15　Keep pilot boat on starboard side.

.16　What is your freeboard?

.16.1　My freeboard ... meters.

.17　Stop in present position and wait for pilot.

.18　Change to VHF channel ... for pilot transfer.

.19　Stand by on VHF channel ... until pilot transfer completed.

.20　Pilotage at ...(name) Pilot Station suspended until ... (date and local time).

.21　Pilotage at ...(name) Pilot Station resumed.

.22　Pilot cannot embark at ... Pilot Station due to ...

.23　Do you accept shorebased navigational assistance from pilot?

.23.1　Yes, I accept shorebased navigational assistance from pilot.

.23.2　No, I do not accept shorebased navigational assistance from pilot.

.23.2.1　I stay in position ... until ...

.24　You may navigate by yourself (or wait for pilot boat at ... buoy).

.25　Follow pilot boat inward where pilot will embark.

6.4.3.2　Embarking/disembarking Pilot 引航员上下船

(The following phrases should normally be preceded by Message Markers "ADVICE" "IN-FORMATION" "REQUEST" "INTENTION" "QUESTION" "ANSWER" .)

(下述语句应加的信文标识为:" ADVICE "" INFORMATION "" REQUEST ""INTENTION""QUESTION""ANSWER" 。)

.1　Stand by pilot ladder.

.2　Rig pilot ladder on port side ... meters above water.

.3 Rig pilot ladder on starboard side ... meters above water.

.4 You must rig another pilot ladder.

.5 Pilot ladder unsafe.

.6 Pilot ladder has broken steps.

.7 Pilot ladder has loose steps.

.8 Pilot ladder has broken spreaders.

.9 Pilot ladder has spreaders too short.

.10 Pilot ladder too far aft.

.11 Pilot ladder too far forward.

.12 Move pilot ladder ... meters aft.

.13 Move pilot ladder ... meters forward.

.14 Move pilot ladder clear of discharge.

.15 Rig accommodation ladder in combination with pilot ladder.

.16 Rig pilot ladder alongside hoist.

.17 Put lights on at pilot ladder.

.18 Man ropes required.

.19 Man ropes not required.

.20 Have heaving line ready at pilot ladder.

.21 Correct list of vessel.

.22 Make lee on your port side.

.23 Make lee on your starboard side.

.24 Steer ... degrees to make lee.

.25 Keep sea on your port quarter.

.26 Keep sea on your starboard quarter.

.27 Make boarding speed of ... knots.

.28 Stop engine until pilot boat is clear.

.29 Put helm hard to port.

.30 Put helm hard to starboard.

.31 Alter course to port, pilot boat cannot clear vessel.

.32 Alter course to starboard, pilot boat cannot clear vessel.

.33 Put ahead engine.

.34 Put astern engine.

.35 Embarkation not possible.

.36 Boarding arrangements do not comply with SOLAS Regulations.

.37 Vessel not suited for pilot ladder.

附录2
人体部位名称（List of Body Parts）

人体正面（Front of the Body）					
1	Frontal region of head	头前额区	19	Central upper abdomen	上腹中央
2	Side of head	颞侧	20	Central lower abdomen	下腹中央
3	Top of head	颅顶	21	Upper abdomen	上腹部
4	Face	脸	22	Lower abdomen	下腹部
5	Jaw	颌	23	Lateral abdomen	侧腹
6	Neck front	前颈	24	Groin	鼠蹊
7	Shoulder	肩	25	Scrotum	阴囊
8	Clavicle	锁骨	26	Testicles	睾丸
9	Chest	胸	27	Penis	阴茎
10	Chest, mid	前胸中部	28	Upper thigh	上股
11	Heart	心脏	29	Middle thigh	中股
12	Armpit	腋窝	30	Lower thigh	下股
13	Arm upper	上臂	31	Knee	膝盖
14	Forearm	前臂	32	Patella	髌骨
15	Wrist	腕	33	Front of leg	胫前
16	Palm of hand	手掌	34	Ankle	踝
17	Fingers	手指	35	Foot	脚
18	Thumb	拇指	36	Toe	脚趾
人体背面（Back of the Body）					
37	Back of head	颅后	47	Spinal column middle	中脊柱
38	Back of neck	颈后	48	Spinal column lower	下脊柱
39	Back of shoulder	肩后	49	Lumbar（kidney）region	腰部
40	Scapula region	肩胛区	50	Sacral region	骶骨区
41	Elbow	肘	51	Buttock	臀
42	Back upper arm	上臂背面	52	Anus	肛门
43	Back lower arm	前臂背面	53	Back of thigh	大腿背面
44	Back of hand	手背	54	Back of knee	腘窝

45	Lower chest region	胸背后区	55	Calf	腓（腿肚子）
46	Spinal column upper	上脊柱	56	Heel	脚跟

<table>
<tr><td colspan="6" align="center">身体器官（Organs of the Body）</td></tr>
</table>

57	Artery	动脉	75	Pancreas	胰脏
58	Bladder	膀胱	76	Prostate	前列腺
59	Brain	脑	77	Rib	肋骨
60	Breast	乳房	78	Spleen	脾
61	Ear	耳	79	Stomach	胃
62	Eye	眼	80	Throat	咽喉
63	Eyelid	眼睑	81	Tongue	舌
64	Gall bladder	胆囊	82	Tonsils	扁桃体
65	Gullet（esophagus）	食道	83	Tooth，teeth	牙
66	Gums	齿龈	84	Urethra	尿道
67	Intestine	肠	85	Uterus，womb	子宫
68	Kidney	肾	86	Vein	静脉
69	Lip，lower	下唇	87	Voice box（larynx）	喉室（喉）
70	Lip，upper	上唇	88	Whole abdomen	全腹
71	Liver	肝	89	Whole arm	全臂
72	Lung	肺	90	Whole back	全背部
73	Mouth	口	91	Whole abdomen	全腹部
74	Nose	鼻	92	Whole leg	全腿

附录 3
常见疾病清单（List of Common Diseases）

1	Abscess	脓肿	48	Immersion foot	下肢水肿
2	Alcoholism	酒精中毒	49	Impetigo	脓疮病
3	Allergic reaction	过敏（变态）反应	50	Insulin overdose	胰岛素过量症（血糖减少症）
4	Amoebic dysentery	阿米巴痢疾	51	Indigestion	消化不良
5	Angina pectoris	心绞痛	52	Influenza	流行性感冒
6	Anthrax	炭疽	53	Intestinal obstruction	肠梗阻
7	Apoplexy（stroke）	中风	54	Kidney stone（renal colic）	肾结石
8	Appendicitis	阑尾炎	55	Laryngitis	喉炎
9	Asthma	哮喘病	56	Malaria	疟疾
10	Bacillary dysentery	杆菌性痢疾	57	Measles	麻风病
11	Boils	疖子	58	Meningitis	脑膜炎
12	Bronchitis（acute）	急性支气管炎	59	Mental illness	精神病
13	Bronchitis（chronic）	慢性支气管炎	60	Migraine	周期性偏头痛
14	Brucellosis	布鲁氏菌病	61	Mumps	流行性腮腺炎
15	Carbuncle	痈（疔疮）	62	Orchitis	睾丸炎
16	Cellulitis	蜂窝组织炎	63	Peritonitis	腹膜炎
17	Chancroid	软性下疳	64	Phlebitis	静脉炎
18	Chicken pox	水痘	65	Piles	痔疮
19	Cholera	霍乱	66	Plague	鼠疫
20	Cirrhosis of the liver	肝硬化	67	Pleurisy	胸膜炎（肋膜炎）
21	Concussion	脑震荡	68	Pneumonia	肺炎
22	Compression of brain	脑压	69	Poisoning（corrosive）	腐蚀剂中毒
23	Congestive heart failure	充血性心力衰竭	70	Poisoning（noncorrosive）	中毒（非腐蚀性）
24	Constipation	便秘	71	Poisoning（barbiturates）	中毒（巴比妥盐类）

25	Coronary thrombosis	冠状动脉血栓形成	72	Poisoning（methyl alcohol）	甲醇中毒
26	Cystitis（bladder inflammation）	膀胱炎	73	Poisoning（gases）	毒气中毒
27	Dengue	登革热	74	Poliomyelitis	脊髓灰质炎（小儿麻痹症）
28	Diabetes	糖尿病	75	Prolapsed inter-vertebral disc（slipped disc）	椎间盘脱出
29	Diabetic coma	糖尿病性昏迷	76	Pulmonary tuberculosis	肺结核
30	Diphtheria	白喉	77	Quinsy	扁桃体周围脓肿
31	Drug reaction	药物反应	78	Rheumatism	风湿病
32	Duodenal ulcer	十二指肠溃疡	79	Rheumatic fever	风湿热
33	Eczema	湿疹	80	Scarlet fever	猩红热
34	Erysipelas	丹毒	81	Sciatica	坐骨神经痛
35	Fits	痉挛小儿破伤风	82	Shingles（herpes zoster）	带状疱疹
36	Gangrene	坏疽	83	Sinusitis	鼻窦炎
37	Gastric ulcer	胃溃疡	84	Shock	休克
38	Gastroenteritis	胃肠炎	85	Smallpox	天花
39	Gonorrhea	淋病	86	Syphilis	梅毒
40	Gout	痛风	87	Tetanus	破伤风
41	Heat cramps	热痉挛	88	Tonsillitis	扁桃体炎
42	Heat exhaustion	虚脱	89	Typhoid	伤寒
43	Heat stroke	中暑	90	Typhus	斑疹伤寒
44	Hepatitis	肝炎	91	Urethritis	尿道炎
45	Hernia	疝	92	Urticaria（nettle rash）	荨麻疹
46	Hernia（irreducible）	难复性疝	93	Whooping cough	百日咳
47	Hernia（strangulated）	绞窄性疝	94	Yellow fever	黄热病

附录 4
船舶信号与甚高频通信实验指导书
Experimental Instructions of Marine Signals and VHF Communication

实验名称：VHF 通信实验

一、实验目的

1. 熟练操作和调节 VHF 话机。
2. 较为熟练地使用中文和标准海事通信用语（英语）进行无线电话通信。

二、实验内容

1. VHF 机的正确调节和频道的恰当选择；
2. 正确使用 VHF 单工工作方式；
3. 使用 VHF 进行呼叫和常规通信的基本程序；
4. 使用 VHF 进行遇险、紧急和安全通信的标准格式；
5. 初步使用和体会 SMCPs。

三、实验要求：使学生初步具备如下能力

1. 熟悉 VHF 机的基本功能及其操作方法；
2. 能够选择恰当的 VHF 频道进行并完成
   常规呼叫和通信（船舶动态、引航、港口、交通管制报告，船—船通信等业务相关通信）；
   遇险、紧急和安全通信；
3. 具备 VHF 值守能力，并能够用英文记录 VHF 通信和广播信息。

四、实验室

雷达模拟器实验室

五、实验模拟场景

某港口附近水域，4 条本船受控于教练台，教练台模拟各不同台站与本船，本船与本船之间按照要求进行通信和联络。

六、实验进程安排

项目	目标	时间安排 (单班 90 min)	组织方法
1.分组和任务下达		10 min	集中布置
2.VHF 机的调节使用	频道和功率选择正确,音量和静噪比调节恰当,信号强度适当	10 min	教师指导、演示
3.呼叫知名船舶台站	呼叫—识别—(更换频道)—信文—结束	20	本船 1 呼叫本船 3, 2-4, 3-1, 4-2
4.呼叫港口 VTS 并报告船舶细节		20	分别进行,1-2-3-4
5.根据虚拟场景完成相应的遇险,紧急或安全通信	格式标准,用语规范,操作正确	20	分别进行,1-2-3-4
6.收听并记录 VHF 广播信息	VHF 值守,信息接收、记录正确	10 min	同时进行

七、注意

1.实验之前必须复习课程第四章有关的内容并阅读本指导书;

2.协调通信,按规定合理地使用频道;

3.使用规范的通信用语;

4.每个学生都应积极参与训练、填写实验报告并于实验结束后提交该报告。

八、实验过程中 4 艘模拟船舶的资料

Ship's name	OWN SHIP 1
Call sign	BONE
Ship's type/CO.,/hull colour	Container Carrier/COSCO/blue
Gross tonnage	39,568 GT
Length overall	295 m
Width	34 m
Draught	12.5 m
Present speed and course	20 knots, 313°
Present position	24°11′.6N,118°1 7′.2E
Last port of call	Singapore
Destination	Xiamen

（续表）

Ship's name	OWN SHIP 2
Call sign	BTWO
Ship's type/CO.,/hull colour	Bulk Carrier/China shipping Co., Lmd./black
Gross tonnage	21,467 GT
Length overall	202 m
Width	26.5 m
Draught	10.8 m
Present speed and course	13 knots, 313°
Present position	24°15'.4N,118°1 1'.6E
Last port of call	Qinhuangdao
Destination	Xiamen

Ship's name	OWN SHIP 3
Call sign	BTRE
Ship's type/CO.,/hull colour	General Cargo Carrier/BLOWN
Gross tonnage	11,302 GT
Length overall	150 m
Width	20.3 m
Draught	9.2 m(F) 9.4 m(A)
Present speed and course	8 knots, 140°
Present position	24°19'.3N,118°1 1'.6E
Last port of call	Xiamen
Destination	Tokyo

Ship's name	OWN SHIP 4
Call sign	BFOR
Ship's type/CO.,/hull colour	Ferry/Xiamen Shipping/White
Gross tonnage	4,500 GT
Length overall	89 m
Width	16.3 m
Draught	4.2 m(F) 4.4 m(A)
Present speed and course	18 knots, 129°
Present position	24°30'.3N,118°05'.6E
Last port of call	Xiamen
Destination	Jinmen

九、实验使用的 VHF 模拟话机听筒和话筒以及控制面板(型号为:IC-M45)示意图

十、VHF 话机各按钮的功能说明

1. 发射状态指示
该指示灯处在面板的左上角,为 TX 字样,显示时表明本设备正在向外发射信号。

2. 按键
是单工工作方式中无线电话机的收/发转换开关,俗称"按住说话键"。
处于话筒的上方,一般会标注"PTT"字样。

3. 电源开关/音量控制旋钮
用于开关本设备,关机时将该旋钮逆时针旋至最小;开机后顺时针旋转则音量增加,逆时针则音量减小。

4. 静噪比调节旋钮
顺时针旋转该旋钮则减小噪声音量,但同时也会对信号音量造成衰减,需要适当调节。

5. 频道选择
本机中调节该旋钮,所选择的频道将出现在的液晶显示屏中。
其他机型中可能使用按键和菜单来选择频道,具体参照其说明书。

6. 16 频道快捷选择键
按照 IMO 有关标准,每种 VHF 话机都应当具有该按键。本机中该按键处于面板的左上角,为一红色按键,按下该按键,则不论频道选择旋钮置于何处,16 频道都将成为当前使用的频道。

7. 双功值守按钮

允许用户在守听 16 频道的同时兼顾守听另外的一个频道。按下该按钮则本话机将以一定的时间轮流值守 16 频道和频道选择旋钮所确定的频道,其中一个频道上接收到信号时话机将守听该频道,并且液晶显示屏上显示该频道。

8. 功率选择按钮

是一个发射信号输出功率的选择按钮,本机中按下该按钮则表明:选择了 25 W 的高输出功率(适用于较远距离通信);弹开该按钮则表明:选择了 1 W 的低输出功率(适用于近距离通信和港内通信)。

其他机型的功率选择按钮也与此类似,大多数机型被选择的功率数值将会在显示屏上显示。

9. 屏幕亮度调节

该按钮分为 3 个档次,每档对应不同的显示屏亮度。用户应根据实际的环境和情况来选择合适的显示屏亮度(如:夜间亮度太大可能会影响视觉瞭望)。

其他机型中可能使用按键和菜单来选择频道,具体参照其说明书。

船舶信号与 VHF 通信实验报告

姓名：_____   学号：_____

专业、班级：_____ 实验时间：_____

实验室：_____ 本船号码：_____

成绩：_____

一、实验的准备

复习已讲授课程,回答下列问题:

1. VHF 机的调节使用

问题 1:如何恰当选择 VHF 通信和值守频道?

问题 2:选择 VHF 机的发射功率的原则是什么?

问题 3:静噪比调节的作用是什么?

问题 4:16 频道的使用应注意什么?

2. 关于 VHF 通信的程序及其使用

问题 1:VHF 一般通信的程序如何?

问题 2:频道已经占用时应如何处理?

问题 3:如果需要呼叫不知名的船舶,如何发起呼叫?

问题 4:海上通信有哪些优先等级?

问题 5：无线电话静默时间是如何规定的？

问题 6：无线电话遇险呼叫程序如何，适用于什么样的情况？

问题 7：无线电话紧急呼叫程序如何，适用于什么样的情况？

二、实验过程记录

按照下列提示内容、使用标准海事通信用语(英语)完成通信,填写通信双方的通话记录并且注明通话的频道。

1. 呼叫已知船名的他船（本船 1 呼叫本船 3；本船 2 呼叫本船 4）
双方识别清楚后转到其他合适的通话频道；
询问彼此的呼号、航向、航速和船位；
结束通信；
回到相应的值守频道。

2. 双方交换角色（本船 3 呼叫本船 1；本船 4 呼叫本船 2）
双方识别清楚后转到其他合适的通话频道；
询问彼此的目的港、船长、船宽和吃水；
结束通信；
回到相应的值守频道。

频道	主叫船	被叫

频道	主叫	被叫

3. 呼叫港口 VTS 并报告船舶细节。

教练台充当港口 VTS,每个本船先后呼叫 VTS,并与 VTS 中心通信。

通信内容记录下表。

本船	厦门 VTS 中心
Xiamen VTS, Xiamen VTS. This is Own ship ( ), Own ship ( ) calling you on channel 8. How do you read me? Over.	Own ship ( ), Own ship ( ). This is Xiamen VTS, Xiamen VTS. I read you _____. Change to channel 17. Over.

4. 根据虚拟场景编制相应的信文，选择合适的频道，完成相应的遇险或紧急通信。

本船 1:人员落水,正在采取救助行动,请附近船只加强瞭望,注意避碰。

本船 2:触碰不明物体,货舱进水,正在下沉,需要拖船救助。

本船 3：2 名船员严重烧伤，正全速前往厦门港，需要立即医疗救助。

本船 4：主机故障，船舶失控，需要立即援助。

通信信文：

_____

_____

_____

_____

_____

_____

_____

5. 收听并记录 VHF 广播信息。

发信台站名称：_____

广播主题：_____

广播时间：_____

广播内容记录：_____

三、实验总结和自我评价

实验一　VHF 无线电话遇险、紧急通信实验

实验目的:

通过实验进一步掌握无线电话遇险和紧急通信的规定和程序,熟悉遇险和紧急信号的使用,掌握 VHF 无线电话对讲机的操作使用。

实验仪器与设备:

VHF 无线电话对讲机两部

实验注意事项:

本实验由于涉及遇险和紧急通信,为了避免出现误报警、扰乱 GMDSS 海上日常通信和遇险安全通信秩序,禁止使用无线电话发信设备进行有效发射。实验通过模拟发射的方法,由通信双方用口语对话进行。

实验要求:

正确使用遇险安全频率,使用遇险呼叫和收妥承认的标准格式进行,通信过程使用英语表达,表达意思要清晰准确。

实验项目:

1. VHF 无线电话遇险通信实验

根据国际无线电规则以及 GMDSS 有关规定,为了维护海上遇险、紧急、安全和日常通信的秩序,所有无线电话通信必须按规定程序来进行,遇险紧急信号的发射必须是在船舶处于遇险和紧急状态下,并且要在船舶负责人的授权下才能进行。

无线电话遇险通信的标准格式:

—MAYDAY YMAYDAY MAYDAY

—THIS IS(遇险船舶识别三次)

—MAYDAY, 遇险船舶识别一次

—遇险报警的内容(包括遇险船位、遇险性质、遇险时间、需要提供的援助,以及其他有助于救助的信息)

—OVER

无线电话遇险报警收妥承认的格式:

—MAYDAY(一次)

—遇险船舶识别(三次)

—THIS IS(本台识别三次)

—MAYDAY RECEIVED（或 RRR 代替 RECEIVED）

—OVER

请以下面例子进行一次无线电话遇险通信的模拟实验：

遇险船：ALPHA；救助船：BELTA

具体过程如下：

"ALPHA" 轮在 23.5N 124.5E 机舱起火，船舶没有能力控制火势，发出呼救，要求提供消防援助；当地刮东北风 4 级。

"BELTA" 轮收到呼救后应答，"BELTA" 轮在距离 "ALPHA" 轮 5 海里方位 095 度的位置，同意以全速前往救助，并将在 20 分钟后到达。

2.VHF 无线电话紧急通信实验

无线电话紧急通信的呼叫格式：

—PAN-PAN PAN-PAN PAN-PAN

—THIS IS（发出紧急呼叫的电台识别三次）

—PAN-PAN 发出紧急呼叫的电台识别一次

—紧急通信的具体内容和要求的援助

—OVER

无线电话紧急呼叫的应答格式：

—PAN-PAN

—发出紧急呼叫的电台识别一次

—THIS IS（进行应答的电台识别一次）

—PAN-PAN RECEIVED

—OVER

请以下面例子进行一次无线电话紧急通信的模拟实验：

发出紧急呼叫的船舶：OCEAN QUEEN

应答电台：HONG KONG MARDEP

事情经过如下：

有一艘名叫 OCEAN QUEEN 的船舶发出紧急呼叫说，她的船上有一名船员严重烧伤，情况危急，需要立即送往医院抢救；船舶位于桂山岛 6.5 海里，方位 125 度的海面上漂航。HONGKONG MARDEP 听到呼叫后进行应答，说是马上派一架直升机前往救助，将在 20 分钟内到达，要求船舶准备好直升机的降落点。OCEAN QUEEN 回答说，前甲板的直升机降落点已经准备好。

实验报告要求：

用英语明语将通信双方的通信内容用对话的格式写出来，并完成思考题。

思考题：

1.遇险紧急通信应该在什么频率上进行？

2.收到遇险紧急呼叫的船舶有什么义务？

3.遇险通信的管制电台在遇险通信结束以后应该做那些工作？

实验二　VHF无线电话日常通信实验

实验目的：

通过实验进一步掌握无线电话日常通信的规定和程序，熟悉呼叫与回答的基本方法，熟练掌握信文标志的使用，掌握VHF无线电话对讲机的操作使用。

实验仪器与设备：

VHF无线电话对讲机两部

实验注意事项：

进行无线电话通信时应该注意的一些问题

（1）若被呼台对发送3次，每次间隔2分钟的呼叫没有应答，呼叫台应该停止呼叫，在过3分钟后再进行这种发送3次，每次间隔2分钟的呼叫。

（2）所有呼叫应该在确认不会对别台产生干扰时进行。

（3）选用工作频率时，应先在此频率上监听适当的时间，确定没有人使用此频率才可以使用此频率。

（4）海上移动业务电台与航空电台的电话通信，在呼叫不通的情况下，可以在5分钟后重复呼叫。

（5）第一项关于呼叫间歇的规定，不使用于遇险和紧急通信。

（6）双方沟通后，如等待时间超过10分钟，应该说明原因。

（7）除遇险紧急情况以外，禁止在呼叫频率上进行无线电话通信。

（8）除遇险紧急和安全通信外，所有在156.8 MHz和2 182 kHz上的呼叫发射不能超过1分钟。

（9）无线电话测试信号不应对别的电台产生干扰，而且不得连续超过10秒钟。

（10）为建立无线电话通信而进行的联络，设备许可时应使用DSC实现。

（11）使用2 182 kHz和VHF CH16进行呼叫时，要避免在无线电话静默时间进行。

（12）使用VHF无线电话进行通信，在能够可靠通信的条件下，为了减少相互干扰，应该尽可能使用小的发射功率。

实验要求：

正确使用呼叫频率进行通信呼叫联系，掌握转换工作频率的方法。呼叫联系上后，在工作频率上重新呼叫，然后进行通信。通信过程要使用英语明语，重要内容的表达要使用信文标志，口语表达要清晰准确。

实验项目：

1.船舶代理业务通信实验

通信双方："安龙江"轮船长　大连外运代理通信的大致情况如下：

"安龙江"轮于2006年12月5日抵达大连港，并于当地时间10点15分在检疫锚地抛完锚，锚位是方位330度，距离黄白嘴灯塔3.5海里；船长根据工作关系向大连外运代理呼叫，报告抵港抛锚情况，同时询问靠泊消息。

大连外运代理要求"安龙江"详细报告船舶抵港油水存留情况和船舶吃水情况，并通知"安龙江"轮12月6日下午16点靠1号突堤的2号泊位，引航员将于明天14点50分上船。预计开始装货时间为12月6日18点。

"安龙江"轮报告的存油水情况如下：重油250吨，轻油100吨，润滑油12 000升，淡水83吨。已作好装货准备，并请大连外运代理推荐一名供应商供应免税烟酒和伙食。

实验报告要求：用英语明语将通信双方的通信内容以对话的形式写出来，并完成思考题：船舶与代理之间的VHF无线电话通信联络通常使用什么频道？

附录 5
常用词汇（Vocabulary）

1. 船舶规范 Ship's regulation

船名 ship's name
呼号 call sign
国籍 nationality
船籍港 port of registry
船舶所有人 ship's owner
船舶所有人地址 ship's owner address
船型 ship's type
船级 class
登记号 official No.
国际海事组织编号 IMO No.
总长度 LOA
宽度 breadth
最大高度 max. height
最大吃水 max. draft
散装舱容 bulk capacity
总吨 gross tonnage
净吨 net tonnage
总载重量 deadweight
水上移动服务识别码 MMSI
账务结算识别码 AAIC
主机种类 type of main engine
主机功率 main engine power
航速 speed
发电机种类 type of generator
重油 F/O
轻油 D/O
滑油 L/O
淡水 F/W fresh water
货舱数量 numbers of hold
压载舱容 ballast tank capacity

2. 船舶结构 Ship's structure

首柱 stem post

首尖舱 fore peak tank

首楼甲板 forecastle deck

油漆间 paint locker

底层舱 lower hold

龙骨 keel

舷侧 top side

舱盖 hatch cover

水密舱壁 watertight bulkhead

大桅 mast

舷梯 accommodation ladder

上层建筑 superstructure

艇甲板 boat deck

罗经甲板 compass flat

海图室 chart room

机舱 engine room

集控室 central controlling room

深舱 deep tank

轻油柜 diesel oil tank

厨房 galley

会客厅 saloon

球鼻首 bulbous bow

防撞舱壁 collusion bulkhead

物料间 store room

二层舱 tween deck

双层底 double bottom

水线间 boot top

舱口围 hatch coaming

货舱 cargo hold

起货机平台 winch platform

主甲板 main deck

尾楼甲板 poop deck

烟囱 funnel

驾驶甲板 navigation deck

驾驶台 bridge

操舵位置 steering stand

尾尖舱 aft peak tank

舵机间 steering gear room

重油柜 fuel oil tank

污油柜 sludge tank

餐厅 mess room

船员房间 crew's cabin

3. 操纵设备 Manoeuvring facilities

锚 anchor

吊杆 derrick

制动器 brake

锚链 anchor chain

锚链舱 chain locker

缆车 winch

自动缆车 tension winch

导向滚轮 guide roller

系缆柱 bitt

尾缆 stern line

倒缆 spring line

引缆 delivery line

锚冠 anchor crown

螺旋桨 propeller

浆毂 boss

定距桨 FPP（fixed pitch propeller）

螺距 pitch

舵叶 rudder blade

舵机 steering gear

主机 main engine

分油机 purifier

应急消防水泵 emergency fire pump

消防总管 fire main

喷淋设备 sprinkler

挡火闸 fire damper

国际通岸接头 international shore connection

防火控制图 fire control plan

消火栓 hydrant

消防水带 fire hose

灭火器 extinguisher

软管 hose

安全销 securing pin

锚杆 anchor shank

起重机 crane

离合器 clutch

锚链筒 hawse pipe

制链器 chain locker

绞盘 capstan

导缆孔 fairlead

系缆桩 bollard

首缆 head line

横缆 breast line

撇缆 heaving line

锚爪 anchor fluke

锚机 windlass

桨叶 blade

尾轴 tail shaft

变距桨 CPP（controllable pitch propeller）

舵 rudder

舵杆 rudder stock

自动操舵 auto pilot

副机 aux-engine

发电机 generator

烟雾探测器 smoke detector

速闭装置 closing device

隔离阀 isolation valve

防护服 protective suit

水枪 giant

消防斧 fire axe

钢瓶 cylinder

喷嘴 nozzle

消防员装备 fireman outfit

4. 安全设备 Safety equipment

消防设备 fire fighting equipment

主消防泵 main fire pump

救生索 lifeline

沙箱 sand box

救生艇 lifeboat

封闭式救生艇 enclosed lifeboat

摇臂 cradle

吊艇钩 boat hook

限位器 stopper

救生筏 liferaft

救生圈 life buoy

救生服 immersion suit

自亮灯 self-igniting lamp

反光带 retro-reflective tape

防护服 protective clothing

手套 gloves

吸油毡 absorbent

拖把 mop

扫帚 broom

消油剂 dispersant

弃船 abandon vessel

登船设施 boarding arrangements

堵漏毯 collision mat

进水 flooding

通用警报 general alarm

防污染设备 anti-pollution material

油水分离器 oily water separator

焚化炉 incinerator

应变部署表 muster list

清除油污 oil clearance

公共广播系统 PA system

点名 roll call

溢油 spill

水密门 watertight door

救生设备 life saving apparatus

消防斧 axe

灭火毯 fire blanket

呼吸器 breathing apparatus

开敞式救生艇 open lifeboat

艇架 boat davit

吊艇钢丝 winch fall

脱钩装置 releasing gear

止荡索 swash line

气胀式救生筏 inflatable liferaft

救生衣 life jacket

静水压力释放器 hydrostatic releaser

安全灯 safety lamp

保暖用具 thermal protective aid

防护鞋 boots

头盔 helmet

锯末 sawdust

桶 bucket

围油栏 oil fence

其他安全设施 other safety items

号笛声 blast

倾覆 capsizing

消防巡逻 fire patrol

烟气 fume

红星降落伞 parachute flare signal

卫生设施 sanitation system

进水 make water

油类记录簿 oil record book

溢流 overflow

污染船 polluter

船舶油污应急计划 SOPEP

数据记录仪 VDR

水密舷窗 watertight scuttle

5. 船舶定线制和报告制 Ship's routing and reporting system

定线制 routing system

分道通航制 TSS（traffic separation scheme）

分隔带 separation zone

通航分道 traffic lane

沿岸通航带 inshore traffic zone

危险品级别 IMO-class

抛弃货物 jettision of cargo

泄漏 leaking

推荐的交通流流向 recommended direction of traffic flow

航行计划 sailing plan

偏航报告 deviation report

危险货物报告 dangerous goods report

报告点 reporting line

基线 reference line

分隔线 separation line

环形道 roundabout

受限区域 restricted area

放艇 launch

抛绳器 line throwing appliance

船位报告 position report

最终报告 final report

航道 fairway

航路点 way point

通航许可 traffic clearance

6. 航行和操纵 Navigating and manoeuvring

漂移 adrift

泊位 berth

双向航路 two-way route

深水航路 deep-water route

警戒区 precautionary area

避航区 area to be avoided

规定的交通流向 established direction of traffic flow

走锚 dragging

登船 embark

预计到达时间 ETA

缠锚 foul(of anchor)

全速 full speed

偏航 lee way

解掉 let go

失控 not under command

恢复 resume

会合地 rendezvous

直航 stand on

编队航行 convoy

航迹向 course made good

最近会遇时间 TCPA

立标 beacon

导标 leading line

侧面标 lateral mark

安全水域标 safe water mark

海上标志 seamark

已设置 established

穿过速度 transit speed

在航 underway

倒出 walk out

登船速度 boarding speed

推荐航路 recommended route

禁锚区 no anchoring area

拖锚 dredging

护航 escort

预计开航时间 ETD

缠螺旋桨 foul of propeller

船首向 heading

下风、上风 leeward/windward

靠泊 moor to

驶向 proceed to

脱浅 refloat

安全航速 safe speed

基点(罗经点) cardinal point

航向 course

最近会遇点 CPA

紧急停车 crash stop

灯船 light vessel

浮标 buoy

孤立危险物标 isolated danger mark

专用标 special mark

雷达信标 racon

航迹 track

转运货物 transshipment

松出 slack

7. 航标 Aids to navigation

灯塔 lighthouse

恢复正常 restored to normal

无灯光 unlit

功率降低 reduced power

已改变 altered

已损坏 damaged

丢失 missing

重新复位 replaced in position

不可靠 unreliable

移位 off station

已毁坏 destroyed

8. 气象和水文状况 Meteorological and hydrological conditions

风向逆转 backing of wind

风向不定 variable of wind

无风 calm

微风 gentle breeze

强风 strong breeze

狂风 storm

主涌 primary swell

涌向 swell direction

波 wave

无浪 calm

轻浪 slight sea

大浪 rough sea

海流 sea current

风向顺转 veering of wind

波速 velocity of wave

轻风 light breeze

和风 moderate breeze

大风 gale

暴风 violent storm

次涌 secondary swell

涌速 swell velocity

波向 direction of wave

小浪 smooth sea

中浪 moderate sea

狂浪 high sea

结冰 icing

9. 港口设施和海岸特征 Port facilities ande coast features

锚地 anchorage

应急锚地 emergency anchorage

防波堤 breakwater

水道 channel

悬崖 cliff

船坞,码头 dock

浮桥 floating bridge

港口 harbour

栈桥,突堤 jetty

管线 pipeline

岸 shore

海湾 bay

泊位 berth

检疫锚地 quarantine anchorage

运河 canal

海峡 strait

珊瑚礁 coral reef

船厂 dockyard

入口 entrance

峡角 headland

船闸 lock

沉船 wreckage

浅滩 shoaling

岸堤 bank

海滩,抢滩 beach

边界 boundary

风压差 leeway

10. 搜寻救助 Search and rescue

搜寻和救助 SAR

联合协调救助中心 JRCC

现场协调人 OSC（on-scene coordinator）

救助协调中心 RCC（rescue coordination center）

搜救单元 search and rescue unit

伤亡 casualty

现场 scene

搜寻起始点 CSP（commence search point）

基点 datum

扇形搜寻 sector search

搜寻速度 search speed

航段 leg

终止搜寻 discontinue searching

起飞 take off

视觉联系 visual contact

海水染色标记 sea maker dye

搜救雷达 SART

全球海上遇险与安全系统 GMDSS

海上救助协调中心 MRCC

初始航向 initial course

搜寻对象 search object

平行搜寻 parallel search

搜寻半径 search radius

继续搜寻 continue searching

幸存者 survivor

无线电测向仪 radio direction finder

数字选择性呼叫 DSC

应急无线电示位标 EPIRB

11. 医疗 Medical section

人体部位和器官 regions and organs of body

颅顶 top of head

颈后 back of neck

脑 brain

眼 eye

耳 ear

唇 lip

扁桃体 tonsil

牙 tooth

肩膀 shoulder

胸 chest

动脉 artery

乳房 breast

肺 lung

肝 liver

肠 intestine

手掌 palm of hand

拇指 thumb

膝盖 knee

脚跟 heel

常见疾病 common diseas

阑尾炎 appendicitis

痉挛 fits

胃溃疡 gastric ulcer

体温过低 hypothermia

流感 influenza

一般症状 general symptom

体温 temperature

呼吸 breathing

出汗 sweating

知觉 consciousness

呕吐 vomiting

出血 bleeding

前颈 neck front

脸 face

齿龈 gums

口 mouth

咽喉 throat

舌 tongue

鼻子 nose

肘 elbow

脊柱 spinal

静脉 vein

心脏 heart

胃 stomach

脾 spleen

腕 wrist

手指 finger

全腹 whole abdomen

踝 ankle

脚趾 toe

皮疹 rash

霍乱 cholera

酒精中毒 alcoholism

中暑 heat stroke

消化不良 indigestion

肿胀 swelling

脉搏 pulse

脑压 compression of brain

精神状况 mental state

疼痛 pain

小便 urine

休克 shock

参考文献

［1］陈宏权. Marine Signals and VHF Communication. 武汉：武汉理工大学出版社，2009.

［2］国际信号规则. 天津：中国人民解放军海军司令部航海保证部，2007.

［3］金永兴. Marine Signals and Radiotelephony. 大连：大连海事大学出版社，2015.

［4］李振华. 船舶信号与 VHF 通信. 大连：大连海事大学出版社，1998.

［5］魏云雨. 船舶信号与 VHF 通信. 大连：大连海事大学出版社，2008.

［6］赵邦良. 船舶信号. 大连：大连海事大学出版社，2003.